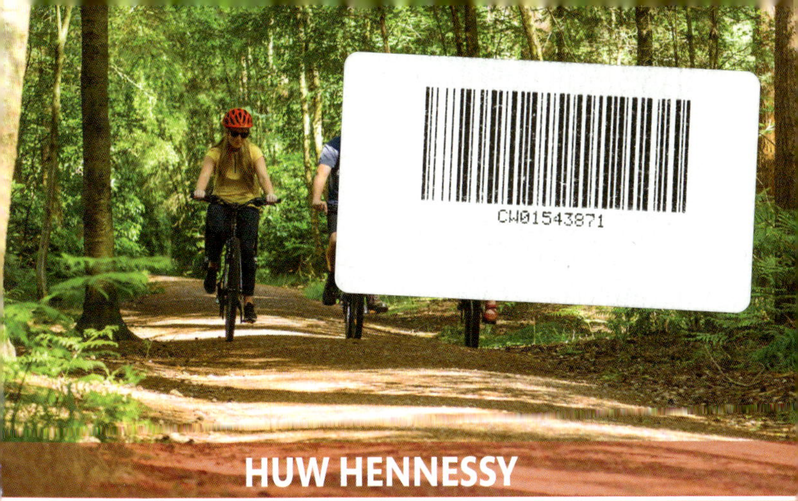

HUW HENNESSY

CYCLING IN EAST ANGLIA

21 HAND-PICKED RIDES

Bradt Guides Ltd, UK
Globe Pequot Press Inc, USA

AUTHOR

Huw Hennessy is a lifelong cycling nut, and since childhood has pedalled as much as possible at every opportunity – from Paris to the Loire Valley after finishing his A-levels to freewheeling down the Andes when updating the Footprint *Colombia Handbook* a few years ago. Since moving to Devon in 2004, he has cycled all over southwest England, including off-road routes across Dartmoor, Exmoor and Bodmin Moor, as well as family favourites such as the Camel Trail and Pentewan Valley Trail. In 2020 he did the Devon Coast to Coast cycle route from Ilfracombe to Plymouth, and has completed the Nello (a 100-mile fundraising pedal for cancer charity, FORCE) eight times over the last 12 years.

Huw is a seasoned travel writer and has written and updated a number of travel guides over many years, including several for Bradt, on St Helena, Mozambique and their first cycling guide: *Cycling in Cornwall & The Isles of Scilly*.

DEDICATION

To Ann and Joe, Dan and Maddie

FEEDBACK REQUEST AND UPDATES WEBSITE

At Bradt Guides we're aware that guidebooks start to go out of date on the day they're published – and that you, our readers, are out there in the field doing research of your own. You'll find out before us when a fine new family-run hotel opens or a favourite restaurant changes hands and goes downhill. So why not tell us about your experiences? Contact us on 01753 893444 or **e** info@bradtguides.com. We will forward emails to the author who may post updates on the Bradt website at bradtguides.com/updates. Alternatively, you can add a review of the book to Amazon, or share your adventures with us on Facebook, Twitter or Instagram (@BradtGuides).

FOREWORD

Rob Marshall, komoot

East Anglia is a wonderful place for a relaxed bike ride, and this book shares some of the area's most beautiful routes, coupled with background features on its history, culture and wildlife. But this book is also unique in that it has teamed up with **komoot** – a route-planning and navigation app that enables users to find, plan and share adventures based on riding type and ability. You can use the komoot smartphone app or komoot.com, and it syncs with practically any GPS device for navigation.

By scanning the QR codes that accompany each route, you'll gain access to an interactive map and detailed route profile: an inch-by-inch breakdown of the surface type alongside an elevation chart. What's more, you can also save the route for offline use. Komoot turns your smartphone into a GPS device, and when you hit 'start' on the ride the turn-by-turn voice navigation will keep you on track, meaning you can pedal in peace and soak up the views without stopping to check the map at every intersection.

Speaking of pedalling and enjoying the scenery, this Bradt guide gives you a wonderful overview of the places you're cycling through and recommendations for where to eat and sleep. Komoot's 'Highlights' (red dots on the komoot map) can boost this intel with tips from the community – suggestions for things that may not appear in the guidebook, like a hidden picnic spot or a section of road loved by local riders.

So go on – it's time to saddle up and enjoy what this region has to offer!

DOWNLOAD A FREE KOMOOT MAPS REGION BUNDLE

Ready to explore more with komoot and Bradt? Create your free komoot account by going to komoot.com/g, then enter the following codes to unlock each regional bundle:

Norfolk: **BRADTNFK**

Suffolk: **BRADTSFK**

Cambridgeshire: **BRADTCBE**

New users only. Offer valid until 31 December 2026.

Sandringham Loop (17.8km)
Royal ride from the manicured grounds of the Sandringham Estate
page 22

Great Bircham Loop (32.9km)
Gorgeous loop taking in a windmill, a stately home & a deer-filled country park
page 30

Wells & Holkham Loop (28.9km)
Diverse ride through salt marshes & across Holkham Hall's magnificent estate
page 38

Thetford Forest (16.6km)
Family-friendly outdoor activity centre offering three mountain-bike trails
page 102

Ixworth Millers' Trail (23.9km)
Bucolic route looping through agricultural Suffolk countryside, passing windmills & water wheels
page 110

Newmarket Jockeys' Trail (45.7km)
Long but diverse route through the wild, windswept Fens & a rolling river valley
page 170

Houghton Mill Loop (28.3km)
Largely off-road riverside route around the peaceful Ouse Valley
page 192

Grafham Water Loop (14.5km)
Scenic loop following the bird-rich shores of this broad reservoir
page 200

Cambridge to Ely (39.1km)
Historic Fenland ride linking two of East Anglia's most distinguished cities
page 182

Moulton Loop (13.1km)
Short loop along the River Kennett offering quaint villages & traditional country pubs
page 164

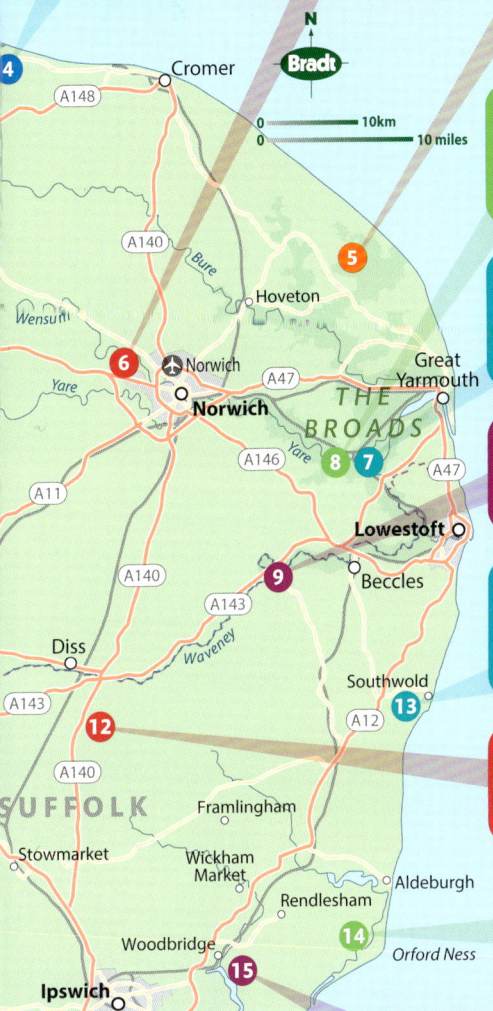

Cley Loop (26.3km)
Inland loop through the Brecks, passing rural villages & a historic watermill
page 46

Marriott's Way (30.8km)
Off-road ride following the tracks of the former Great Eastern & Midland & Great Northern railways
page 62

Northern Broads: Hickling to Horsey Loop (32.9km)
Wildlife-rich ride exploring Norfolk's northern Broads
page 54

Southern Broads Loop (34.7km)
From picturesque Reedham, this circular route explores a string of sleepy Suffolk villages
page 82

Reedham Broads Loop (38.4km)
Leisurely loop through the Norfolk Broads, exploring an assembly of exquisite churches
page 72

Bungay Saints Trail (32.5km)
Rural ride through the heart of north Suffolk visiting medieval churches known collectively as 'The Saints'
page 92

Walberswick to Southwold Loop (31.3km)
Charming route bookended by these two popular resorts, exploring the fringes of Dunwich Forest
page 130

Eye to Debenham Loop (34.4km)
Diverse loop taking in historic towns, medieval churches & a vintage railway
page 120

Orford Loop (33.9km)
From nautical Orford, this route takes in a medieval church, a watermill & dense woodlands
page 138

Lavenham Loop (20.7km)
Gentle route from this historic market town, following the trickling River Brett
page 156

Sutton Hoo & Rendlesham Forest Loop (35.2km)
Diverse loop offering a quirky mix of Anglo-Saxon treasures, glorious coastline & off-road mountain-bike trails
page 146

CONTENTS

INTRODUCTION..10
CYCLING: THE ESSENTIALS..12
HOW TO USE THIS BOOK...18

01 SANDRINGHAM LOOP 22
Start/end: Sandringham **Distance:** 17.8km **Time:** 1–1½hrs
Difficulty: ① **Highlights:** Historic Royal Sandringham Estate and Castle Rising, churches, woodlands and picturesque villages

02 GREAT BIRCHAM LOOP 30
Start/end: Great Bircham **Distance:** 32.9km **Time:** 3hrs
Difficulty: ① **Highlights:** Rolling country lanes, through pretty villages and arable farmland; past Bircham Windmill, Houghton Hall and Deer Park

03 WELLS AND HOLKHAM LOOP 38
Start/end: Wells-next-the-Sea **Distance:** 28.9km **Time:** 2hrs
Difficulty: ① **Highlights:** Holkham Nature Reserve, AONB coastal dunes and wildfowl nature reserve; off-road trails and historic country estate, Holkham Hall; detour to site of Warham, Iron Age fort; Wells-next-the-Sea, resort and sandy beach on Holkham Bay

04 CLEY LOOP 46
Start/end: Cley Marshes Nature Reserve **Distance:** 26.3km
Time: 2½hrs **Difficulty:** ① **Highlights:** Cley coastal marshes and heath, Letheringsett Watermill, Holt Country Park and passing near to the North Norfolk Railway at High Kelling

05 NORTHERN BROADS: HICKLING TO HORSEY LOOP 54
Start/end: Hickling Broad Visitor Centre **Distance:** 32.9km
Time: 3½hrs **Difficulty:** ① **Highlights:** Hickling Broads Nature Reserve, Horsey coastal sand dunes and seal colony, Horsey Windpump, a huge Tudor barn and a rare medieval church

06 MARRIOTT'S WAY 62
Start/end: Norwich/Aylsham **Distance:** 30.8km **Time:** 3hrs
Difficulty: ① **Highlights:** Along the peaceful Wensum Valley, following the route of the former railway line from Norwich to Aylsham, dotted with Victorian steam memorabilia

07 REEDHAM BROADS LOOP 72
Start/end: Reedham Ferry **Distance:** 38.4km **Time:** 4hrs
Difficulty: ① **Highlights:** Farmland, marshes and villages of the lower Yare Valley, historic churches and riverside Reedham overlooking the Broads

08 SOUTHERN BROADS LOOP 82
Start/end: Reedham Ferry **Distance:** 34.7km **Time:** 4hrs
Difficulty: ② **Highlights:** Peaceful Broads waterways and farmland, historic churches, windmills and stately gardens

09 BUNGAY SAINTS TRAIL 92
Start/end: Bungay **Distance:** 32.5km **Time:** 3½hrs **Difficulty:** ②
Highlights: Bungay, ancient market town; historical churches in isolated hamlets and a World War II aviation museum

10 THETFORD FOREST 102
Start/end: High Lodge, Thetford Forest **Distance:** 16.6km
Time: 2hrs **Difficulty:** ② **Highlights:** Forestry woodland; off-road cycling trails over level or gently rolling terrain; multi-activity centre, from high-wire adventure to climbing walls and more

11 IXWORTH MILLERS' TRAIL 110
Start/end: Ixworth **Distance:** 23.9km **Time:** 2½hrs **Difficulty:** ①
Highlights: Historic windmills, a watermill, an Elizabethan manor and vineyard, and a wetland nature reserve

12 EYE TO DEBENHAM LOOP **120**
Start/end: Eye **Distance:** 34.4km **Time:** 3½hrs **Difficulty:** ①
Highlights: Historic market town Eye, chic Debenham, Wetheringsett vintage railway and mid-Suffolk's rolling golden meadows

13 WALBERSWICK TO SOUTHWOLD LOOP **130**
Start/end: Walberswick **Distance:** 31.3km **Time:** 3½hrs **Difficulty:** ② **Highlights:** Walberswick and Southwold, traditional seaside resorts; heath and countryside, picturesque villages and a historic windmill

14 ORFORD LOOP **138**
Start/end: Orford **Distance:** 33.9km **Time:** 3½hrs **Difficulty:** ①
Highlights: Historic Orford, arty Snape Maltings, a medieval church and a watermill, plus an optional red-graded MTB forest trail

15 SUTTON HOO AND RENDLESHAM FOREST LOOP **146**
Start/end: Sutton Hoo **Distance:** 35.2km **Time:** 4hrs **Difficulty:** ②
Highlights: Anglo-Saxon treasures at Sutton Hoo, Shingle Street beach, mountain biking in Rendlesham Forest

16 LAVENHAM LOOP **156**
Start/end: Market Square, Lavenham **Distance:** 20.7km **Time:** 2½hrs **Difficulty:** ① **Highlights:** Lavenham, one of the best-preserved medieval towns in East Anglia; sleepy villages and rolling agricultural countryside

17 MOULTON LOOP **164**
Start/end: Moulton **Distance:** 13.1km **Time:** 1½ hrs **Difficulty:** ①
Highlights: Rolling meadows and woods, Fen villages, a stud farm, a medieval bridge and three great country pubs

18 **NEWMARKET JOCKEYS' TRAIL** **170**
Start/end: Moulton **Distance:** 45.7km **Time:** 4½hrs **Difficulty:** ②
Highlights: Sleepy villages, rolling meadows, pristine stud farms, and Newmarket – world capital of horse racing

19 **CAMBRIDGE TO ELY** **182**
Start/end: Cambridge–Ely **Distance:** 39.1km **Time:** 4hrs
Difficulty: ② **Highlights:** Historic Cambridge University colleges, Anglesey Abbey, Ely Cathedral, Cam riverside path and Wicken Fen

20 **HOUGHTON MILL LOOP**.............................. **192**
Start/end: Houghton Mill **Distance:** 28.3km **Time:** 3hrs
Difficulty: ① **Highlights:** Historic Houghton watermill, riverside villages, and the Busway–Cycleway eco-route through Fen Drayton Lakes RSPB Nature Reserve

21 **GRAHAM WATER LOOP** **200**
Start/end: Marlow Park, Grafham Water **Distance:** 14.5km
Time: 1½hrs **Difficulty:** ① **Highlights:** Lakeside trail fringed by wooded countryside; nature reserves and watersports

ACCOMMODATION..**206**
BIKE HIRE..**218**
FURTHER INFORMATION **222**
ACKNOWLEDGEMENTS **226**
INDEX.. **228**
INDEX OF ADVERTISERS..**231**

INTRODUCTION

Like a snail's shell clinging to the side of England, East Anglia is a vast flatland protruding out into the North Sea. Despite its proximity to London and the Midlands, and its continental ferry links, East Anglia is one of the quietest regions in the country, with Ipswich and Norwich the only cities in its heartland. The ancient kingdom of the Angles is also its oldest inhabited region, from Palaeolithic times to Viking and Roman invasions; its wetlands irrigated by canals and windmills, its villages enriched with hundreds of medieval churches.

East Anglia is also one of our most scenic regions, with perhaps more varied landscapes than it gets credit for, with its broads, fens and marshes, forests and beaches. From Holkham Bay on the north coast to the otherworldly Shingle Street in the south of Suffolk, its extensive coastline has miles of gloriously wild and windswept beaches. You'll also find some great British seaside resorts here too, though; from loud and lively Great Yarmouth to arty Walberswick, genteel Orford, and Southwold's gloriously quirky pier.

↑ Cyclists on Jesus Green, Cambridge (Andy333/S)

The Norfolk Broads are another of the region's most popular holiday destinations, for drifting along on a narrowboat or traditional wherry. Their reed beds and marshes are also among the richest areas in the country for birds and other wildlife: the spectacular crane and the dazzling swallowtail butterfly among its many rarities. Then there are the Brecks, one of the driest areas in the UK, with low-lying sandy heaths and forests, including Thetford Forest and Grime's Graves Iron Age mining site. All said and done, though, it is true that much of East Anglia is flat or if not, gently undulating between river valleys and waterways. But rather than dismiss this level landscape as dull and monotonous, it should be relished for its tranquillity, particularly when bathed in sunlight under wide *Constable* skies.

Most importantly for the purposes of this book, the flat terrain here is ideal cycling territory: you could spend hours exploring its narrow, country lanes, where you'll meet little traffic but explore sleepy villages, with historic windmills, traditional local pubs and stunning medieval churches.

East Anglia is blessed with hundreds of kilometres of cycle routes, part of the National Cycle Network, managed by SUSTRANS. These clearly signposted routes enable cyclists to explore the countryside on quieter roads and cycle paths, including off-road trails through country estates, forests, heathland or former railway lines. The coastline too, with its sand dunes, marshes and windswept beaches, has been incorporated into two long-distance cycle paths. The Norfolk Coastal Cycleway runs for 160km from King's Lynn to Great Yarmouth, continuing south as the Suffolk Coastal Cycle Route for another 142km from Dunwich to Felixstowe. They are also part of the National Cycle Network, combining routes 1, 30, 42 and 41. Not all of this coastal route is actually on the coast, however, partly because of the historic erosion that has been eating away at the east of England for hundreds of years. But the routes hug as close to the coast as is possible, with plans currently underway in Norfolk to re-route some sections in order to avoid the increasing traffic in the region (for the latest progress, visit ⌀ norfolk.gov.uk and search for Norfolk Coastal Cycleway). While there's nothing even slightly mountainous in East Anglia, there are plenty of challenging trails for MTB (mountain bike) fans. The Peddars Way, for instance, follows a former Roman Road, largely comprising off-road trails, spanning 79km from Knettishall Heath northwest to Holme-next-the-Sea. It also links to the Icknield Way, an even longer 274km multi-user route, running southwest from Knettishall Heath to the Chilterns.

So, all you need to do now is to choose a route, grab your helmet, and jump on your bike. Happy cycling!

CYCLING: THE ESSENTIALS

CHOOSING YOUR BIKE There's a wide and ever-increasing range of bicycles on the market today, including BMX, cyclocross, gravel bikes and fatbikes (great fun on sandy beaches). The routes in this book are suitable for the five most common and popular types (detailed here), and each chapter specifies which of these is the most suitable for that route.

Road bike Also known as a racing bike, usually with drop handlebars and made with lightweight material, such as aluminium or carbon fibre. Ideal for speed and for longer distances on road, but with its narrow tyres and less robust frame than a mountain bike it's not so practical off-road on uneven surfaces. Touring bikes are sturdily built road bikes, with racks for carrying panniers.

Mountain bike Strong frames, with suspension on the front and/or back wheels designed for absorbing the rough and tumble of MTB trails. Their chunky wheels and deeply treaded tyres give good grip on rough terrain off-road, but their weight and wide wheels make them less suitable for long-distance rides.

Hybrid A cross bike, with the speed of a road bike and the strength and gearing of a mountain bike. Hybrids are extremely popular, versatile and are the single most useful bike for most of these routes. They're comfortable, sturdy and strong, with lighter frames and thinner wheels than most mountain bikes, and so are better for long distances.

Gravel bike Essentially a cross between a road bike and a mountain bike, the increasingly popular gravel bikes are designed to go faster on all types of terrain. They are lighter and more aerodynamic than conventional mountain bikes, so are also good for longer rides. Most have drop handlebars, some with suspension, and a wide range of wheel widths and tyre treads are available, to suit your preferred ride.

E-bike Electric bikes come in different shapes and styles, usually as hybrids but there are e-mountain bikes and even e-folding bikes too. They're great for getting up hills; most have automatic power mode to give you an instant start or a manual override setting. You'll need to factor in the battery charging time for each ride. They're not cheap but prices may come down as their popularity grows, and as the search continues for greener energy sources, will we all be riding solar-powered e-bikes sometime soon?

MAINTENANCE Keeping your bike in good working order is essential. Before every ride, take a few minutes to do the **M-Check**: a step-by-step assessment of the bike in the shape of the letter **M**. Start from the rear wheel up to the saddle, down to the pedals, up to the handlebars and back down to the front wheel:

1. Rear wheel: make sure it is firmly attached to the forks and turning freely. If using quick-release levers, check they are properly locked (facing backwards to avoid snagging on branches, etc). Run through the gears to make sure they're all working correctly.
2. Spokes: make sure they are all equally tight; pluck each one to check they sound about the same.
3. Tyres: check for possible splits, bulges and tears and remove any material stuck in the tread, which could cause a puncture. Ensure the tyres are inflated to the correct pressure (usually marked somewhere on the wall of the tyre).

4. Brakes: apply the rear and front brake in turn to make sure each grips the wheel firmly under forward pressure. Check there is nothing obstructing the brake pad and that it is not worn or loose.

5. Saddle: check that it is firm and that the seat post is not raised above the limit line. If needed, adjust the height and tighten the saddle with an Allen key or spanner. To measure your correct saddle height, you should be able to sit steadily on your bike, with the tips of your toes on the ground and your legs nearly straight.

6. Chain: keep it clean and oiled (though not too much oil as this can pick up dirt and debris, which can damage the chain set).

7. Pedals: spin them to make sure they rotate freely. Check that the cranks are firm and don't wobble or creak.

8. Front wheel stem: check that the handlebars and front wheel do not move independently from side to side. Do this by holding the front wheel between your knees and trying to twist the handlebars (not too hard or that will loosen them!). Tighten the stem bolt and handlebar clamp with an Allen key.

9. Headset: make sure it is correctly firm. Grip the head tube with one hand and squeeze the front brake with the other, and then try to shake the headset from side to side to make sure there is no loose movement or clicking sounds.

10. Frame: check for possible cracks or structural damage; this might occur at the joint between the head tube and the frame, and where the saddle post joins the frame.

11. Front wheel: apply the same tests as for the rear wheel.

EQUIPMENT AND ACCESSORIES For shorter rides, all you really need is a bicycle pump, a bell and a lock if you might be stopping for a break along the way.

For longer distances, the following are also useful:
- puncture repair kit
- lights (if on a long ride)
- toolkit (multi-tool with built-in spanners and Allen keys saves space)

- tyre levers
- disposable gloves (to keep oil off your hands if the chain comes off, etc)
- fluorescent reflectors (ie: armbands, spoke bars, ankle straps).

If you have any problems with your bike during a ride, there's a list of local cycle-hire and repair shops on page 218.

WHAT TO WEAR As with the equipment, for short rides you don't need much; the only essential item, whether you're going off-road or not, is a bike helmet. In addition, for longer rides, the following are also useful:
- sturdy shoes
- loose-fitting clothing (including a lightweight cagoule even in summer, as the weather is unpredictable here, as it is anywhere in the UK; bright colours are good for visibility, but a word of warning: midges love them too!)
- gloves
- sunglasses or cycling goggles
- overshoes and gaiters (for muddy mountain biking and/or very wet weather)
- padded cycle shorts
- and, definitely last, stretch lycra tops and leggings (strictly optional, or banned for anyone over 40, according to my cycling buddies!).

TAKING YOUR BIKE ON PUBLIC TRANSPORT Greater Anglia (✆ 0345 600 7245 – option 0; 🌐 greateranglia.co.uk), is the main train operator covering East Anglia. Bikes can be taken on trains, but they're usually limited to two bikes per train and advanced booking is advisable in summer months. On some routes at peak times, including those covering London and Cambridge, only fold-up bikes are allowed on board.

First Norfolk and Suffolk Bus (🌐 firstbus.co.uk), who operate bus services covering most of East Anglia, will also take fold-up bikes, but the limited space available is shared with pushchairs and wheelchairs, so it is unreliable. If you're planning to hire a bike, however, the local buses

can be useful for getting to some of the more remote parts of this sparsely populated region, where there's no nearby train station.

For general information about bus and rail travel across the whole region, including Cambridgeshire, contact the UK travel portal, Traveline (⌀ 0871 200 2233; ⌀ traveline.info).

Details of local services, including the innovative Guided Busway Cycleway from Cambridge to St Ives (⌀ thebusway.info), are included in the relevant chapter. Note, though, that some of the bike routes in this book are in remote locations, far from train stations, or even buses. So, sorry to say this, especially in today's era of climate change concern, but cars are often the best option to get to the start point.

SAFETY Cycling is generally a safe and fun form of transport, but is not without its potential risks and hazards. East Anglia is criss-crossed by a huge network of quiet backroads, which our routes follow wherever possible. Unfortunately, by contrast, its A-roads and larger B-roads are often heaving with fast-moving traffic, for which reason it's usually better

↑ The Holkham Estate is a great destination for cyclists of all ages and abilities (Holkham Estate)

to go early in the morning or the middle of the day to avoid commuter traffic. This is particularly the case for several routes, such as the Southern Broads Loop (page 82), the Newmarket Jockeys' Trail (page 170) and the Ixworth Millers' Trail (page 110), which cross several A-roads.

Following these guidelines, based on the Highway Code, will make your ride even safer for all:

- Be considerate to other users, taking extra care around those who may be short-sighted or blind, people in wheelchairs or other mobility vehicles.
- Use your bell when necessary to signal to others you are approaching, don't startle people by shooting past on narrow paths without warning.
- Ride single file on narrow roads and paths.
- Give way to walkers, wheelchair users and horse riders, leaving plenty of room when passing each other in either direction.
- On shared paths and roads, show extra caution if cycling at high speeds.
- Take extra care at junctions, bends and entrances, and signal when turning on to another road if other road users are nearby.
- Cyclists must follow the same traffic regulations as other users, including red lights, one-way roads and give-way lines.
- Narrow and high-banked country lanes muffle the sound of approaching vehicles, so listen out for traffic at all times, especially on blind hills and corners.
- Be alert to parked cars on narrow roads in case doors open suddenly in front of you.

MOUNTAIN BIKING There are only two MTB trails in this book: in Thetford Forest (page 102) and Rendlesham Forest (page 146), plus a detour along the Viking Trail, just off the Orford Loop (page 138). If you'd like more information about the grading system used on mountain biking trails around the UK, see ⌀ forestryengland.uk/article/mountain-bike-trail-grades-and-safety.

HOW TO USE THIS BOOK

This book features 21 rides all across East Anglia, from Grafham Water in Cambridgeshire, up to Wells-next-the-Sea and Cley on the north coast, down to Sutton Hoo in the south of Suffolk. As a pocket-sized guide to a sack-sized region, I can't pretend to have included all of its cycle routes, which must number in the hundreds, with new ones being added all the time – especially with the boom in online apps, such as komoot which we have used here. But they're my personal favourites, opening up many corners of the countryside that were new to me, and which I hope will appeal to others too.

The routes range from 8km to 45km, offering anything from an hour's ride to a whole day out on your bike. They are aimed to appeal particularly to beginners, families and leisure cyclists. We've also included several mountain bike routes here – not as long as the Peddars Way, but with lots of gnarly bumps, berms and rollers to get you bouncing happily out of the saddle.

All but two of the routes are loops, making travel arrangements easier, and most of the start and end points are in picturesque towns, villages, historic sites or wildlife reserves, which are worth exploring in their own right, either before or after the ride. Most of the routes are on well-established trails, wherever possible following the excellent National Cycle Network (NCN), but also with tailor-made tweaks, detours and extensions, exploring lesser-known backways.

Several of the trails could be combined with others nearby, including the **Sandringham** and **Great Bircham** loops (Routes 1 and 2), the **Reedham Broads Loop** (Route 7) on one side of the River Yare, with the **Southern Broads Loop** (Route 8) across the other side via the chain ferry, and the **Moulton Loop** (Route 17) with the **Newmarket Jockeys' Trail** (Route 18). If you feel energetic you could do both back to back, or stop overnight between rides (nearby accommodation is listed in the back of the book, page 206).

THE ROUTES For each ride, an **information panel** details the start and end point, distance in kilometres and approximate time to complete the route

BEST FOR:
Families: 3, 6, 10, 21
History and heritage: 1, 2, 7, 9, 11, 12, 14, 15, 16, 19, 20
Off-road adventure: 3, 6, 10, 13, 15
Wildlife: 2, 3, 4, 5, 8, 19, 20, 21

(depending on your fitness and number of stops along the way). Each has a **difficulty rating** (① easy or ② moderate) and a **scenic rating** (Ⓐ pleasant/interesting; Ⓑ great; Ⓒ superb), as well as an **overview of terrain** – whether the route is on- or off-road, if the path is surfaced, if any major hills are included, etc. I've also listed which bikes are best suited to each ride.

At the end of each route chapter, you'll find information about getting to the start point, the nearest tourist office and public toilets, and recommended cafés, pubs and restaurants (including bike-friendly places that have cycle racks and parking spaces).

MAPS Each chapter includes a map outlining the route and points of interest along the way, plus suggestions for relevant Ordnance Survey (OS) maps. We have also teamed up with **komoot**, the route-planning and navigation app, with a customised digital map for each route. Simply scan the QR code (or use the numerical reference code) at the beginning of the route to gain access to a 'zoom-able' map and detailed insights, including an elevation profile, way type and surface information, as well as photos of highlights and key junction signage. See page 3 for more on komoot.

ACCOMMODATION See page 206 for a list of suggested hotels, B&Bs, hostels and campsites. Covering a reasonable price range, most of these are on or close to one or more cycle routes, and many have cycle storage facilities. Some of the routes are a way from towns and villages, but even the remotest corners often have nearby holiday cottages and cyclist-friendly campsites, with glamping pods, safari tents and shepherds' huts becoming an increasingly common feature of the countryside.

The **Camping and Caravanning Club** (⌀ campingandcaravanningclub.co.uk; see ad, page 217) has a handful of campsites across East Anglia, including one in Sandringham near routes 1 and 2; and holiday lettings agents, such as **Original Cottages** (⌀ originalcottages.co.uk; see ad, page 217) have hundreds of properties across the region. We have also included the nearest tourist information office within each chapter which will have details of local accommodation or may offer an on-site booking service. Finally, **Visit East of England** (⌀ visiteastofengland.com) is the official tourism portal for Norfolk and Suffolk, with comprehensive accommodation listings and reviews.

CYCLE-HIRE SHOPS At the back of the book (page 218) is a list of cycle-hire and bike-repair shops covering East Anglia, with a number to indicate which routes they are closest to. Most of these shops have a range of adult and children's bikes for hire, as well as toddler seats, tagalongs and trailers (for children and pets!); some also have bikes adapted for wheelchair users. Hire charge usually includes essential equipment, such as helmet, pump and lock. Some companies will drop off and collect hired bikes, usually up to a range of about 10km.

OPENING HOURS This book was researched and written in the summer and autumn of 2021, when many hotels, restaurants and other businesses were still recovering from the most recent Covid lockdown. We have therefore left out opening hours to avoid confusion, but where possible have provided websites/Facebook pages so you can check when they'll be open during your visit. All the establishments listed were still open for business at the time of going to press.

THE BRADT STORY

In the beginning

It all began in 1974 on an Amazon river barge. During an 18-month trip through South America, two adventurous young backpackers – Hilary Bradt and her then husband, George – decided to write about the hiking trails they had discovered through the Andes. *Backpacking Along Ancient Ways in Peru and Bolivia* included the very first descriptions of the Inca Trail. It was the start of a colourful journey to becoming one of the best-loved travel publishers in the world; you can read the full story on our website (bradtguides.com/ourstory).

Getting there first

Hilary quickly gained a reputation for being a true travel pioneer, and in the 1980s she started to focus on guides to places overlooked by other publishers. The Bradt Guides list became a roll call of guidebook 'firsts'. We published the first guide to Madagascar, followed by Mauritius, Czechoslovakia and Vietnam. The 1990s saw the beginning of our extensive coverage of Africa: Tanzania, Uganda, South Africa, and Eritrea. Later, post-conflict guides became a feature: Rwanda, Mozambique, Angola, and Sierra Leone, as well as the first standalone guides to the Baltic States following the fall of the Iron Curtain, and the first post-war guides to Bosnia, Kosovo and Albania.

Comprehensive – and with a conscience

Today, we are the world's largest independently owned travel publisher, with more than 200 titles. However, our ethos remains unchanged. Hilary is still keenly involved, and **we still get there first**: two-thirds of Bradt guides have no direct competition.

But we don't just get there first. Our guides are also known for being **more comprehensive** than any other series. We avoid templates and tick-lists. Each guide is a one-of-a-kind expression of an expert author's interests, knowledge and enthusiasm for telling it how it really is.

And a commitment to wildlife, conservation and respect for local communities has always been at the heart of our books. Bradt Guides was **championing sustainable travel** before any other guidebook publisher. We even have a series dedicated to Slow Travel in the UK, award-winning books that explore the country with a passion and depth you'll find nowhere else.

Thank you!

We can only do what we do because of the support of readers like you – people who value less-obvious experiences, less-visited places and a more thoughtful approach to travel. Those who, like us, take travel seriously.

TRAVEL TAKEN SERIOUSLY

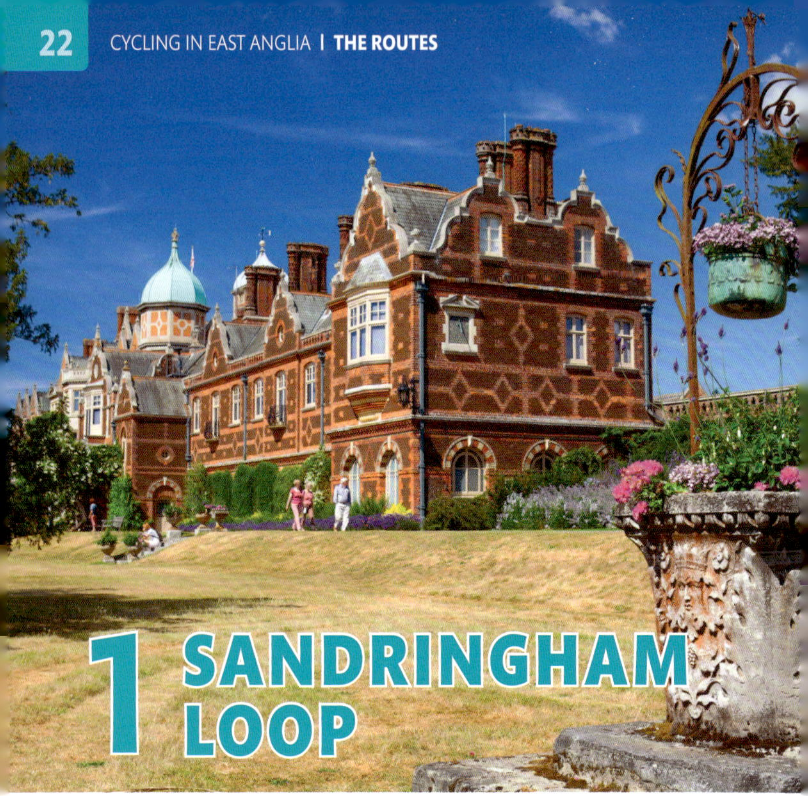

1 SANDRINGHAM LOOP

START/FINISH	Sandringham House Visitor Centre
DISTANCE/TIME	17.8km/1–1½hrs (extension: 8.9km round trip, 1hr)
DIFFICULTY/TERRAIN	① Gently undulating; all on minor roads, apart from a short stretch on the B1443
SCENIC RATING	⑧ Historic Royal Sandringham Estate and Castle Rising, churches, woodlands and picturesque villages
SUITABLE FOR	Hybrid, e-bike or road bike
NCN ROUTE	NCN1
MAPS	OS Explorer 250 (1:25 000)
KOMOOT REF	531500886

↑ Sandringham House (Radomir Rezney/S)

This rural, royal ride meanders around the manicured grounds and farmland of the Sandringham Estate. From Sandringham Stud – the royal stables – we go down the tree-lined King's Avenue and out into the countryside, past fields fringed with wildflowers, ancient burial mounds and historic churches in picturesque villages.

A short optional extension hops down to Castle Rising, a lovely old village a few kilometres south of Sandringham, with its Norman castle and church and its medieval almshouses.

THE ROUTE

Start at the courtyard in front of ❶ **Sandringham Visitor Centre**. Here, even among all the tourist trappings, the site has a regal feel, from the immaculately trimmed verges to the royal crests stamped on every available surface. Turn left on to Scotch Belt, the broad main avenue through the estate, then right at the T-junction. On the right are the **Norwich Gates**, the grand wrought-iron gateway adorned with heraldry which marks the formal entrance to Sandringham House. Follow the Hillington Road around to the right, then take the second left on to the wide, tree-lined King's Avenue. A short way along on the left are the royal stables, **Sandringham Stud**, with the statue of champion racehorse Persimmon (1895–1908) on the front lawn. Owned by the Prince of Wales

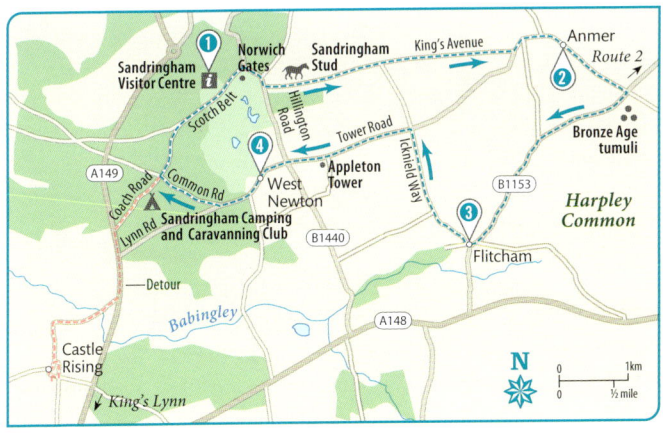

(the future King Edward VII), Persimmon won seven out of his nine races, in a short career lasting from 1895 to 1897; and subsequently produced a prize-winning pedigree.

Continue along the straight and level avenue, through fields fringed with purple field scabious, ox-eye daisies and scarlet poppies. At first glance, these colourful borders seem to be merely decorative features, in line with the neatly mown verges and trimmed hedgerows typical of this pampered landscape. But as you cycle past and look closer, you might also spot little game birds scuttling through the hedgerows, and plastic feed bins among the plants. It turns out that these are 'wildlife corridors', part of the Sandringham Farm's organic and environmental practices (see box, page 25).

After around 4km, King's Avenue winds left and right, coming into the little farming village of ❷ **Anmer**. Pass the church on the right and social club on your left, and notice the unusual, bare wooden village sign on the left, depicting a scout on one side and a Roman centurion on the other. The scout denotes the area's connection with the Scout Association, as hosts to jamborees in the 1950s. The Roman soldier relates to a battle between the Romans and Boudicca – queen of the Norfolk-based Iceni tribe – which took place in nearby woods (Anmer Minque).

Leaving Anmer, turn right at the crossroads after about 1km, and on to the B1153. Across the fields on your left are several **Bronze Age tumuli**, lying close to the Peddars Way, the Roman road running all the way from Norwich up to Hunstanton on the northwest coast. These grass- and bracken-covered 'bowl barrow' burial chambers are around 3m tall, with nine in total dotted around **Harpley Common**, near Anmer (Route 2 (page 30) passes closer to the mounds).

Follow the road winding across Harpley Common and then gently downhill into ❸ **Flitcham**, about 5km from Anmer. Flitcham is a pleasant little village, tucked in the valley on the edge of the Sandringham Estate, just off the busy A148. There are no special sights to hold you up here, although the church of St Mary has some 12th-century features, but most of it is 19th-century restoration. Coming into the village, follow the road around to the right, then right on to Church Road, towards the church.

Before you reach the church at the end of the road, however, take the next right on to the Icknield Way, signposted Sandringham. Continue along this single-track road through the fields, slightly uphill, taking the third turning on the left at a crossroads, after a couple of kilometres, heading west towards West Newton.

Carry on along Tower Road, leading to a tall, red-brick water tower above the trees ahead on the left. **Appleton Tower** and its huge, 32,000 gallon water tank were built in 1877 for the Sandringham Estate, to replace its old and unsanitary water supply. Contaminated water was thought to have been the cause of the Prince of Wales and his son falling ill with typhoid. It is now a Landmark Trust holiday property (page 206).

NATURE-FRIENDLY FARMING

If you notice the wide banks of wildflowers bordering various fields around Sandringham, they're not just for decoration. As explained above, these 'wildlife corridors' are planted around arable fields as part of the estate's agroforestry programme. Together with the planting of trees, including cider apple, quince and walnut alongside the wildflowers, the aim is to develop habitats for insects and birds, such as pheasants and partridges, which consume pests. This reduces the need for insecticides and the tree roots restrict soil erosion and run-off, which in turn improves the nutrient content of the soil in the adjacent arable fields, leading to better crop yields. The classic organic win-win scenario, in fact.

The Prince of Wales has led the drive to make Sandringham Home Farm organic since he took over the 8,500ha estate in 2017, however, it is not the only wildlife-friendly farm in East Anglia. The **Nature Friendly Farming Network** is a UK-wide organisation that supports farming in partnership with nature, and which counts some 132 farmer members across the region. NFFN member farmers come from a wide range of backgrounds, with large and small farms, using both organic and conventional working methods, but all are passionate about keeping our countryside – including its wildlife – healthy and thriving. Visit ⌘ nffn.org.uk for more details – it's free for farmers and public supporters to join and help raise awareness of better food and farming.

Passing the water tower, now hidden behind trees from close up, continue downhill to the crossroads with the B1440. Take care crossing this road, and go straight ahead on to Lynn Road, into ❹ **West Newton**. This village on the Sandringham Estate has tidy rows of neatly tended cottages, with a traditional butcher's and village store opposite the church, on the right. Keep going through the village, straight ahead at the next crossroads, then take a right fork on to Common Road, returning to the dense woods of the Sandringham grounds, where we started this ride. Follow this lush avenue, lined with mature trees and ornamental rhododendrons until you reach another crossroads, after about 1km. Turn right here on to Donkey Pond Hill, climbing steadily up to Scotch Belt, the broad avenue flanked by wide lawns. Continue right here for another few hundred metres until you return to the Sandringham Visitor Centre on your left.

EXTENSION: CASTLE RISING

If you've still got some energy and an hour or so to spare, a short backroad route leads from Sandringham to Castle Rising, a medieval village with one of the best-preserved Norman castles in England.

Starting from the last crossroads at the end of our main ride (the meeting point of Common Road and Double Lodges Road), turn left down Coach Road, where we turned right up Donkey Pond Hill. Pass the Sandringham Camping and Caravanning Club (page 210) on your left, and go downhill through the trees to a T-junction. Take the path on the left, just before the T-junction (signposted NCN1, King's Lynn), dismount and walk across the *very busy* A149, via the central island. The cycle path continues to the left, parallel to the road, but soon winds to the right – thankfully away from the roaring traffic. This quiet lane, shaded by oak trees, goes over the River Babingley, which runs through The Wash and joins the Great Ouse near King's Lynn. If you notice ruins in the middle of the marshy meadows on the right, they're the remains of the 14th-century church of St Felix, now derelict but on a site claimed to be Norfolk's first Christian mission.

Follow the lane winding left around woods, and join Old Hunstanton Road as you come into **Castle Rising**. At the T-junction with Lynn Road are two of the village's most important historic buildings. On your left is

↑ Castle Rising is one of England's best-preserved Norman castles (Kev Gregory/S)

Trinity Hospital: a two-towered brick quadrangle of almshouses, built in 1609 (occasionally open to the public, but closed at the time of writing). Opposite is the parish church of **St Laurence**: a massive stone church, originally dating from the Norman era, but mostly restored in more recent times. Its stained-glass windows are magnificent; if it is not open, go around the back of the church to see the intricately carved stone doorway and the stunning west window above.

To get to the castle itself, follow the Lynn Road around to the right and then left to the entrance. The historic Norman castle (⌀ castlerising.co.uk) is hardly visible from the road, unfortunately, hidden behind moated earth mounds and a gated perimeter. But it is well worth the entrance charge (a reasonable £5 at the time of writing), for its massive, stone keep, and for the views from the gatehouse, over the village and the river valley beyond. To return to Sandringham, retrace the same route, though if you're in need of refuelling try the Black Horse Inn next to the church or the Unique Tearooms behind the pub.

THE ESSENTIALS

GETTING THERE By **car**, Sandringham is just under 14km northeast of King's Lynn, via the A149; or 28km west of Fakenham, off the A148. The 35 Lynx **bus** goes from King's Lynn to the Sandringham Visitor Centre, with regular daily departures, taking just under half an hour. The nearest mainline **train** station is at King's Lynn, which is on the Great Northern Line, around 2 hours from London King's Cross.

WHERE TO EAT

✕ **Terrace Café** Sandringham PE35 6EH; ⌀ 01465 544548; ⌀ sandringhamestate.co.uk. This casual café, with picnic tables on the lawn in the Sandringham Courtyard Visitor Centre, serves take-away snacks, light lunches, cakes & pastries. For a posh blowout, the Sandringham Restaurant in the main house does a luxurious afternoon tea (⌀ 01485 544112; advance booking essential, no children under 12) **£–££**

✕ **Black Horse Inn** School Rd, Castle Rising PE31 6AG; ⌀ 01553 631333; ⌀ theblackhorseinncastlerisingnorfolk.com. In the heart of this lovely, historic village, this gastropub serves some seriously good nosh. The menu does the staple pub favourites, including fish & burgers, but with stylish extras, as well as a range of tapas starters & sumptuous desserts. **£££**

✕ Unique Tearooms Castle Rising PE31 6AF; 🔗 01553 631211; **f** Castle Rising Tea Rooms. With a walled garden, tucked behind the Black Horse pub in this lovely old village, these tearooms do b/fasts, lunches & afternoon teas, with fantastic homemade cakes, pastries & savoury snacks; they also do take-aways & their store sells more of their delicious goodies. **££**

FACILITIES AND FURTHER INFORMATION The Sandringham Visitor Centre (🔗 sandringhamestate.co.uk) has an information office, toilets, café, cycle racks and pay-and-display car park. There are also toilets in Castle Rising in the pub, café and the castle.

ℹ King's Lynn Tourist Information Centre Saturday Market Pl, King's Lynn PE30 5DQ; 🔗 01553 763044; 🔗 visitnorfolk.co.uk. The main tourist office for northwest Norfolk, this walk-in centre provides details about local accommodation, activities, events & what's on where.

GREAT BIRCHAM LOOP | CHAPTER 2

START/FINISH	Great Bircham
DISTANCE/TIME	32.9km/3hrs
DIFFICULTY/TERRAIN	① Level or undulating on minor country roads (one long stretch of ups and downs from Shernborne to Anmer)
SCENIC RATING	⑧ Rolling country lanes, through pretty villages and arable farmland
SUITABLE FOR	Road bike, hybrid or e-bike
NCN ROUTE	NCN1
MAPS	OS Explorer 250 (1:25 000)
KOMOOT REF	578938402

The more northerly of two loops near Sandringham, this route starts from the picturesque village of Great Bircham. Following country lanes through grassy commons and arable farmland, we also pass Ingoldisthorpe and Shernborne, with highlights including a working windmill, prehistoric burial mounds, a stately home and a country park of rare white fallow deer. Other wildlife you might well see en route include brown hares, one of Norfolk's most distinctive species, especially when they're up to their mad March boxing antics. During my research ride last summer, I spotted seven lolloping along – too fast for me to grab my camera, unfortunately.

THE ROUTE

Starting from ❶ **Great Bircham**, an attractive little village between Sandringham and Fakenham, go right from the stores, up to the war memorial on the little triangle, then left on to Snettisham Road. About 800m on the right is Mill Lane, leading after another 100m to the 19th-century **Bircham Windmill** (⌖ birchamwindmill.co.uk), which has been restored and is fully functioning today. They sell their own stone-ground flour in the bakery, and there's also a tearoom and a museum.

Returning to the Snettisham Road, turn right and on to a long straight stretch, a former Roman road, climbing slightly uphill through the fields for about 5km. After a couple of kilometres, we cross the **Peddars Way**, another ancient route, running from the Suffolk border up to the Norfolk coast, near Hunstanton. Just as we start coming downhill towards the coast,

← Restored Bircham Windmill is still functioning today (Richard Bowden/S)

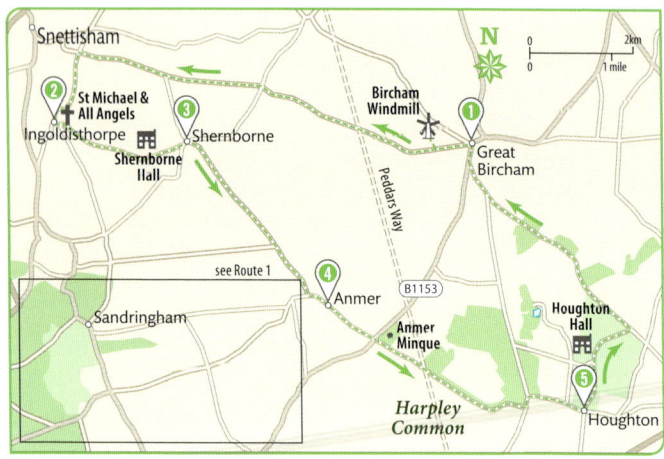

turn left on to St Thomas's Lane (NCN1), on the outskirts of Snettisham. You might notice the elegant spire of the village church peeking above the fields on the right.

Continue southwards down St Thomas's Lane and into ❷ **Ingoldisthorpe**, another appealing little rural village, noted for its **church of St Michael & All Angels**. Take the second turning on the left, on to Shernborne Road, and left again down a gravel path, to visit this medieval church, with a squat and apparently slightly lopsided tower. The local story about the 'Leaning Tower of Ingoldisthorpe' is that when the builder was accused of shoddy workmanship, he simply replied 'Only God is perfect!' The angle, today at least, is only minor, and is more noticeable from the churchyard behind the main entrance. If the church is open, though, have a look inside; the 19th-century stained-glass windows are impressive, particularly those in the east-facing windows of the south aisle.

Returning to the main road, continue to the left along Shernborne Road, past the primary school. After a further 2km or so through open fields, we reach ❸ **Shernborne**, passing the handsome **Shernborne Hall**, with Dutch-style gables, behind the farm on your left. Coming through the village, pass the church by the triangle on your left, and turn right, signposted Anmer.

From here, it's another 4km or so through undulating countryside, predominantly arable fields, to the quiet little village of ❹ **Anmer** (which is also on Route 1 (page 24), if you wanted to combine the two rides). The surrounding countryside is notable for its **Bronze Age burial mounds**, including several that we're about to pass. Leaving Anmer, carry on straight ahead at the crossroads with the B1153: look out for traffic. Crossing the Peddars Way again, notice three rounded mounds in the common on your right. About 3m high and overgrown with grass and bracken, these 'bowl barrow' burial mounds date from the Bronze Age, with nine in total dotted around here on Harpley Common. They have all been excavated long ago, producing fragments of pottery, bone and charcoal. Local lore claims that treasure remains buried here, which is why rabbits don't burrow in them. Treasure or not, it is the case that there aren't many rabbit burrows on the common (though in case you're thinking of bringing a trowel with you, they are protected scheduled monuments).

The woods on the other side of the road here also have historic importance: known as **Anmer Minque**, they were believed to have been the scene of a battle between Boudicca, queen of the Iceni, and the Romans (see box, page 36). Anmer village commemorates the battle with a Roman centurion depicted on one side of its sign, on the left as you come into the village. Continue along this straight road for another couple of kilometres, passing through arable fields. Several fields are bordered with wide bands of wildflowers, known as 'wildlife corridors' (see box, page 25).

At the end of the road, turn left at the T-junction and right soon after, to ❺ **Houghton**, with its neat rows of whitewashed cottages matching the gateway opposite to **Houghton Hall** (⌀ houghtonhall.com). Standing at the end of a long, tree-lined drive on the left, this Palladian mansion was built by the former prime minister, Sir Robert Walpole, in the 1720s. With bricks dismissed as inadequate and with no suitable stone available locally, Walpole spared no expense on his palatial home and transported stone all the way from North Yorkshire. Now the residence of the Marquess of Cholmondeley (direct descendant of Sir Robert), Houghton Hall is open to the public, with its exhibitions of contemporary sculpture and historic model soldiers. The surrounding parkland is also open to visitors, with a

herd of more than 1,000 deer, including rare white fallow deer, which you might see as you cycle past the perimeter of the grounds.

Turn left at the far corner of Houghton Park, on to an unmarked side road (Lime Kiln Lane), running slightly uphill alongside the park. Carry on straight, then left at the top of the road, in front of a red-brick farmhouse, on to Crow Lane. Follow this straight road for about 1km, back to Great Bircham. Join Lynn Road, continuing right at a narrow fork, leading shortly to the centre of the village.

↑ Houghton Hall (SuperStock)

THE ESSENTIALS

GETTING THERE By **car**, Great Bircham lies between Fakenham, 17.3km to the east via the A148 and B1454, and Hunstanton on the coast, just over 17km northwest via the A149 and B1454. By **bus**, the nearest service is the Lynx bus 21 from King's Lynn, just under 24km southwest, which takes around 35 minutes. The nearest mainline **train** station is also at King's Lynn, which is on the Great Northern Line, around 2 hours from London King's Cross.

BOUDICCA

Dubbed the Warrior Queen, for her AD60–61 uprising against the occupying Romans, Boudicca led the Iceni tribe into battle in woods known as Anmer Minque, just outside the village of Anmer, midway along this cycle route. When Boudicca's husband and former Iceni leader Prasutagus died, the Romans took over rule of the Iceni, a Celtic tribe based in East Anglia. Outraged by the Romans' subsequent torture of Boudicca, and their rape of her daughters, the Iceni rebelled. They inflicted widespread defeat of the Romans across much of southern England, including in present-day Colchester, London and St Albans. Thousands died, but the Iceni were eventually conquered by a Roman army led by governor Gaius Suetonius Paullinus. Boudicca is thought to have poisoned herself, rather than face capture; the site and date of her death, however, remain unknown.

Archaeological discoveries across East Anglia have included, most famously, the Anglo-Saxon burial ship at Sutton Hoo (page 147), as well as a Bronze Age timber circle, dubbed **Sea Henge**, off the Norfolk coast near Hunstanton. A major Iron Age and early Roman site named the 'Boudicca Temple' was also found in the outskirts of Thetford in 1973, with remains including a rich hoard of gold and silver jewellery. The finds are now in the Norwich Museum (⌖ museums.norfolk.gov.uk), which has a useful exhibition covering this fascinating period in East Anglian history.

Several museums across East Anglia have collections of Iceni and Roman artefacts from this fascinating period of the region's early history, including the Museum of Norwich and Sutton Hoo.

WHERE TO EAT

✕ Bircham Stores Great Bircham PE31 6RJ; ✆ 01485 576006; ❂ Bircham Stores & Cafe. A take-away deli, village store & café with a cosy walled garden, this one-stop-shop is open daily for b/fast, brunch & afternoon tea. Offering delicious freshly made food & using local ingredients, including Norfolk crab, seafood & salmon, plus wines, beers & smoothies. The chatty & friendly owner is full of local knowledge & tips. ££

✕ Bircham Windmill Tea Rooms & Gallery Great Bircham PE31 6SJ; ✆ 01485

578393; birchamwindmill.co.uk. This historic & beautifully restored windmill is a good stop-off for light lunches & cream teas, with freshly baked bread & cakes made from its stone-ground flour. **£**

The King's Head Hotel Great Bircham PE31 6RJ; 01485 578265; thekingsheadcountryhotel.co.uk. This restored Edwardian inn is now a boutique hotel & the only pub in the village, with an à la carte menu or good pub grub at the bar, including burgers, fish & chips & hearty sandwiches. It's also open early for b/fast. **£–££**

The King William IV Heacham Rd, Sedgeford PE36 5LU; 01485 571765; thekingwilliamsedgeford.co.uk. This lovely old country inn by the roadside at the western corner of this route loop serves above-average pub grub, with belly-busting favourites as well as 'light bites' & daily chef's specials. There are 4 separate dining areas, including a large back garden, handy for keeping an eye on your bike. **££**

FACILITIES AND FURTHER INFORMATION

The nearest toilets are in cafés and pubs en route, and also at Bircham Windmill and Houghton Hall. There is no car park in Great Bircham village, but plenty of roadside parking – there are also a few spaces in front of Bircham Stores on Lynn Road.

King's Lynn Tourist Information Centre Saturday Market Pl, King's Lynn PE30 5DQ; 01553 763044; visitnorfolk.co.uk. The main tourist office for northwest Norfolk, this walk-in centre provides details about local accommodation, activities, events & what's on where.

3 WELLS AND HOLKHAM LOOP

START/FINISH	Wells-next-the-Sea
DISTANCE/TIME	28.9km/2hrs (including 4km detour)
DIFFICULTY/TERRAIN	① Level or undulating, mostly on minor roads and about 25% off-road on gravel farm tracks and shared paths
SCENIC RATING	☺ AONB coastal dunes and wildfowl nature reserve, off-road trails and historic country estate, with a detour to an Iron Age fort
SUITABLE FOR	Sturdy hybrid with off-road tyres, gravel bike or similarly robust e-bike
NCN ROUTE	NCN1
MAPS	OS Explorer 251 (1:25 000)
KOMOOT REF	578980037

↑ Holkham's wide, stately avenues are perfect for easy riding (Holkham Estate)

WELLS AND HOLKHAM LOOP | CHAPTER 3

With its wide, sandy beach and wooded dunes sheltering Wells-next-the-Sea, Holkham Bay is one of Norfolk's most popular holiday destinations. On this short but diverse ride, we set off from the dunes, through the reeds and salt marshes of the Holkham Nature Reserve and across Holkham Hall's magnificent landscaped estate. Circling inland, we take a short detour to the remains of an Iron Age Fort at Warham then head back to the coast, bumping and bouncing along off-road cross-country trails.

THE ROUTE

Start from ❶ **Beach Road car park**, at the far end of Beach Road by the dunes. Follow NCN1/Norfolk Coast Path signs in the far corner of the car park along a flat, sandy track sheltered by a high bank of wooded dunes.

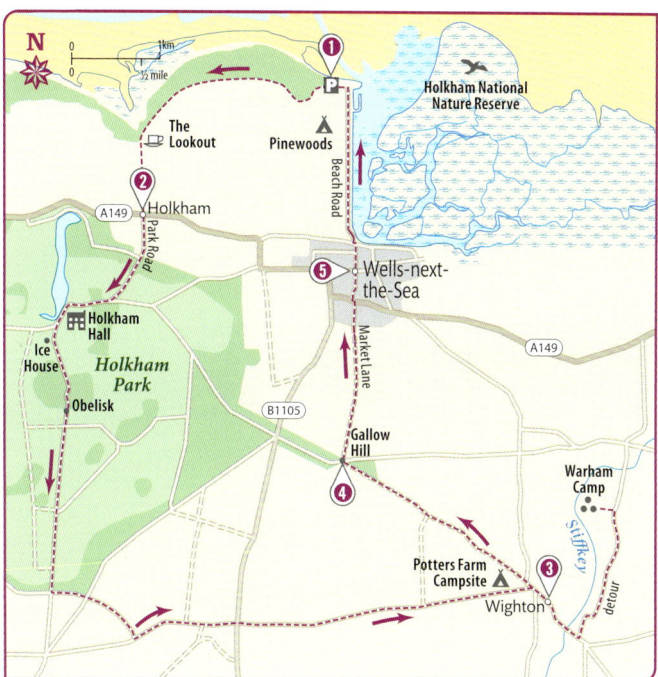

Go carefully on this loose sand and be considerate of others, looking out for holidaymakers crossing the dunes. As the path winds left inland, after a couple of kilometres, you come to a clearing and a car park. On your left is **The Lookout café**, which does what it says: looking out over the Holkham National Nature Reserve with footpaths into the reserve and bird hides, signposted opposite (see box, page 43).

Continuing left past the café, through the reed beds and marshes, we come to ❷ **Holkham**, a smartly groomed village, with matching brick cottages flanking the Holkham Estate. Carry on straight ahead at the crossroads with the A149 (watch out for traffic), past the Victoria Inn on the right and a Great War memorial on the left. The tree-lined Park Road leads up to **Holkham Hall** (⌀ holkham.co.uk): a magnificent 18th-century mansion built in Palladian style, by Thomas Coker, inspired by his travels in Italy. With its honey-coloured brick façade, the hall looks out over extensive landscaped grounds, with a deer park, ornamental lake and walled gardens. Today, the hall and its 10,000ha estate are privately owned by Coker's descendant, the Earl of Leicester. The grounds are free to visit

↑ Holkham National Nature Reserve is one of the largest reserves in England (Holkham Estate)

and the house is also open to the public, with magnificent marbled interior including classical artworks and sculptures. They also hire out bikes, with a network of paths around the estate, including our route on the NCN1.

Go through Holkham's grand wrought-iron gateway; humble cyclists have to dismount and walk in via the side entrance. Follow the wide, paved avenue around to the right of the house and past the lake on your right, with signposts for the South Gate (approx 4km). Keep alert for others here; although it is wide, it's a shared path and it gets busy here during holidays. The wide, stately avenue passes the thatch-roofed **Ice House** to the right, and goes up to the **Obelisk**. This towering limestone monument stands some 24m tall on the highest point in the estate, with superb views across the grounds. It was the estate's first project, completed in 1729 to mark the beginning of building works. Carry on straight past the Obelisk, rolling downward now to the South Gate exit.

Turn left out of the gate and on to a minor road running alongside Holkham's perimeter walls. Go straight ahead at the crossroads on the corner of the estate and left at the next junction (signposted Wighton

2 miles). Continue straight at the next crossroads and, after a few kilometres, down into ❸ **Wighton**, a little farming village by the River Stiffkey. As you come into the village, you can either continue on the main route back to the coast or take a short detour first to Warham Camp (page 44). Also, just to the south of Wighton, is the historic Anglican shrine of Walsingham Abbey, while nearby is the terminus of the Wells & Walsingham Light Railway, the steam train that runs from Wells down to Walsingham. It's about 4km from here to Little Walsingham, down Whey Curd Road (on the NCN1) on the other side of the village.

Otherwise, to continue on our main route, turn left at the triangle as you come into Wighton, following the NCN1 and passing Potters Farm Campsite (page 209) on your left. This return section of the route is off-road cross-country to the outskirts of Wells. It's traffic-free, apart from the occasional tractor; uphill at first, nothing that steep or tricky, but you'll be glad now if you've got MTB suspension and grippy tyres. The signpost here is also marked Rough Track. Actually, it's paved at first but after passing the cemetery on the right it certainly does get bumpy and flinty.

Carry on straight ahead at a wide clearing, where a side path goes left to disused farm buildings. Continue uphill for another 500m or so, coming to a crossroads between the trees, with the pretty red-brick Cuckoo Lodge on the right. This area is known as ❹ **Gallow Hill**, thought to be a former execution site, but there are no remains here now. Cycle carefully on the sharp flinty track, as I learned to my cost with a slashed back tyre – my only puncture on all 21 research rides! From here on, though, the trail finally levels off and slopes down towards the coast, back to Wells. You're rewarded here too with great views over the coastal dunes to the sea – punctuated here and there on the horizon with spiky ranks of wind turbines.

Keep on straight, now joining Market Lane, a narrow, grassy path. After approximately 200m, you reach the outskirts of ❺ **Wells-next-the-Sea**, as the path joins the paved road, passing Alderman Peel High School on your right. This last stretch of the route winds through the busy little town centre, including narrow alleys, so take it slowly and keep alert for other users. At the T-junction with Burnt Street, turn left then first right down Plummers Hill, an alleyway running alongside Buttlands, a smart

HOLKHAM NATIONAL NATURE RESERVE

Stretching from Burnham Norton in the west to Blakeney in the east, Holkham National Nature Reserve covers more than 3,700ha along the north coast, and is one of the largest nature reserves in England. With its wide, sandy beach, forested dunes and windswept marshes, it is also one of the most stunning stretches of coastline in the UK. Jointly managed by the Holkham Estate and Natural England, the reserve comprises a mix of natural and managed habitats, including pine-forested sand dunes, salt marshes, scrub and reclaimed grazing marsh. It is home to a rich array of flora and fauna, including many rare species. Birdlife is particularly abundant, with wildfowl, waders and seabirds, marsh harriers, kestrels and owls.

Cycling through the reserve, from Wells down to Holkham Hall and gardens, you'll pass the tall bank of dunes and cross the sheltered reeds and marshes that stretch to the east and west. If you want to break your journey and explore its secluded corners on foot, one of the best points of access is from The Lookout café, which we pass en route to Holkham, with footpaths allowing a circular route through the dunes. Follow the Norfolk Coast Path signs from here, leading westward to two viewing platforms: the first is around 200m along a boardwalk through the dunes and the other is another 250m further to the west, both giving magnificent panoramic views across the beach and around the bay. There are also two bird hides: the George Washington hide connects to the first viewing platform, and beyond that is the Joe Jordan hide – both hides provide great views southward over a pond and marshes towards the Holkham Estate. Note that access to the viewing platforms and hides is on foot only, as there are steps and areas of soft sand.

residential square with a couple of nice-looking pubs. Carry on straight across the square and over the staggered crossroads to Clubbs Lane. Continue ahead, then left and right along another narrow lane, Tunns Yard, finally coming out to a T-junction by the harbourside.

Turn left here, then immediately right up Beach Road, past the amusement arcade. In stark contrast to the off-road gravel trails behind us, we're in the heart of the seaside bustle now, passing the miniature railway and Pinewoods holiday camp (page 209) on your left, and finally back to the Beach Road car park. If the weather is fine and you feel like having a dip, there are paths across the dunes to the gloriously wide and sandy beach.

DETOUR: WARHAM CAMP

To visit this historic site, considered the finest Iron Age earthworks in East Anglia, continue through Wighton, passing the Carpenter's Arms on the left. Cross over the river, and take the first left, up a narrow lane, signposted Warham. After about 1km at the brow of the hill, turn left on to a side track. There's no signpost to the camp, just a notice on a gate by the roadside on the left. You can wheel your bike through here and along a grassy track leading after about 200m to another gate at the entrance to the camp. This second gate is locked, but with access on foot via a stile.

Lying in the middle of the field here is a large, rounded earthwork, about the size of a football pitch and some 5m tall, with two concentric moats. The camp was built by the Iceni tribe more than 2,000 years ago. Although it is called a fort, it is not known whether the site was used for military purposes, as a trading centre, or possibly both. Pottery unearthed in excavations here has been dated back to 200BC; Roman pottery has also been found nearby, suggesting they had used the site after the Iceni. With its hilltop setting by a bend in the River Stiffkey overlooking the surrounding, low-lying area, the fort must have had considerable defensive strength. Even today, standing on top of the overgrown mound, you can see for miles all around, including the coast, where more clusters of wind turbines can also be seen.

To continue on the main route, return to Wighton and follow the directions above.

THE ESSENTIALS

GETTING THERE By **car**, Wells-next-the-Sea is 47km northeast of King's Lynn, off the A148, via Flitcham, Great Bircham and Stanhoe, though it is probably quicker to continue eastward on the A148, turning north through

Cranmer and Egmere. Alternatively, it is 61km northwest of Norwich, via the A148 and B1454. By **bus**, the number 36 Coastliner from Fakenham takes just under half an hour. The nearest mainline **train** stations are at King's Lynn and Norwich, on the Great Northern Line from London King's Cross. King's Lynn is a slightly shorter route, at just under 2 hours, and Norwich about 2 hours 10 minutes.

WHERE TO EAT

Wells Crab House Seafood Restaurant 30–40 Freeman St, Wells-next-the-Sea NR23 1BA; 01328 710456; wellscrabhouse. co.uk. Highly rated for its seafood, this family-run little restaurant near the quayside specialises in locally sourced produce, from smoked eels to lobster & Brancaster oysters, plus steaks & veggie dishes. Very popular year-round, with booking ahead advisable; take-away also available. **££–£££**

Courtyard Café Holkham Hall, Wells-next-the-Sea NR23 1AB; 01328 713111; holkham.co.uk/stay-eat/courtyard-cafe. They offer a good selection of hot & cold snacks & drinks, salads, cakes & sandwiches in this casual café at Holkham Hall's main visitor centre, close to our cycle route. Indoor tables or outside in the courtyard. **£**

Three Horseshoes 69 The St, Warham NR23 1NL; 01328 710547; warhamhorseshoes.co.uk. This cosy 18th-century country inn just off the southeast corner of the route overlooks the green in the historic village of Warham, 1km north of Warham Camp, with its walled back garden very popular on sunny afternoons. The menu focuses on pub classics, particularly meat pies, puddings & Sun roasts plus a couple of veggie options. The bar stocks several local ales, including Woodforde's & Adnams, as well as a wine list including a decent selection available by the glass. **££**

FACILITIES AND FURTHER INFORMATION Public toilets are available in Wells-next-the-Sea, on Beach Road (by the playground) and at Holkham Hall.

Wells-next-the-Sea TIC Staithe St, Wells-next-the-Sea NR23 1AN; 01328 710885. Handy little centre in the town, around the corner from Wells Bike Hire, offering information on lots of local attractions, accommodation & booking for boat trips. Open seasonally; check the website for the latest opening hours.

4 CLEY LOOP

START/FINISH	Cley Marshes Nature Reserve
DISTANCE/TIME	26.3km/2½hrs
DIFFICULTY/TERRAIN	① All on minor back lanes or B-roads; level going or undulating, with a couple of moderate hills around Holt
SCENIC RATING	⑧ Coastal marshes and heath, Letheringsett Watermill, Holt Country Park and passing near to the North Norfolk Railway at High Kelling
SUITABLE FOR	Hybrid, road bike or e-bike
NCN ROUTE	NCN1
MAPS	OS Explorer 251 (1:25 000)
KOMOOT REF	491444217

↑ Cley's pretty windmill overlooks the River Glaven (Helen Hotson/S)

Tucked behind dense marshes on the north coast between Wells-next-the-Sea and Sheringham, Cley (pronounced *Cly*) is the starting point of our inland loop along the Glaven Valley through the Brecks: dry heathland that occurs across East Anglia. En route, we pass picturesque rural villages, including Glandford, with its quirky Shell Museum, and the historic watermill at Letheringsett, before winding north back to Cley, with its superb RSPB reserve, Georgian townhouses and converted windmill.

THE ROUTE

Start from the ❶ **NWT Cley Marshes Visitor Centre** just outside Cley. Turn left out of the reserve, on to the A149 coastal road to Cley; not as busy as some around here, but stay alert for traffic. Follow the High Street through ❷ **Cley-next-the-Sea** town centre. If you want a peek at **Cley Windmill**, turn right on to The Quay, where the High Street winds inland to the

CYCLING IN EAST ANGLIA | **THE ROUTES**

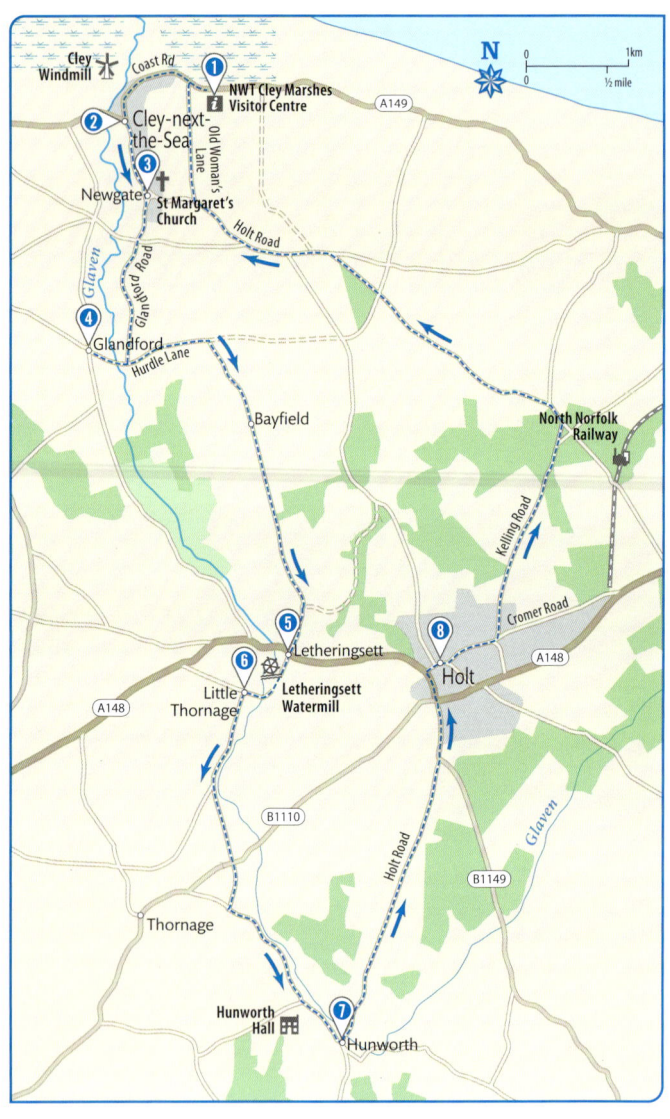

left. At the end of the road, with great views over the marshes to the sea, the Grade II-listed early 19th-century mill still has its sails but it is no longer used to grind flour. It has now been converted into a five-storey guesthouse (page 206).

Returning to the High Street, keep going to the right and at the junction where the coast road winds right, carry on straight ahead and on to Holt Road. Shortly after, you'll come to ❸ **Newgate**, with its pretty village green, overlooked by the Three Swallows pub on your left, and the Grade I-listed **St Margaret's Church** behind – one of the grandest medieval churches along the north coast, with a lofty nave and elaborate stone and stained-glass work. Go down the right-hand side of the green, heading south towards Glandford. Carry on ahead at the crossroads after 400m or so, following the course of the River Glaven on your right.

After about 1km you come to a T-junction, outside ❹ **Glandford**, a pretty little village worth a detour with a lovely old church, arty café (page 53) and the **Shell Museum** (⌀ shellmuseum.org.uk), with a huge natural history collection, including thousands of seashells as well as artworks and other fascinating bits and bobs.

Back on the main route, turn left at the T-junction of Glandford Road and Hurdle Lane, now joining the NCN30. After a long but moderate climb, the road levels out, then winds around to the right, and downhill through Bayfield into ❺ **Letheringsett**. At the staggered crossroads with the A148, go straight ahead. It's only a narrow two-lane road, but take care here – it's safer to get off and walk across, on to Riverside Road. Just after the crossroads, opposite a converted barn, a short lane on the right leads to **Letheringsett Watermill**, the only working watermill remaining in Norfolk. Watermills have stood here on the River Glaven since at least 1086, as first mentioned in the Domesday Book. The current, four-storey mill dates from 1802, and was comprehensively restored to working order in 1987. Today, it still grinds flour and also serves as the village shop, selling fresh produce, homemade cakes and pastries.

Back on Riverside Road, continue straight ahead; the road then turns right and over a ford across the River Glaven – usually too deep to cycle through safely – but there is an adjacent footbridge. A short way after the

NWT CLEY MARSHES

Apart from being an ideal hub for this cycle route, Cley Marshes is also a superb nature reserve: the oldest reserve, in fact, owned by the Norfolk Wildlife Trust, opened in 1926. With the addition of the Salthouse Reserve to the east in 2012, the combined site comprises 300ha of freshwater and saltwater marshes, reed beds, pools and water meadows, spanning the coast from the west to the east of Cley. It attracts a huge number of birds, including many rare breeding species, such as pied avocets, bitterns and marsh harriers, as well as exotic recent visitors, including spoonbills – now settling in the UK – and snow buntings. Besides birds, the reserve is rich with insects, plants, amphibians and sea life, including porpoises, with plenty to be seen here all year round.

Access to the reserve is directly across the road from the visitor centre, with footpaths leading through the tall reeds, pools and scrapes (shallow depressions often used by birds as feeding areas for their young). It has six bird hides, four of which are wheelchair-accessible via boardwalks, and a circular walk taking around 2 hours. The reserve also offers a range of guided walks, as well as special events and workshops at the Aspinall Centre behind the main visitor centre.

↑ Cley Marshes is a good place to spot pied avocets (Erni/S)

ford, turn left at the triangle by the little cluster of cottages in the hamlet of ❻ **Little Thornage**. Heading southwards again now, take the next left-hand turn at the fork signposted Hunworth and Briston, go straight ahead at the crossroads with the B1110, and left again at the T-junction.

After another couple of hundred metres, cross over another ford. There's only a narrow footbridge here, but this ford is much smaller than the last and safe to cycle through. Coming into ❼ **Hunworth**, follow the road around to the left, in front of **Hunworth Hall**, an early 18th-century country house, with a grand façade including six bay windows and pilastered doorway. The house itself is not open to the public, but it sometimes opens its gardens – renowned for their manicured, Dutch-style topiary – for open days in support of the Norfolk Churches Trust.

Turn left at the triangle, Hunworth's green, and out of the village, now heading back north towards Holt. This B-road winds uphill through the fields on quite a straight stretch for several kilometres. Coming into ❽ **Holt**, at the roundabout on the A148/Holt Bypass, cross over to the cycle/footpath on the right and go down an underpass: an otherwise gloomy tunnel, decorated with colourful artwork for the Holt Mural Project. Out of the tunnel, continue on the cycle path to the right, then join the Norwich Road. Turn right after around 200m on to the High Street, keeping alert for shoppers, traffic and parked cars in the town centre.

Holt is an attractive and lively little town, with some fine Georgian architecture lining its High Street, side alleys and courtyards. Most notably, as you turn left halfway along the High Street, is Byfords Café & Deli (page 53), which is thought to be Holt's oldest surviving building. With its decorative brick and flint façade, it has been immaculately preserved as a virtual living museum. At the T-junction, turn right on to Albert/Bull streets, past the defiantly non-Georgian Holt Vinyl Vault vintage record shop on your left: this former post office is now proudly labelled Punk Office.

Continue straight on Cromer Road and, after about 500m, turn left on to Kelling Road, leaving Holt and aiming north again through the fields. Continue straight for another couple of kilometres, turning left at the T-junction with Bridge Road. Carry on straight for another kilometre, ahead at a crossroads signposted Cley, then straight ahead at the fork soon after, signposted Kelling and Cley. The road winds right now through a little copse, signposted Cley/NCN30.

Approaching Cley again, we're treated to a nice downhill run back to the coast, after about half an hour of gentle climbs. Beyond the wide band of marshes, a sliver of sea is visible on the horizon, along with the glinting spikes of wind turbines offshore, seemingly omnipresent along this stretch of the north coast. Coming into Newgate, on the outskirts of Cley, turn right on to Old Woman's Lane, which diverts around the town centre. After another 1km, uphill and then down, you reach a T-junction back on Coast Road, behind the marshes. Turn right here – taking care crossing the traffic – and arrive after 200m or so back at the Cley Marshes NWT Visitor Centre.

THE ESSENTIALS

GETTING THERE By **car**, Cley is easily accessible either from Norwich (43km to the southeast) or King's Lynn (59km southwest). From Norwich, take the B1149 north, via Horsford and Saxthorpe, crossing over the A148 just before Holt. From King's Lynn, head north on the A148, turning left after 50km on to the B1156/Holt Road at Sharrington, and right again after 54km on to Blakeney Long Lane. By **bus**, it's a bit of a schlep, taking nearly 2 hours from Norwich, with a change of bus (44A/X44) to Cromer, then CH1 to Cley. From King's Lynn, it's worse: three buses also taking just under 2 hours, via Fakenham and Wells/Grove Road.

By **train**, the nearest mainline stations are at King's Lynn and Norwich, on the Great Northern Line from London King's Cross. King's Lynn is a slightly shorter route, at just under 2 hours, and Norwich is about 2 hours 10 minutes on a good day.

WHERE TO EAT Besides the cafés listed here, which are either on the route or close by, Cley has several good pubs and restaurants, as well as its renowned Smokehouse (cleysmokehouse.com), which is something of a foodie hotspot, with great charcuterie, cheeses, fish and pies. It's not cheap but it's excellent-quality food, predominantly locally sourced and sustainably resourced.

✖ **Cley Marshes Visitor Centre Café** Coast Rd, Cley-next-the-Sea NR25 7SA; ℘ 01263 740008; ⌖ norfolkwildlifetrust.org.uk. Besides its tasty snacks, cakes, soups & sandwiches, the best thing about this café is its open-air terrace, giving wide-open views over the marshes. **£**

✖ **Art Café** Manor Farm Barns, Glandford NR25 7PJ ℘ 01263 741711; ⌖ art-cafe. org. This great little vegetarian café is just off the cycle route in Glandford, around the corner from the Shell Museum. Apart from its delicious locally sourced food, open for b/fast, lunch & afternoon tea, it also brews great artisan coffee from beans roasted 'just over the farmyard', plus its gallery and shop features local artworks & an eclectic range of unusual objets d'art. At the time of writing, it's open Wed to Sun. **£**

✖ **Byfords Café & Deli** 1–3 Shirehall Plain, Holt NR25 6BG; ℘ 01263 711400; ⌖ byfords. org.uk/cafe. Housed in a beautifully preserved Georgian building, Byfords is an all-in-one café with indoor & outdoor tables, deli, B&B & self-catering apartment, right in the centre of town. It's open all day for b/fast, lunch, afternoon tea & dinner & specialises in great local produce, including Cley smoked fish, Norfolk sausages & cheeses. **££**

FACILITIES AND FURTHER INFORMATION

ℹ **NWT Cley Marshes Visitor Centre** Cley-next-the-Sea NR25 7SA; ℘ 01263 740008; ⌖ norfolkwildlifetrust.org.uk/home. In the absence of an official tourist information centre in Cley itself, the NWT is a great source of local information, with staff on hand upstairs in the bookshop, which sells a good range of guidebooks & maps, as well as a virtual murmuration of ornithological titles. Toilets on site.

5 NORTHERN BROADS: HICKLING TO HORSEY LOOP

START/FINISH	Hickling Broad Visitor Centre
DISTANCE/TIME	32.9km/3½hrs
DIFFICULTY/TERRAIN	① Virtually level the whole way, on minor backroads and a few short unpaved lanes
SCENIC RATING	⑧ NWT Hickling Broads Nature Reserve, coastal sand dunes, seal colony, Horsey Windpump, a huge Tudor barn and a rare medieval church
SUITABLE FOR	Hybrid, e-bike or road bike
NCN ROUTE	NCN30
MAPS	OS Explorer 40 (1:25 000)
KOMOOT REF	533447172

↑ Sunrise over Hickling Broad (SuperStock)

NORTHERN BROADS: HICKLING TO HORSEY LOOP | CHAPTER 5

Spanning the coastal hinterland between Great Yarmouth and Sea Palling, Norfolk's northern Broads are home to historic treasures, including a Tudor Great Barn, a windpump and a 13th-century church. The star attraction, though, is of course, the wildlife: in particular, the cranes at Hickling Broad NWT and the seals at Horsey Gap. Hickling, which comprises the Broads' largest expanse of open water, lies on the northern edge of the Broads National Park, one of the richest wildlife regions in the UK.

This out-and-back ride is all about exploring a peaceful corner of the Norfolk Broads, linking with nature trails, boat tours and beaches. The route winds through quiet rural backroads, all on the NCN30, so it's a relaxing ride to suit all abilities.

THE ROUTE

Starting from ❶ **NWT Hickling Broad**, turn left out of the visitor centre on to the rubbly, unpaved road, past the FAITH animal rescue centre on your left, and up to the T-junction with Stubb Road. Turn left here and follow this long, straight road all the way to another T-junction, with the Greyhound Inn on the right.

Turn right past the pub and go through ❷ **Hickling**. It's a pretty and peaceful village, with several thatched cottages along the main road and St Mary's Church surrounded by fields at the end on the right. Leaving Hickling, the flat lane winds through arable fields and towards the coast. Pass **Hickling Hall**, a grand manor house hidden behind high brick walls and sheltering pine trees on the left. Follow the road around to the right, signposted Sea Palling.

After about another 3km, you come to a T-junction, turning right here on to Stalham Road and heading towards ❸ **Sea Palling**. It's only about 1km to the sea from here, but the coast is lined by a tall bank of sand dunes. Coastal dunes are common along the Norfolk coast, all the way from Great Yarmouth to The Wash; they provide a range of important benefits to the landscape, not least as a natural barrier against erosion and flooding. Nevertheless, and despite defensive concrete walls being added alongside the dunes, this stretch of coastline has been wearing away at the rate of around 5m a year, for the last 30 years and more.

As one of the many coastal towns that are under threat from the forces of nature, Sea Palling is a typical example. If you want to take a short (200m)

detour here, turn left at the triangle and down Beach Road to the seafront, still on the NCN30. The road ends in a humpback hill across the dunes; beyond, the sandy beach stretches for miles north and south. Huge storms broke through the dunes here in 1954, killing seven people and washing away many houses. Since then, its sea wall has been reinforced with rock armour and huge quantities of sand added to the beach. Unsurprisingly, perhaps, given its ongoing battle with the elements, this is a low-key resort, with a few slightly forlorn cafés, a huddle of holiday chalets and an amusement arcade. For now, they're holding on in defiance, so come and see it while you can.

To continue on our route, return to the main road and turn left towards ❹ **Waxham**, a historic hamlet about 1km south of Sea Palling. Coming into the village, follow the road around to the right, in front of the huge, thatched barn that gave the village its name. Measuring 55m in length, it is the biggest barn in East Anglia. The Woodhouses, one of the wealthiest families in Waxham in Tudor times, built **Waxham Barn** as a manorial hall in around 1570. According to local lore, they had it constructed specifically to be a few feet longer than the former largest barn in the area, nearby in Paston, supposedly in order to assert their superiority. Having survived mostly undamaged for 300 years, after winter gales in 1987 destroyed much of the roof, the barn was bought by Norfolk County Council. It was

HICKLING'S CRANES

Common cranes (*Grus grus*) used to be native to the UK, but these tall, elegant birds became extinct 400 years ago. In 1979, however, a pair of cranes was spotted here on Hickling Broad, with a local farmer reporting the 'biggest bloody herons' he had ever seen. The delighted Norfolk Wildlife Trust jumped at the opportunity to welcome back the long-lost cranes and a careful breeding programme began nearby in Horsey. It was a slow process, however, and it wasn't until 2003 that cranes nested again at Hickling. Today, they are one of the iconic birds of the northern Broads. Although precise figures are not known, visitors to the NWT site have often reported as many as 50 gathered together in the undisturbed marshes.

Besides cranes, Hickling Broad is home to many other marsh birds, raptors and waders, also including the bittern (*Botaurus stellaris*), whose booming call can sometimes be heard through the dense reeds, though an actual sighting of this shy bird is a rare treat.

Ongoing work to encourage and protect all the wildlife here includes the building of more waterways through the marshes. The circuits of pathways through the reed beds and boat trips across the broad provide some of the best opportunities in Norfolk for birdwatching. For cyclists returning here after a day out on the road, sit, watch and listen to the wind rustling the reeds, alert to the echoing boom of a bittern or the reflection of a crane gliding over the water: sheer bliss!

repaired and restored in the 1990s, and is now a Grade I-listed building protected by the Norfolk Historic Buildings Trust. It's open during the week (free entry), unless under hire for a function. To make a short loop around the rest of the village – a derelict but peaceful little backwater, certainly in contrast to poor, battered Sea Palling – take the next turning on the left, Church Road. Follow it around to the left, past the crumbling St John's Church and the similarly abandoned Waxham Hall, until you return to the main Waxham Road.

Turn left, past Waxham Barn again, and carry on down the coast. After following the coastal road for another 3km or so, alongside sheep-grazing meadows, we come to ❺ **Horsey Gap**, an easily overlooked little spot, but one of the best sites for spotting seals along Norfolk's east coast. Turn left as the road bends to the right, down a rough track to the National Trust nature reserve, with a little food shack in the car park at the end of the lane. The gloriously soft, sandy dunes are a haven for a broad range

↑ Horsey Gap is well known for its resident seals (Kev Gregory/S)

of protected wildlife, including little terns, ringed plovers and nightjars, fritillary butterflies and natterjack toads. The show stealers, though, are the grey seals. Large numbers are regularly spotted here, bobbing offshore or on the sandy beach itself. Between November and March, in particular, hundreds of seals gather here, raising their pups. They're irresistibly cute but also extremely sensitive to human intrusion, so visitors are advised to keep their distance.

From the reserve, return to the main road and turn left. Pass Poppylands café (page 61) on your right, then wind right and left through ❻ **Horsey**. If you're as big a fan of old churches as I am, it's worth taking a short detour to Horsey's lovely old, thatch-roofed **All Saints Church**. It's down a little lane on the left after a couple of hundred metres on the way back from the windpump. With parts dating back 1,000 years or more, it's one of the region's more unusual churches, with an octagonal belfry. Inside, slightly musty and cobwebbed, is a charming gallery of old photographs and pictures; it's virtually a local museum, including drawings of barn owls and other birds that have nested in the tower over the years.

Shortly after the village, you'll come to **Horsey Windpump** on the right; with the mill's tall sails reflected in the side channel off Horsey Mere, it's a classic East Anglian scene. Now owned by the National Trust, the current mill was built in 1912, but records show that there have been mills here or nearby since the 1700s. It is open to the public, with 360° views from its upper tower over the Broads and the coast. There are footpaths and guided nature tours from here into the Broads and to the coast; there's also a little food shack by the waterside, and toilets. From here, we retrace our route back to Hickling.

THE ESSENTIALS

GETTING THERE By **car**, NWT Hickling Broad is about 4km from Stalham, off the A149 between Stalham and Caister-on-Sea. From Hickling village, follow the 'brown badger' signs to the reserve, via Stubb Road. It's not near any public transport service: the only options are the X6 or 704 **buses** from North Walsham to Hickling village, then to cycle from there (only fold-up bikes allowed on board).

↑ Horsey Windpump (Peter Kiernan/Broadland Cycle Hire)

WHERE TO EAT

The Greyhound Inn The Green, Hickling NR12 0YA; 01692 598306; greyhoundinn.com. On the junction of Stubb Rd leading to Hickling Green wildlife centre, this traditional country pub has a front terrace & a walled cottage garden behind. There's also an open fire on cold evenings. The bar stocks local & guest real ales & the menu features local produce (including Cromer crab in the summer), with hearty pub favourites, veggie options, lunchtime Sun roasts, snacks & sandwiches. **££**

Poppylands Tearoom Waxham Rd NR29 4EQ; 01493 393393; Poppylands. This quirky roadside café with outdoor tables between Horsey & Waxham Barns is embellished with an eccentric collection of 1940s memorabilia, including a mock-up lookout guard, vintage car & a craft room full of retro knick-knacks. The Ration Book menu is nostalgic too, with Blitz Breakfasts, Air Raid Sandwiches & even a Winston Churchill Toasted BLT. **£**

Nelson Head Horsey NR29 4AD; 01493 393378; thenelsonhead.com. This tiny old village inn overlooks the Broads just outside Horsey. With a garden across the road (or sit inside by the fireside snug), the bar stocks a good selection of local ales & ciders. The menu includes local pork & fish dishes, including beer-battered fish finger butty, steaks, burgers, salads & Posh Beans on Toast among a few veggie options. **££**

FACILITIES AND FURTHER INFORMATION There are toilets at NWT Hickling Broad, Horsey Windpump and in pubs and cafés en route.

NWT Hickling Broad Visitor Centre Stubb Rd, Hickling NR1 1RY; 01692 598276; norfolkwildlifetrust.org.uk. The nearest official tourist information centre to Hickling is quite a way from here in Great Yarmouth (01493 846346; great-yarmouth.co.uk), so your best bet is the visitor centre here in Hickling, run by friendly & knowledgeable staff who will help with local information – particularly, of course, anything related to the wildlife here on the Broads.

6 MARRIOTT'S WAY

START/FINISH	Outskirts of Norwich to Aylsham (Bure Valley Railway)
DISTANCE/TIME	30.8km/3hrs
DIFFICULTY/TERRAIN	① Mostly level or slightly downhill; mostly on unpaved cycle paths, with a few short road sections and minor junctions – ideal for families with older children
SCENIC RATING	⑧ Along the peaceful Wensum Valley, following the route of the former railway line, dotted with Victorian steam memorabilia
SUITABLE FOR	Hybrid bike with grippy tyres, gravel bike or sturdy e-bike
NCN ROUTE	NCN1 and NCN33
MAPS	OS Explorer 237 (1:25 000)
KOMOOT REF	496518955

↑ The Marriott's Way follows the tracks of the former Great Eastern and Midland and Great Northern railway lines (Visit Suffolk)

MARRIOTT'S WAY | **CHAPTER 6**

This off-road ride follows the tracks of the former Great Eastern and Midland and Great Northern railway lines, now a converted leisure trail between Norwich and the historic market town of Aylsham, through tunnels of trees, between arable fields speckled with poppies and cornflowers. Named after William Marriott, one of the leading railway engineers in the great Victorian steam era, the Marriott's Way winds northwards along the Wensum Valley, crossing the river several times over old railway bridges, before heading east to Aylsham. From here, either backtrack to Norwich or stop overnight before continuing the next day along the Bure Valley Path to Wroxham, gateway to the Norfolk Broads.

The trail is very popular with visitors, particularly here in the suburbs, so be alert to walkers, joggers, horseriders, Segway scooters and fellow cyclists. It's also worth noting, possibly for another day's activity, that the first part of the Marriott's Way, up to the crossing over the A1270 just north of Thorpe Marriott, is on the Walsingham Way (walsinghamway.blog), a 60km footpath from Norwich to Walsingham near the north coast. The route was launched in 2021, inspired by historic pilgrimage routes to the Shrine of Our Lady of Walsingham, dating from 1061 (see Route 4, page 46).

The Marriott's Way has been designated a protected county wildlife site, with the Wensum river valley a 'wildlife corridor', promoting the diversity of wildlife in the surrounding woodlands, water meadows and fens. The wide verges, cuttings and embankments, formerly cut back to keep the way clear for trains, are important habitats for a thriving array of wildflowers. Primroses, orchids, wild strawberries and wild roses are among around 100 plant varieties that flourish here. The lush vegetation provides a rich habitat for a variety of birds and animals. Among the more exotic but elusive species are otters, Chinese water deer and grass snakes. If you keep your eyes peeled, you might spot kingfishers darting over the water, kestrels hovering overhead, and hares bounding through the fields.

Look out too for reworked remnants of the former railway line. Dotted alongside the path are lengths of old rail tracks, sleepers and concrete blocks imaginatively turned into seats, hitching posts and sculptures. These public works of art include handy waymarkers alongside the benches every mile along the route; some sculpted pieces have been inscribed with poems and other words of wisdom. So, you can check your progress, have a rest and let literature inspire you to jump back in the saddle.

THE ROUTE

Start at the entrance to the Marriott's Way, on ❶ **Marl Pit Lane**, off the A1074 ring road roundabout on the western outskirts of Norwich. As

64 CYCLING IN EAST ANGLIA | THE ROUTES

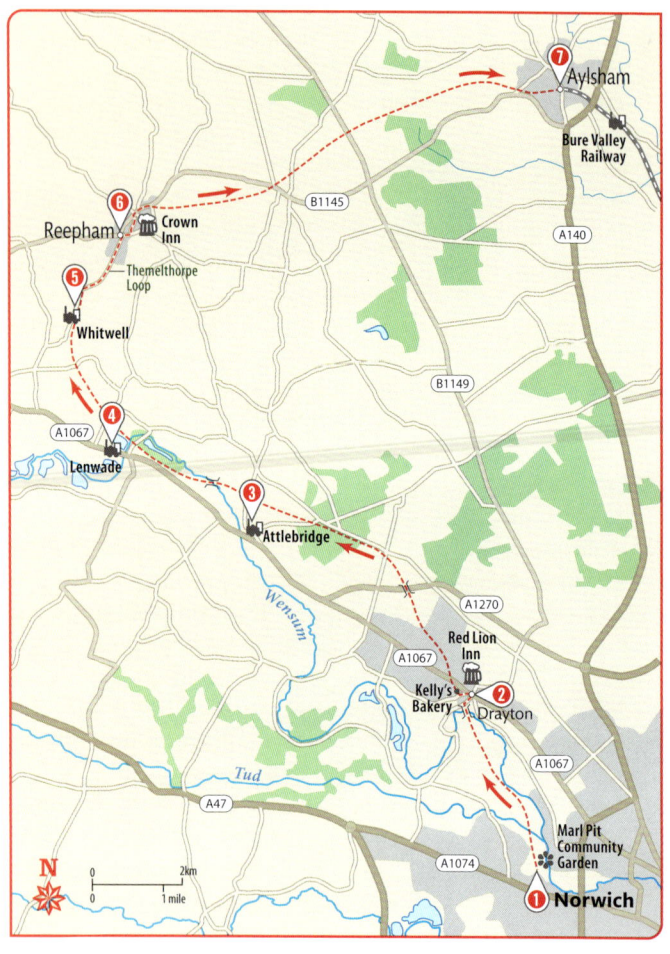

you join the path, on your right is the **Marl Pit Community Garden**, a sustainable gardening and environmental group, with Marriott's Way/NCN1 signs alongside to guide you on your way (the NCN1 is signposted from here to Reepham, where we join the NCN33 all the way to Aylsham).

Within a few minutes, we're out under the trees and into the countryside. For the first 6km or so the track is mostly a firm mix of sandy gravel, but in wetter weather and with the aforementioned tree cover it can get slippery, so go carefully, particularly on bends and inclines.

Leaving Norwich behind, the River Wensum can be glimpsed occasionally through the trees on your right. We also cross a small tributary, the River Tud, after about 1km; just beyond on the left is the Gunton Lane recreation area, which is a popular spot for paddling in the shallows and picnicking by the riverbank. The trail runs quite straight for this first stretch, under the shade of mature broadleaved trees, including oak, beech, chestnut and lime. After about 4km, we approach ❷ **Drayton**. The Wensum loops west across our path just before this suburban village, so we cross the river over an **A-frame railway bridge** – one of the few of its kind remaining in Norfolk, with its riveted iron struts and girders. The bridge surface is covered in rubberised matting which, despite a warning sign that it's unsuitable for cyclists, shouldn't cause any problem in dry weather, but could be slippery when wet.

Soon after the bridge, we zigzag down to Costessey Lane, on the outskirts of Drayton, turning right here and up to a T-junction, opposite the Red Lion Inn. Turn left and left again almost immediately, at the triangle, on to Taverham Road. A short way up this road, after Kelly's Bakery on the right, rejoin the path on the right – look out for the familiar NCN1 sign. Take care here too as the path descends a steep, rubbly slope back to the old railway line. A few hundred metres further on, the path crosses the A1067/Fakenham Road. There are traffic lights at the pedestrian crossing here, so it's safer to dismount to cross at the lights. From here, for another 5km or so, the path is more mud than gravel, particularly along the shady stretches under the trees. After rain it can get wet and mucky here, so you might have to walk in places. Between the trees the countryside opens up on both sides, with arable fields and meadows speckled with wildflowers, including the ubiquitous poppies, as well as blue bugloss and meadow crane's-bill.

After a further 1km there's a gated road crossing, so it's better to dismount here and walk across. Shortly after that we go over the A1270 on a new footbridge, after which the Walsingham Way diverts off to the

↑ Attlebridge station (Huw Hennessy)

left, followed soon after by another gated road crossing. There are quite a few more of these crossings en route – none are on major roads, but it's always worth checking before you cross any road and dismount if unsure, particularly if you're cycling with children.

About 3km after the A1270 crossing, we reach ❸ **Attlebridge**, a former station on the old Midland and Great Northern Line. The original station house has been converted into a private property and B&B, with a campsite behind (page 208). It has kept many of its original outdoor features, though, including the railway crossing gates and signals.

Turn right briefly on to the road here, then first left after about 100m to rejoin the path, back into open fields crossing the River Wensum again over a low bridge. A couple of kilometres past Attlebridge, the old station yard at ❹ **Lenwade** has been built over with industrial estates hidden behind trees and high walls. Emerging from this wooded cutting, we cross another railway bridge, and into a lush area of River Wensum flood meadows to the left and right. Some of these ponds are open to the public and others belong to the Angling Club. Besides the anglers' stocks of carp, pike and tench, these tranquil waterways are a great wildlife habitat, with otters, deer, kingfishers, wildfowl, owls and other birds, as well as butterflies and dragonflies.

A further 3.5km from Lenwade is ❺ **Whitwell**, the next former station that has been preserved along the line. The old Whitwell and Reepham Railway (⌀ whitwellstation.com) here has been lovingly maintained, with open days and steam rallies, and they're fundraising for ongoing work to restore and reopen the former line to Reepham, to run alongside the Marriott's Way. It's an unashamedly nostalgic site, with a fleet of vintage carriages and steam engines on display in the old station yard, as well as a railway museum, café and gift shop.

After Whitwell, the Marriott's Way route splits in two, with one route winding to the west, on the Themelthorpe Loop. This 8.5km section of the old railway joined two rival lines, the Midland and Great Northern with the Great Eastern Railway, for goods trains going from Norwich city to Norwich Thorpe station. However, we're taking the shorter route to Reepham here, avoiding what is quite a muddy stretch (we have had quite enough mud already!).

Leaving Whitwell and Reepham station, turn right on to the Whitwell Road. Pass a Camping and Caravanning Club site on your right and after about 1km you reach ❻ **Reepham**, an attractive old market town. Carry on straight into the town centre, along Whitwell Road, running into School Road and passing Reepham High School on your left. Turn right at the crossroads and into Market Place, Reepham's main square and historic centre, lined with Georgian townhouses, some of which are now shops – there's also a café/deli and a smart boutique hotel. Cross over the square and along Church Hill to Reepham's parish church, with a noticeboard proclaiming that it's 'Three Churches in one Churchyard'. There are in fact two complete and functioning churches within the walled grounds here: St Michael's and St Mary's are similar in age and size, with square towers and arched windows. Alongside St Michael's, a stump of wall is all that remains of an earlier church, All Saints. It was engulfed by a fire in 1543 and then demolished in 1796 but is still fondly preserved here, like an old tooth! St Mary's, dating probably from the 1200s, is now the town's main parish church, while the adjacent St Michael's is thought to have been built subsequently, in the late 1300s.

Go around Church Street, beside the churchyard wall, and up Ollands Road (next to a Spar convenience store on the corner), a quiet road

↑ Two for one: the churches of St Michael's and St Mary's, Reepham (Jules & Jenny/WC)

winding uphill out of town. Turn left by the junction with the Crown Inn on your right, then right at the T-junction with a Co-op opposite. A short way up this road (B1145) on the left is the old Reepham station. This is where the Themelthorpe Loop rejoins the main path, so if you want to check it out, it has a great little café, The Station Café (page 71) and a bike shop, adjacent in the station yard. Otherwise, continue along the B1145 for another 100m or so and, just after the turning on the left to Wood Dalling Road, turn right back on to the Marriott's Way. Look out here for the steep steps made out of old railway sleepers: there's only about a dozen steps but unless you're on a sturdy bike and bouncing with confidence, it's probably wiser and safer to get off and walk.

From here all the way to Aylsham (approx 10km), the way is straight and mostly through open countryside, under East Anglia's famously big skies. The Marriott's Way has joined a different National Cycle route now, the NCN33, and we're also on a different railway line, the Great Eastern. It's all off-road with just a few gated crossings over minor roads, so it's nice and relaxing cycling. This open landscape also offers better chances of spotting wildlife: not only songbirds, such as linnets and yellowhammers in the hedgerows, but also the glorious trill of skylarks high overhead, that classic anthem of the British summer countryside. Barn owls are also often seen here during daylight hours, surprisingly perhaps for a mainly nocturnal bird. Their flight is smooth and silent, so they're easy to miss, but there's no mistaking the pale round face and forward-staring eyes, as they skim low over the fields, alert for prey.

The path is firmer now too, with the exception of one short and narrow muddy stretch between hedgerows and trees after going under Cawston Bridge. The path soon widens out, and turns to firm pink and then grey gravel as you approach ❼ **Aylsham**. Here, the farmland gives way to residential suburbs, and you're more likely to come across dog walkers and others, so time to get back into urban alert mode. As you come into the town centre, the path joins the road by a mini-roundabout (with a Tesco superstore on the left). Cross over via the pedestrian crossing and follow the sign down to the right to the **Bure Valley Railway**

WILLIAM MARRIOTT

The man whose name was taken for the Marriott's Way, William Marriott (1857-1943) was an engineer and traffic manager of the Midland and Great Northern Joint Railway, the line that the converted off-road path follows from Norwich to Themelthorpe. A man of prodigious energy and versatility, Marriott worked at the railway for some 40 years, from 1884 until his retirement in 1924. During his remarkable and long-lasting career, he designed bridges, locomotives, mailbag collection devices and a whole host of engineering projects. He was born in Basel, Switzerland, where his father was an English professor at Basel University. Marriott subsequently became an orphan and moved to Bideford, Devon, and was educated both in England and abroad.

The William Marriott Museum in Holt station, north Norfolk (Cromer Rd, Holt NR25 6QA), where he also worked, houses artefacts of Marriott's many engineering works and other memorabilia of railway's great steam era. There is also a mile marker dedicated to him on the Marriott's Way at six miles, just after Thorpe Marriott. The plaque depicts a Number 45 locomotive steaming along the line towards Melton Constable: a fitting symbol for a true railwayman, often called the 'Father of the M&GN'.

(⌀bvrw.co.uk). There's a café here, and a car park, so it's a good place to end this route if you are getting a lift.

Alternatively, as mentioned in the introduction to this route, stop overnight in this pleasant old market town, then carry on the next day to Wroxham to explore the Broads. Bikes can be taken on the miniature train (subject to space availability; £3.50 charge per bike at the time of writing). Or, if you still have the energy in your legs you can cycle along the Bure Valley Path, which runs alongside the railway line for approximately 14km to Wroxham (⌀broads.co.uk/media/bure_valley_path_cycle_map.pdf).

THE ESSENTIALS

GETTING THERE By **car**, Norwich is 114km northeast of Cambridge, via the A11, or 190km from London, on the M11 and A11. By **train**, there are regular direct services from Cambridge, taking from about 1 hour 10 minutes, or around 2 hours from London, Liverpool Street station. Returning from Aylsham, Norwich is approximately 21km south, via the A140; by **bus**, the X44 is a regular, direct service, taking around 30 minutes. From Wroxham to Norwich, there are regular buses (12 Network Norwich), taking about half an hour, as well as direct trains, taking about 40 minutes.

WHERE TO EAT

The Sidings Café Whitwell & Reepham station, Whitwell Rd, Reepham NR10 4GA; 01603 871694; whitwellstation.com. This licensed café-restaurant at the station with indoor tables as well as an outdoor area among all the nostalgic railway carriages, next to the cycle path, serves full meals as well as snacks, pizzas, cakes, sandwiches, & hot & cold drinks. **£**

The Station Café Station Rd, Reepham NR10 4LJ; 01603 920707; Reepham Station Cafe. This popular café is just what its name says: housed in the old station on the outskirts of Reepham, right by the end of the Themelthorpe Loop of the Marriott's Way. There's seating inside the old station house, as well as outside tables on the platform & in the front station yard. They serve b/fasts, light lunches, burgers & salads, snacks, freshly baked cakes & pastries. **£**

Bread Source 13 Red Lion St, Aylsham NR11 6ER; 01263 733733; breadsource.co.uk. This great little artisan bakery is in the centre of Aylsham, about 5 mins by bike from the station. They bake a wide range of breads, as well as take-away cakes, pastries, buns, pizzas, sandwiches & freshly brewed coffee (closed Sun & Mon). **£**

FACILITIES AND FURTHER INFORMATION There are public toilets in Reepham and Aylsham, and facilities en route at the Red Lion pub in Drayton and Whitwell station. At the start of the route there's plenty of roadside parking nearby in residential streets, such as Hellesdon Road, opposite Marl Pit Lane.

Aylsham Heritage Centre Market Pl, Aylsham NR11 6EH; 07919 962814. As the tourist information centre in Norwich is now sadly closed, this local heritage centre has a good range of leaflets & other tourism literature & their staff are happy to help with enquiries (though they do not make accommodation bookings); alternatively, the **Bure Valley Railway** at Aylsham station (page 69) may also be able to provide useful tips & directions.

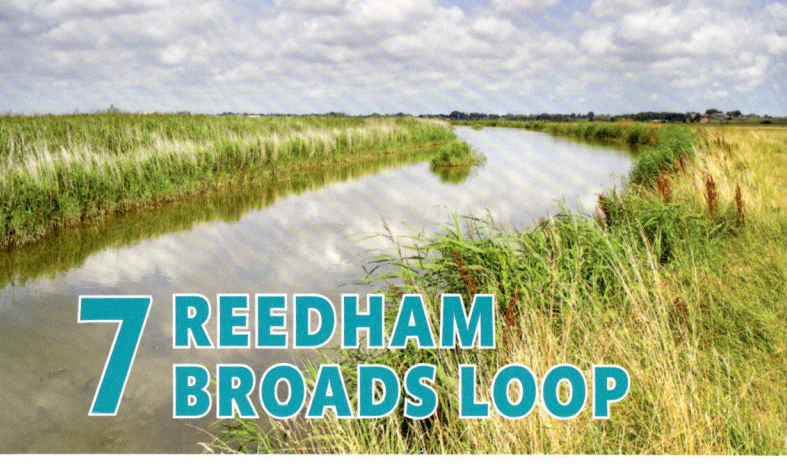

7 REEDHAM BROADS LOOP

START/FINISH	Reedham Ferry
DISTANCE/TIME	38.4km/4hrs (including 3km detour to Tunstall Church)
DIFFICULTY/TERRAIN	① All on minor roads and back lanes, mostly flat with a few short and moderate inclines
SCENIC RATING	Ⓐ Farmland, marshes and villages of the lower Yare Valley, historic rural churches and Reedham's riverfront overlooking the Broads
SUITABLE FOR	Hybrid, e-bike or road bike
NCN ROUTE	The nearest is NCN1, to the west
MAPS	OS Explorer OL40 (1:25 000)
KOMOOT REF	579480117

This leisurely loop through the Norfolk Broads could be subtitled the Holy Tour, for its angelic assembly of exquisite churches, particularly those of Moulton St Mary and Wickhampton, with their magnificent medieval murals. If that sounds a tad pious, though, for balance we also pass a couple of waterside pubs, an artisan brewery, and a family-friendly animal adventure park. Starting from Reedham, we set off clockwise from the north bank of the River Yare, through sleepy villages, including Limpenhoe, Freethorpe, Tunstall and Halvergate. Winding back via the hamlet of Wickhampton,

↑ The River Yare winds through the Broads (Steven Bramall/DT)

REEDHAM BROADS LOOP | CHAPTER 7 | 73

we return to Reedham's picturesque waterfront, with pleasure boats drifting across the horizon, through the Broads.

The route ties in with Route 8 (page 82), which explores the southern Broads, across the river via Reedham Ferry.

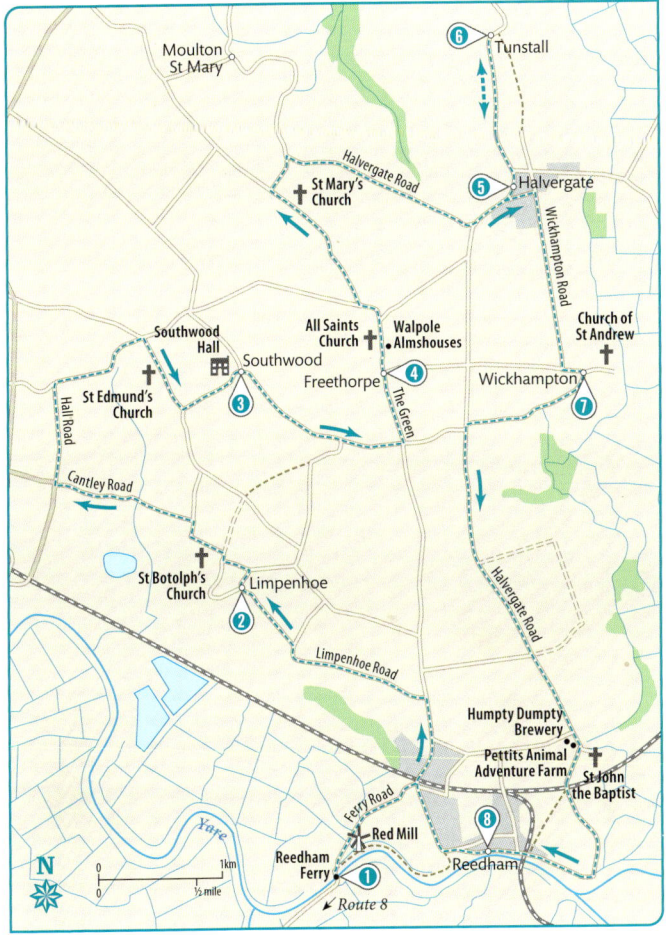

THE ROUTE

Start from ➊ **Reedham Ferry**, the only remaining chain ferry in operation in Norfolk, just outside Reedham village on the north bank of the River Yare. The short crossing here is also the only vehicular river crossing between Norwich and Great Yarmouth, which saves motorists on this virtual island in the Broads from having to make a long detour instead. There has been a ferry here since the 1770s, if not earlier: it was originally horse-powered or manually operated, with a diesel engine fitted only in 1950. The ferry runs daily from early till late; there is no need to book and it can carry up to three cars, plus bikes.

From the ferry, turn right past the Reedham Ferry Inn and across the grazing marshes towards Reedham station. With waterways lining both banks of the river here, waterbirds are plentiful too, with mallards, swans, and maybe a kingfisher, if you're quick enough to spot the flash of iridescent blue over the water. Overlooking the river on the right are the remains of the mid 19th-century **Red Mill**, a former drainage mill (see box, page 79). As with many windmills in the Broads, this mill is now a holiday home, shorn of its sails and painted black, despite its name.

↑ Reedham Ferry is the only remaining chain ferry in operation in Norfolk (SuperStock)

Coming to a junction on the outskirts of Reedham, after about 1km, carry on ahead, uphill and across Reedham railway bridge. After 800m, turn left on to Limpenhoe Road, through the fields for another kilometre or so, running into Reedham Road. Then, just after the winds to the right at a triangle in front of a farm, turn left towards ❷ **Limpenhoe**, still on Reedham Road. Going through the village, there's more wiggling to and fro, even more than the River Yare, which meanders just out of sight beyond the railway line on your left. But, like the river, you're also going roughly northwestwards. Firstly, the Reedham Road winds to the right at a little triangle, after around a further kilometre. Turn left at the T-junction a couple of hundred metres later, on to Freethorpe Road, next right on to Well Road for a short distance, then left at the next junction on to Church Road, through the centre of the quiet hamlet of Limpenhoe. There are no shops or pub here, just **St Botolph's Church**, standing in the grassy churchyard on the left. It seems quite a large and ornate church for such a small village but is a typical feature across this part of Norfolk, with lots of impressive churches in sleepy but formerly wealthy villages. St Botolph's was founded in the 11th century but today its only surviving Norman feature is the decorative stone doorway on the north side, now filled in.

Carry on past the church and, just after the road winds to the right, turn left on to Cantley Road. Continue straight for about 1km, then right at the crossroads, now heading northwards on Hall Road. At the next crossroads, after about another 1km by Manor Farm, turn right on to Cow Meadow Road, signposted Southwood. Turn right again at the next crossroads, then look out for a tiny footpath among the high hedgerows on your right after about 200m. Here, almost smothered between the trees, are the ruins of **St Edmund's**, a tiny, medieval church which was abandoned 150 years ago, when Southwood parish was merged with Limpenhoe. There's little of the original, thatch-roofed building visible now. It's almost completely enveloped in ivy and is dangerous to explore inside, through risk of falling stonework. But the tiny churchyard, with gravestones still tended, is a peaceful little lost world.

Back on the main road, continue right, then left at the triangle after 1km, leading up to ❸ **Southwood**. Turn right at the T-junction here, but

you might notice to the left **Southwood Hall**, a huge, Grade II-listed, 18th-century thatched barn now used for weddings and private functions.

Continue to the right and shortly we come to ❹ **Freethorpe**. Turn left at the T-junction on to The Green, the main road through the village. It's a pretty place, with several older buildings, including the **Walpole Almshouses**, a row of well-preserved Victorian almshouses a few hundred metres up The Green on the right, with a plaque stating that they were 'erected by Richard Henry and Harriet Vade-Walpole for the use of six poor widows of the parish of Freethorpe 1873'. The finest historical building in Freethorpe, however, is **All Saints Church**, a little further up the road on the left. Most of this lovely little church is medieval, possibly including its rare round tower, though much of the interior is Victorian reproduction.

Continuing north through the village, we join Reedham Road, towards **Moulton St Mary**. Before this village, though, another really special little church is tucked off the road about 1km beyond Freethorpe. On the right, down a rough track towards Manor Hall Farm, is **St Mary's Church**, on the left just before the farm. This tranquil church hidden amid farm meadows

↑ St Mary's Church just outside Moulton St Mary is a real historic treasure (Jim Laws/A)

is a historic gem. Its squat round tower with a conical rooftop is barely taller than the thatch-roofed nave. The real treasure, however, lies inside, with a stunning collection of wall paintings, some of which date from the 14th century. Remarkably preserved, the ochre and grey paintings depict St Christopher, the Ten Commandments and biblical scenes, titled the Seven Works of Mercy. Together with the wall paintings at Wickhampton, which we visit later on, these are some of the finest examples of medieval church art in the area, if not in the whole country.

Continue to the right up Reedham Road, which winds around to the right, then turn right before you reach the village of Moulton St Mary – carefully as this road can get busy – on to Halvergate Road. Carry on up this road, slightly uphill and through open meadows, until you reach ❺ **Halvergate**, turning left at the T-junction and through the village, with the tall, towered church of St Peter and St Paul on your left. This is another sleepy little village, with no shop or school and just one pub, the Red Lion, on the far side of the village, on the road to Great Yarmouth.

A worthwhile detour from here, particularly if you're into old churches, is to ❻ **Tunstall**, about 1.5km up the road. Pass the church on your left, keep left at the triangle, with a war memorial and village sign (note the medieval spellings on the back: Halfriate and Tunestalle), and straight ahead at the fork on to Tunstall Road, as the main road winds right on to Marsh Road. Keep going for about 1km until you come to the church nestled among the trees at the end of the road. The main nave of this 14th-century church is roofless and in ruins, but the inside chapel is opened for occasional services. It is usually locked, but there's a key at Manor Lodge, the second house on the right a couple of hundred metres back along the Halvergate Road.

From Tunstall, we begin looping back southwards to Reedham. So, firstly return to Halvergate, this time turning left at the triangle before the church, and right at the crossroads, on to Wickhampton Road. After about 1.5km on this narrow, tree-lined back lane, turn left at the T-junction, leading to ❼ **Wickhampton**, with its ancient **church of St Andrew**, which contains what may be even more impressive murals inside, including what look like dancing skeletons, depicting 'the three living and the three dead',

as well as St Christopher and the Seven Acts of Mercy. From the church, return to the junction by the Wickhampton village sign, turning left here on to Low Road, then left again at the T-junction on to Halvergate Road. This carries on straight and gently rolling through open fields, passing **Pettits Animal Adventure Park** on the left, followed by the **Humpty Dumpty Brewery** opposite: a combination likely to keep the whole family happy.

After the brewery, if you can stand one more church – worth it, I promise – take the left fork leading up a gravel path to **St John the Baptist**. The church dates back some 700 years, but sadly was gutted by fire in 1981. Since restored, it now features two stunning modern stained-glass windows, a rarity in this traditional region. The abstract, glowing blue and yellow designs possibly represent the church rising from the ashes, or Jesus's resurrection – or both!

From the church, take a narrow, unpaved footpath to the left, over a railway level crossing (dismount and walk your bike through the gates); take the left fork down a short but steep footpath (also safer to walk your bike down), leading to the pretty waterfront at ❽ **Reedham**, with a couple of pubs, post office, deli and tearoom. To return to the ferry crossing,

↑ St John the Baptist church features two spectacular modern stained-glass windows
(Alan Reed/A)

continue along the waterfront, turn right, following signs to the station, then turn left before the station, and back down Ferry Road.

THE ESSENTIALS

GETTING THERE Reedham lies between Norwich and Great Yarmouth, in the heart of the Broads. By **car**, it's just over 27km from Norwich, via the A47 and the B1140. By **train**, there's a regular direct service on greateranglia, taking around 20 minutes.

WINDMILLS OF THE BROADS

Asked to pick one identifying feature of East Anglia, most people would instantly say windmills. With their ribbed sails and conical towers, they stand out on the horizon as if floating across the area's equally iconic Broads.

When they were first introduced into the marshy wetlands of the Broads some 200 years ago, it was as drainage mills, or windpumps, to counter the repeated flooding that wiped out livestock, particularly sheep, which made East Anglia one of the wealthiest regions in England. By the mid 19th century there were some 400 windmills in Norfolk alone. With the Industrial Revolution replacing wind and water power with coal-fired steam engines, however, the mills rapidly declined.

Today, nevertheless, there are still thought to be around 60 mills of one sort or another still in Norfolk, including several around the Reedham area. Some have been converted into holiday homes, such as the Red Mill, near Reedham, mentioned above. Many are now protected as listed buildings and scheduled monuments, most notably the Berney Arms Windmill, considered one of Norfolk's best-surviving marsh windmills, just off this cycle route, on the Weavers' Way. The only way to get to this remote mill is on foot – either via a 5km walk across the marshes from Halvergate, or around 0.5km from Berney Arms request-stop station on the Norwich–Great Yarmouth Line. If you feel like giving your bike a break, a visit is highly recommended. At the time of writing, the mill was closed for maintenance works (see ⌀ english-heritage.org.uk/visit/places/berney-arms-windmill for updates).

WHERE TO EAT

✕ Reedham Ferry Inn Ferry Rd, Reedham NR13 3HA; 📞 01493 700429; 🖱 reedhamferry.co.uk. Part of a visitor complex comprising the Reedham Ferry opposite & adjacent campsite with its own fishing lakes (page 210), this popular family pub is well placed to cater for a whole range of visitors. Its restaurant looks out over the Broads & there are outdoor tables by the waterside, with great views of passing river traffic. The menu is traditional, good-quality pub grub, including 1 or 2 vegan dishes, homemade desserts & Sun roasts. The bar stocks local ales, including Woodforde's of Woodbastwick, as well as Reedham's own Humpty Dumpty Brewery. **££**

✕ Red Lion Inn Marsh Rd, Halvergate NR13 3QB; 📞 01493 700317; **f** The Red Lion Halvergate. This 18th-century thatched inn is a quiet & friendly traditional local, the only pub left in the equally tranquil Halvergate village. The bar stocks several local real ales, including Wolf, Humpty Dumpty & St Peter's, & the food is decent, no-frills, traditional pub grub. **£**

✕ Cannell's By The River Reedham; 📞 01508 520994; 🖱 cannellsfarmproduce.co.uk. This local farm shop, deli & patisserie has a couple of outdoor tables in front, right in the middle of Reedham's buzzy but laidback riverfront. Serving delicious homemade cakes, pastries, quiches, freshly made sandwiches & snacks, fresh coffee, tea & fruit juices, you can eat in or take away – all produce is very reasonably priced. **£**

FACILITIES AND FURTHER INFORMATION
The only public toilets en route are in Reedham station.

ℹ Broads National Park Reedham Quay, Reedham NR13 3TE; 📞 01493 701867; 🖱 broads-authority.gov.uk. This tiny kiosk on Reedham's riverfront, opposite the post office, is mostly geared up for holidaymakers on boats. They're also knowledgeable about the whole Broads area, with a selection of leaflets available too (open Easter–end Oct daily).

JOIN
THE TRAVEL CLUB

THE MEMBERSHIP CLUB FOR SERIOUS TRAVELLERS
FROM BRADT GUIDES

Be inspired
Free books and our monthly
e-zine, packed with travel tips
and inspiration

Save money
Exclusive offers and special
discounts from our favourite
travel brands

Plan the trip
of a lifetime
Access our exclusive concierge
service and have a bespoke
itinerary created for you
by a Bradt author

Join here:
bradtguides.com/travelclub

Membership levels to suit all budgets

Bradt GUIDES

TRAVEL TAKEN SERIOUSLY

8 SOUTHERN BROADS LOOP

SOUTHERN BROADS LOOP | CHAPTER 8

START/FINISH	Reedham Ferry
DISTANCE/TIME	34.7km/4hrs
DIFFICULTY/TERRAIN	② Paved road, mostly flat with a few moderate dips and climbs; mostly on quiet, traffic-free country lanes, largely following NCN routes; a couple of busy A-road crossings, including one over the A143 via a footbridge
SCENIC RATING	⑧ Peaceful Broads waterways and farmland, lovely old churches, windmills and historic stately gardens
SUITABLE FOR	Hybrid, e-bike or road bike
NCN ROUTE	Partly on NCN1, 30 and 31
MAPS	OS Explorer 40 (1:25 000)
KOMOOT REF	580361816

Similar to Route 7, this circular route south of Reedham winds around sleepy rural villages and down to the River Waveney, on the Suffolk border. From Reedham, we go through the elegant market town of Loddon, on to the riverside villages of Ellingham and Geldeston, then back north via stately Raveningham Hall, with its historic vegetable gardens and remodelled 18th-century park. Also like the Reedham route, we manage to fit in a few historic churches en route too.

THE ROUTE

Start from ❶ **Reedham Ferry** on the north bank of the River Yare, taking the chain ferry across the narrow river crossing. Carry on down Low Road, keeping your eyes peeled for wildlife here in these riverside meadows. Deer and hares are quite common, but birds in particular love the marshes, from clouds of croaking rooks to leggy herons stalking along the riverbanks. Or even surprise nocturnal predators: on my early morning ride here last summer, I was stunned when a creamy white barn owl suddenly appeared just feet in front of me, wheeling to and fro across the road, silently flapping its long wings as it skimmed low over the fields.

← Loddon, on the banks of the River Chet (Alun John/A)

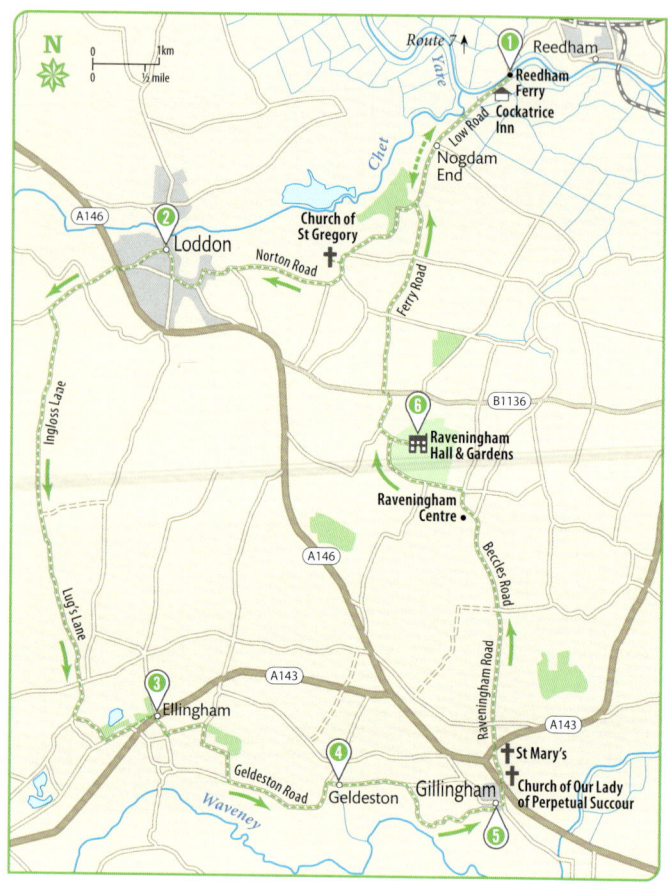

After about 300m, pass the old Cockatrice Inn on your left, now a B&B but still with the former pub's stained-glass window. Shortly after that, by the little triangle in Nogdam End, carry on straight ahead, now on Ferry Road. Turn right at the fork, about 800m later, signposted Loddon and right again at the next unmarked fork, downhill. Just as the road winds to the left, take a short detour to the right for about 100m along a rough farm track, leading to the **Church of St Gregory**, Heckingham. Standing on a grassy rise overlooking the River Chet, this cute little thatch-roofed Norman church has an unusual octagonal tower, and its arched doorway is embellished with stunning carved motifs.

Returning to the main road, turn right after a couple of hundred metres to rejoin Norton Road, then carry on for about another 3km, mostly downhill and winding to the right, leading into ❷ **Loddon**. This handsome town on the banks of the River Chet has a handful of Georgian townhouses lining its High Street, and main square, including the former Town Hall, now a hair salon. It's a bustling old market town, now largely a commuter hub for nearby urban centres. It's also popular with visitors, for access to the Broads from its 'staithe' moorings and for its watermill, now used as a well-being centre. To get to the waterfront and watermill, it's only a short detour: continue along the High Street, past the square and down Bridge Street, which crosses the River Chet after a few hundred metres, with the mill on your left and the marina on the right.

Otherwise, turn left off Bridge Street on to George Lane (NCN31), leading out of town and up to the A146. Cross this busy road – with

↑ The Norman Church of St Gregory has an unusual octagonal tower (Richard Hayman/S)

care! It's only a right–left wiggle around this dog-leg crossroads on to Mundham Road opposite, and there's a shortcut path across the corner of the A-road, so you can avoid the traffic to turn left here. Follow this quiet farm lane for about 1km, through poppy-fringed fields, then left up Ingloss Lane (now joining the NCN1), and straight ahead, continuing southwards into Lug's Lane.

Eventually, after about a 5km gloriously long stretch through wide and rolling countryside, we cross Rectory Road at another dog-leg crossroads, this time left then right on to Loddon Road. Take the next left on to Home Farm Road and left again at a T-junction on to Old Yarmouth Road, coming into ❸ **Ellingham**, another largely commuter town by the River Waveney, one of the three main rivers feeding the Norfolk Broads (besides the Yare and the Bure). As the road bends right, take the shared cycle/footpath on the left which cuts alongside the A143, then crosses it after a few hundred metres. There's a traffic island in the middle of the road, but it's safer to dismount and walk across this busy road, continuing left on to Church Road through the suburbs.

After about 300m take the first left on to Mill Road, then the second right after about 600m on to Mill Lane, signposted Geldeston and Gillingham. As Mill Lane bends right, it carries on as Braces Lane, which shortly comes to a T-junction (back on to the NCN1), winding along Geldeston Road and Station Road to ❹ **Geldeston**, another quiet little village by the River Waveney. Coming into the village, pass Locks Lane on the right leading to the waterside Locks Inn community pub and Three Rivers Pitch and Paddle boat hire (⌀ threeriversboathire.co.uk), turn right at the crossroads on to The Street (still on the NCN1), past the Wherry Inn on the left, opposite the village hall – two lovely age-worn, rural buildings.

Pass the Dunburgh Farm Shop & Café on the right and soon after, take the right fork along Dunburgh Road, leading into King's Dam, which bends left and up to a T-junction. Turn right here, then left at the crossroads, on to Loddon Road towards ❺ **Gillingham** (back on to the NCN31). A couple of hundred metres up the road, before you reach the A146, turn left up Kenyon Row, then immediately right along Forge Grove, through the modern housing estate, leading to a tiny footpath between the trees at the end of the cul-de-sac (signposted NCN31) on to a footbridge – this time thankfully crossing over another *very* busy A-road!

Follow the footpath down to the left, past the **Church of Our Lady of Perpetual Succour** on your right. This twin-towered Catholic church looks like it would be more at home overlooking a Mediterranean piazza than here on this leafy lane. It's a privately owned 'Chapel of Ease', built in 1898 by the Kenyon family of nearby Gillingham Hall, and is only open for Sunday morning mass. As if one grand church in this secluded nook

THE BROADS NATIONAL PARK

Spanning some 300km² across Norfolk and Suffolk, the Broads boast the greatest biodiversity of all of the UK's national parks, with 28 designated Sites of Special Scientific Interest (SSSIs) among its fens, woodlands and coastal dunes. It became a national park only in 1988, but now receives nearly 8 million visitors a year, making it the country's fourth most popular national park.

The Broads' waterways attract a huge number of visitors on pleasure boat holidays. Kayaking and surfing are also available for those looking for something more energetic. There are also plenty of land-based family-friendly attractions on offer, including BeWILDerwood, near Wroxham, Pleasurewood Hills theme park near Lowestoft and the Dinosaur Adventure in Lenwade. And not to forget, of course, its quiet back lanes and NCN National Cycling routes – ideal for cyclists.

For a more tranquil wildlife-watching experience, though, there are many nature reserves, including Hickling Broad (page 57), Horsey (page 59), Ranworth Broad and Strumpshaw. With secluded bird hides, pathways and boardwalks, these superb natural havens offer the chance of encountering rare species – from bitterns and water voles to swallowtails, Britain's rarest butterfly, found only in Norfolk. For its wealth of wildlife, the Broads is worth visiting year-round – from migrant birds in spring and autumn, to nightjars churring on heathland on warm summer nights, to newly born seal pups coming ashore at Horsey throughout the coldest winter months.

For more information, check out ⊘ visitthebroads.co.uk.

wasn't enough, adjacent is Gillingham's parish church of **St Mary's**, mostly a 19th-century restoration of the 12th-century original. Next to that are the ruins of the 15th-century **All Saints Church**, with Commonwealth War Graves in its churchyard. And yes, that's us done for churches today.

Follow the cycle path for around 200m through the trees and coming also to our last busy road crossing. It's the A143 again, and still very busy, so walk across and rejoin the cycle path continuing on the other side, winding right and immediately left on to Raveningham Road. Follow this road for several kilometres through the fields, then left at a narrow fork (still on the NCN31). A short way up Beccles Road on the left is the **Raveningham Centre**, part of the Raveningham Estate. This vintage bric-a-brac emporium and café (page 90) is scattered around a barnyard

↑ Raveningham Hall dates to the mid 1700s (John Fielding)

and duck pond. It's a wonderfully eccentric spot, completely unexpected here in the middle of nowhere, but altogether a perfect pit-stop after the previous long empty stretch.

Continue left out of the Raveningham Centre, then left again shortly at a crossroads, still on Beccles Road, winding around to the right and coming to the entrance on the right to ❻ **Raveningham Hall & Gardens** (⌖ raveningham.com). The hall dates from the mid 18th century and is a Grade II-listed building, home to the family of Sir Nicholas Bacon, descendants of the Elizabethan statesman Sir Francis Bacon (1561–1626). The extensive estate is run as a working farm: mostly crops but also with cattle and sheep. The gardens are open, usually from spring to autumn, with Victorian kitchen gardens, as well as an arboretum and lake, and not forgetting its tearoom, although this is only open to visitors to the gardens (admission £5/free adults/under 16s).

From Raveningham, continue right up Beccles Road, to a T-junction with Yarmouth Road. This is only a B-road but cycle carefully for the short zigzag left and then immediately right up Ferry Road (still on the NCN31). After a couple more kilometres, we come back to the crossroads with Loddon/Norton Road we passed earlier en route to Loddon. Continue straight ahead, moderately uphill, returning soon to Reedham Ferry. There's no set timetable for the ferry, but it will soon float across if it's not already on the south bank of the river. Nothing is rushed here on the Broads, though. And while you're waiting, who knows – maybe you'll spot an owl, hovering over the marshes on its dusk hunt for prey.

THE ESSENTIALS

GETTING THERE Reedham lies between Norwich and Great Yarmouth, in the heart of the Broads. By **car**, it's just over 27km from Norwich, via the A47 and the B1140. By **train**, there's a regular direct service on greateranglia, taking around 20 minutes. The Reedham Ferry (reedhamferry.co.uk/chain-ferry) across the River Yare runs daily from early till 22.00; single fares, at time of writing: £1 pedestrian with cycle; £4.50 car.

WHERE TO EAT

The Terrace 2 Church Plain, Loddon NR14 6EX; 01508 521932; theterraceatloddon.co.uk. Housed in a former bank, with a garden & terrace overlooking the town square, this hip café-bistro serves b/fast, lunches & light teas. They serve hot & cold snacks, salads, jacket potatoes & sandwiches, including several options for vegans & special dietary needs. **££**

Locks Inn Locks Ln, Geldeston NR34 0HW; 01508 830033; thelocksinn.com. This welcoming local community-run pub in Geldeston has an idyllic setting by the banks of the Waveney, serving local ales & good honest pub grub, including burgers (meat or vegan), pasta & sandwiches. They also do occasional live music nights & storytelling in their riverside beer garden. **£**

The Ravenous Café Raveningham Centre, Beccles Rd NR14 6NU; 01508 243104; The Ravenous Café. Inside this rambling emporium of vintage rugs, second-hand clothing & assorted bric-a-brac around the corner from Raveningham Gardens, this ace little café serves delicious homemade cakes, snacks, salads & sandwiches, with outdoor tables in the yard, next to the duck pond. £

FACILITIES AND FURTHER INFORMATION There are public toilets in Loddon, by the riverside just off Bridge Street. It's more practical to start on the north side of the river, as there's a pub (Reedham Ferry Inn), campsite and more parking space here, but no such amenities on the other side (except for a small car park).

Norfolk Broads Information Centre Beccles Library, Blyburgate, Beccles NR34 9TB; 01502 523442; broads-authority. gov.uk. This is the nearest information centre, just south of Gillingham, in Suffolk, with a selection of guidebooks & maps for sale, plus leaflets & local information. There is also an information kiosk on Reedham waterfront, via the Reedham Ferry.

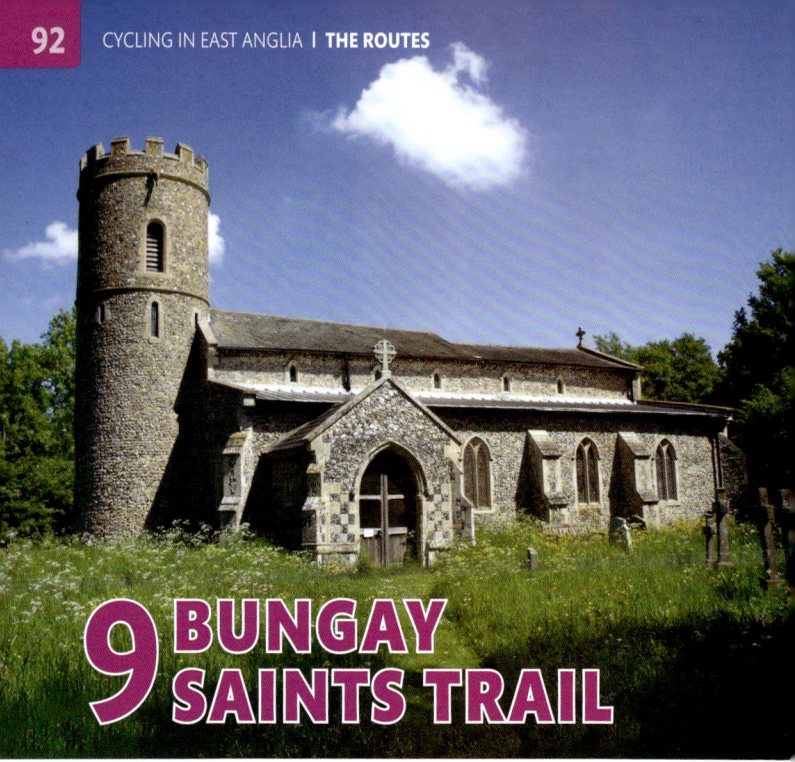

9 BUNGAY SAINTS TRAIL

START/FINISH	Bungay
DISTANCE/TIME	32.5km/3½hrs
DIFFICULTY/TERRAIN	② On quiet country lanes and B-roads, level or undulating, no busy junctions
SCENIC RATING	⑧ Ancient Bungay, market town; historical churches in isolated hamlets amid rolling farmland, and a wonderful World War II air museum
SUITABLE FOR	Road bike, hybrid or e-bike
NCN ROUTE	Between the NCN30 to the north and NCN1 to the east
MAPS	OS Explorer 231 (1:25 000)
KOMOOT REF	583376035

↑ All Saints Church, South Elmham – one of 12 medieval churches in this region known as 'The Saints' (David from Colorado Springs/WC)

BUNGAY SAINTS TRAIL | **CHAPTER 9**

This rural route through the heart of north Suffolk visits eight of the 12 medieval churches known collectively as 'The Saints', which lie between Bungay and Halesworth. From Bungay, we loop south to Ilketshall and Elmham (which between them give their names to all the Saints), then back via the aviation museum outside Flixton.

As you may discover for yourself, the route is quite fiddly in parts. Some of the Saints churches are hidden down isolated cul-de-sacs or side lanes, now cut off from their nearest villages, which have drifted away over the years. Directions for the short detours are included so you can visit all of these historic churches, or keep to the main trail if you simply want to enjoy the wide-open countryside, under the vast Suffolk skies.

THE ROUTE

Start from Priory Lane car park in the centre of ❶ **Bungay.** Nestled inside a loop of the River Waveney, this lively little market town dates back to Roman days, but also has a vibrant modern cultural scene, with several galleries, an arts centre and theatre. Turn left out of the car park down Priory Lane and right at the T-junction, on to St Mary's Street. It's a one-way road going the other way here, but only for around 50m, so walk your bike along the pavement, leading to the right fork with Upper Olland Street, which takes us out of town. Carry on downhill, past shops and suburbs, and at the foot of the hill carry on straight ahead, as the road runs into Flixton Road (B1435). Note a windmill on your left, at the end of Southend Road, now sailless and converted into a private house. At the crossroads shortly after the windmill, continue ahead on to St Margaret's Road, taking care crossing the B1062. The road winds gently uphill, through a tunnel of trees and then levels out at the top as we emerge into open countryside.

Carry on straight ahead at the next junction, after about 1km, signposted St Margaret's (with a little yellow Saints Trail church symbol on the signpost). Pass the handsome red-brick Elm Farm on your left, bordered by arable fields. At the T-junction shortly after Elm Farm, turn left on to Low Street to see our first Saints church: ❷ **St Margaret**, set back from the road on the right on the way into the village of Ilketshall St Margaret. This beautiful church dates from the 11th century, with a round tower and fine stonework around arched windows, though much of what we see today

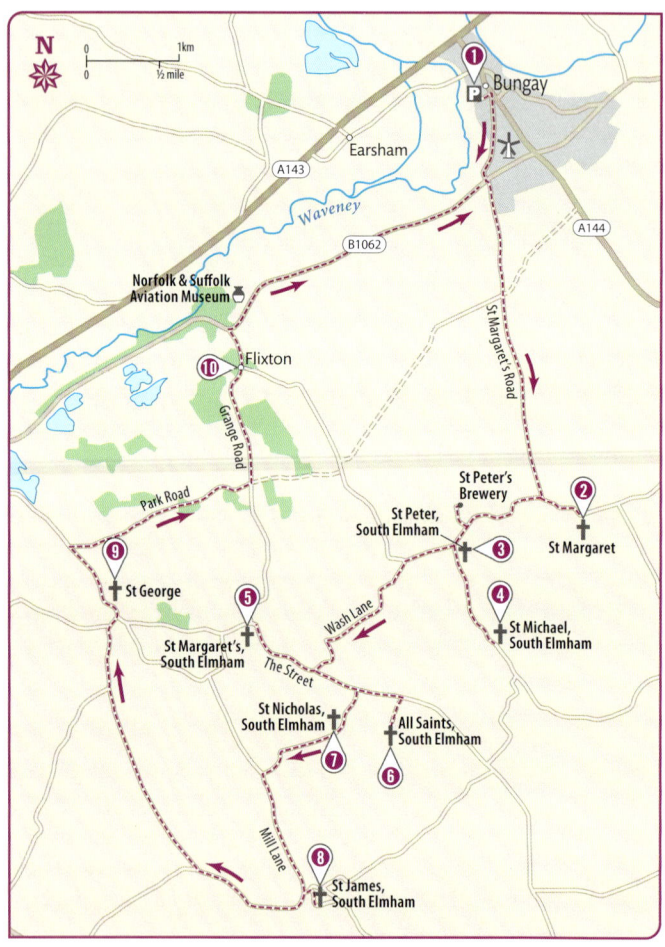

inside and out has been restored. The village itself, just beyond, is a hamlet with a few farm cottages clustered around the village hall.

Back to the T-junction, continue straight ahead, westwards towards the Elmhams. Pass the lovely pink-washed, thatched Charity Cottage on your right and a little further on the right is the entrance to **St Peter's Brewery** (⌖ stpetersbrewery.co.uk), one of Suffolk's best-known craft breweries. Whether you like your real ale or not, it's worth a peek even if only for its impressive 13th-century Great Hall in front. Today, the moated St Peter's Hall is a restaurant and function venue; the brewery also run tours, which shed more light on its long history (not to mention beer tasting too).

Just after the brewery, we come to a fork leading left to our next couple of churches, both in tiny hamlets of the same name: first, just around the corner on the left, is the cute little ❸ **St Peter, South Elmham**. With its crenelated square tower, this solid little church, with parts dating from the 13th and 14th centuries, looks over one of the smallest parishes in East Anglia, with a scattering of half a dozen or so houses between here and the stream at the bottom of the road. Carry on down the same road for about 1km, coming next to ❹ **St Michael, South Elmham**: the elegant 14th-century church has a homely, red-brick floored interior and is tucked away down a gravel track on the left, amid fields. Its hamlet has the poignant unique status as Suffolk's only 'Thankful Village' – no soldier from here was killed in World War I (there are only 32 such villages in the whole of the UK). If you felt like having a rest here, though, a message on the sundial outside wards off any such behaviour: 'Why stand gazing? Be About Your Business!'

Duly admonished, return to the fork, and turn left on to Wash Lane, signposted Flixton and Homersfield. Follow this winding lane through the fields, over a couple of streams and, finally coming to a triangle, between two more Saints: All Saints, South Elmham, out on its own in the empty countryside off to the left; and St Margaret's, South Elmham, on the right in the village of the same name. Both of these churches are optional detours off our main route, which heads further south between them. This is where it gets fiddly! Hopefully, at least to tackle each of these in some semblance of logical order, firstly we head to the right along The Street and into ❺ **St Margaret's, South Elmham**. One of only three Saints with what looks and feels like a real village, St Margaret's has a pretty wrought-iron village sign, on a narrow ribbon of green on the left in front of the village hall. A row of farm cottages stand face to face alongside, as if for solidarity. As

↑ A 19th-century stained-glass window in the church of St Margaret's, South Elmham (geogphotos/A)

with all the other Saints, there's no pub or shop here, but like many other villages around the whole country, there is a phone box on the right as you come into the village that now serves as a free exchange bookstall.

Back on the route, return through the village and past the triangle where we turned off earlier. About 1km further along the road, take the second turning on the right, leading shortly to ❻ **All Saints Church, South Elmham**. The smallest of the Saints and hidden behind tall trees off the end of a tiny lane, this is one of the pick of the bunch, particularly for its peaceful setting here among the fields. With a round tower and more flint cladding, All Saints is another Victorian restoration. Nevertheless, there are some stunning details of its medieval origins that are worth exploring. Look out in particular for the stained-glass depictions of saints Ursula and Dorothy, the font and the carved bench adjacent. There's little else nearby to keep this lonely church company today, apart from a farm and a holiday-home barn, but it is remarkably well preserved.

Returning towards the triangle once more, take the first turning to the left, then, after heading south for about 500m, we reach ❼ **St Nicholas, South Elmham**. In case you have lost count: six Saints done, two to go! After a few hundred metres we pass through St Nicholas: its church was demolished long ago and the masonry reused for other buildings including, possibly, St Peter's Hall, at the brewery.

At the T-junction with Mill Lane, turn left and after about 1.5km at a bend in the road, we come to ❽ **St James, South Elmham**. As elsewhere, the church here is out of the village so, as Mill Lane comes to the junction with The Street, instead of following it around to the right, turn left here and then right on to Church Lane. The church stands on a grassy rise, tucked between the houses down a footpath on the left. It looks a simple little church from outside, but inside are several medieval wonders that make it special, including a Norman font with a magnificently carved wooden lid, a carved wooden rood screen, and two small round windows flanking the royal arms on the west wall, which may be Saxon.

OK, one more church left to see – heading north again now, back towards Bungay, return to The Street and turn left for around 2km, then turn right at the fork, signposted St Cross. Carry on still straight, coming into the village at a forked junction. St Cross, South Elmham is another tiny little hamlet, again with the church tucked down a side road. To add to all the other complications with names and convoluted routes, the church here is actually called ❾ **St George**, not St Cross! To get there, take the lane on the right after the road through the village bends left and crosses the River Beck. With its solid, tall tower and high arched roof, this is the biggest Saints church and maybe for that reason alone the grandest. Inside, its main medieval feature is its font; in the graveyard, though, is the church's main claim to fame: the grave of Canadian writer Elizabeth Smart (1913–86), whose novel *By Grand Central Station I Sat Down and Wept* has been credited as an inspiration for The Smiths. It might not match Jim Morrison's gravestone in Père Lachaise Cemetery, Paris, but among the Saints, her simple grey headstone has something of a cult following.

Continuing right up Fox Hill from St Cross, after about 700m turn right: a sharp turning on to Park Road. Follow this level road for a couple of kilometres until you reach a crossroads, then turn left on to Grange Road and down through a small wood at the foot of the hill to ❿ **Flixton**. There's not much to see in the village itself; as with the Saints villages, there's no pub or shop, just a smattering of modern bungalows and older farmhouses. Flixton's sky-high attraction (excuse the pun), however, is just around the corner. As you leave Flixton, by the triangle with the village sign, turn right on to the B1062. The road is not generally that busy, but more than we have been used to, so keep alert.

A few kilometres along this road, we come to the **Norfolk and Suffolk Aviation Museum** (⌘ aviationmuseum.net), next to the Buck Inn. This collection of World War II RAF and USAAF aircraft is laid out on a field and hangar, together with other military memorabilia, a museum, café, gift shop and toilets. Entry is free; it's run by a very welcoming and knowledgeable team of volunteers, and makes for an interesting contrast to all those venerable churches. Continuing to the right after the museum, we pass a random but curious string of sites in a row on the left: the BUGS play café and swimming school, followed by the Stow Fen Brewery, the Milk Shed farm shop and café, and just after that, finally, the Three Willows

Garden Centre – all of which might feel like a bustling metropolis after emerging from the secluded Saints' backwaters.

Finally, reaching the outskirts of Bungay, another 1km further along the B1062, we return to the same crossroads where we set out, en route to St Margaret's. This time, turn left back up the Flixton Road, which leads into Upper Olland Street, and left up St Mary's Street to Market Place. Having slogged your way through all those 'dry' villages, see below for a couple of watering holes within staggering distance, where you can slake your thirst at last!

THE ESSENTIALS

GETTING THERE By **car**, Bungay is midway between Lowestoft – just under 25km to the east, via the A146 and A143 – and Norwich, 25km to the north via the B1332. By **train**, the best connection from London is the direct service from London Liverpool Street to Norwich, which stops at Beccles, about 15 minutes' drive east of Bungay, or Diss, around 25 minutes' drive southwest of Bungay. By **bus**, there are direct services to Diss, Beccles and Norwich.

↑ The Norfolk and Suffolk Aviation Museum (Tanya Dedyukhina/WC)

THE SAINTS

Dotted across the wide, flat and remote farmland between Bungay and Halesworth, are 12 medieval churches and the memory of another two, collectively known as The Saints. They are divided between two rural districts: with St Andrew, St John, St Lawrence and St Margaret in Ilketshall, directly south and east of Bungay; and All Saints, St George, St James, St Margaret, St Mary, St Michael, St Peter and St Cross in South Elmham, adjacent to the west. In addition are St Nicholas, long since demolished, its site just marked by a cross, and the remote ruins of South Elmham Minster, in the parish of St Cross. Apart from these two, all the other Saints remain in use – remarkable considering their isolation and sparse local population. Only one, All Saints, South Elmham, has been made formally redundant, and is now cared for by the Churches Conservation Trust.

Although none of the Saints may be deemed historically or architecturally important, each has its own charm. Visiting them by bike is a challenge of finding your way around the winding back lanes and battling the gusty wind that often sweeps across the flat countryside. Their attractions are subtle: a finely carved stone doorway here or a translucent stained-glass window there, amid quiet hamlets mostly without even a pub or a shop.

And it's interesting to compare this scattering of old churches across backwater countryside with, for instance, Norwich to the north. This historical city has 31 medieval churches out of a former total of 57 – the most of anywhere in northern Europe. So, perhaps we should appreciate the Saints for what they are not, and for their mere survival in such lonely outposts.

WHERE TO EAT

The Fleece Inn St Mary's St, Bungay NR35 1AX; 01986 897079; thefleeceinnbungay.co.uk. This 15th-century inn stands in the centre of Bungay, right on our cycle route, & with a cosy walled courtyard behind (handy for parking bikes via the rear entrance). Its snug bar serves a good range of local & guest ales & its menu is strong on local produce, including wild boar, venison & goat from Masebrook Farm, & fresh fish from Scaled-Up Fish. They also host occasional live music. **££**

✖ Earsham Street Café 11–13 Earsham St, Bungay NR35 1AE; ✆ 01986 893103; 🖰 earshamstreetcafe.co.uk. Just off Market Pl, this great café-deli is a favourite with cycling clubs, with bike racks in their covered courtyard garden. It's a lovely place for kicking back & enjoying their home cooking, with daily specials often including Lebanese dishes, salads, soups, cakes & sandwiches (vegans & special diets well catered for). Open for b/fast, lunch & afternoon tea. **£**

✖ Buck Inn 8 The St, Flixton NR35 1NZ; ✆ 01986 892382. Newly refurbished this 19th-century half-timbered pub just outside Flixton is right on our route next to the Norfolk and Suffolk Aviation Museum. Its restaurant is best known for the good-value carvery & the bar stocks a decent selection of wines & beers, including local ales from Stow Fen Brewery, just up the road. **£**

FACILITIES AND FURTHER INFORMATION There are public toilets in Bungay, on Cross Street, just off Market Place, as well as toilets at Flixton's Aviation Museum and the adjacent Buck Inn.

ℹ Bungay Community Library Wharton St, Bungay NR35 1EL; ✆ 01986 892748; 🖰 suffolklibraries.co.uk. There is an information point here in Bungay's main library, with a selection of leaflets & brochures – staff are also available to help with local enquiries. The Museum on Broad St is also a helpful source of information.

10 THETFORD FOREST

START/FINISH	High Lodge, Thetford Forest
DISTANCE/TIME	16.6km/2hrs (plus two extensions: Shepherd's Trail and Heritage Trail, just under 5km each)
DIFFICULTY/TERRAIN	② Mid-range MTB trails, with two optional easy detours, including the wheelchair-friendly Heritage Loop
SCENIC RATING	⑧ Forestry woodland – off-road cycling trails over level or gently rolling terrain
SUITABLE FOR	Mountain bike (or sturdy hybrid for the easy Shepherd's Trail, suitable for beginner MTB riders, or the wheelchair-accessible Heritage Trail)
NCN ROUTE	All routes are off-road on MTB trails
MAPS	OS Explorer 225 (1:25 000)
KOMOOT REF	583475008 (Shepherd's Trail: 536622311; Heritage Trail: 536625756)

Deep inland, straddling the Norfolk–Suffolk border, the Brecks form the driest region in the country, with sandy heathland and low-lying forests. They're a great place for cycling, along quiet lanes and off-road forest trails. Possibly best of all for cyclists is Thetford Forest, a family-friendly outdoor activity centre with a host of activities on offer including three mountain bike trails, suitable for both beginners and proficient MTB riders.

This route follows the moderate-rated Beater Trail, with the option of combining it with the easy Shepherd's Trail. There is also the wheelchair-friendly Heritage Trail, with a smooth, level path exploring the forest's long history.

THE ROUTE

Starting from the ❶ **High Lodge Visitor Centre**, go across the sides of the Badger and Nightjar car parks with sandwich boards marking the start of the **Beater** (moderate) and the red-graded (difficult) **Lime Burner** trails. The various cycle trails and footpaths are well signposted throughout the forest – blue signs for the Beater Trail. After 100m or so, the level sandy

← Thetford Forest's MTB trails are suitable for all levels (High Lodge/Forestry England)

trail comes to a road. Turn right here and briefly on to the road, watching out for traffic (which is restricted to 15mph on forest roads), then left back into the forest. After about another 100m, the Beater peels away from the Lime Burner Trail and continues, meandering gently between the trees.

The path narrows to single track here, and remains so for most of this trail. The way is easy so far, with just a few knobbly tree roots and muddy puddles to look out for here and there. Only overtake if there is room and the way ahead is clear, having rung your bell or called out as appropriate. If, on the other hand, you're taking it easy or stop to admire the view, keep a lookout over your shoulder or pull over off the path as the forest is hugely popular with cyclists, including families with children of all ages. Apart from the odd careering cyclist, the forest is gloriously peaceful, its under-canopy floor carpeted in bracken, with the occasional butterfly and dragonfly flitting to and fro during the warmer months.

After about 1km, just after crossing the road again at the top end of the trail, we come to the first of the Beater Trail's three technical MTB sections –

❷ **The Tightrope**, a series of zigzags and mild berms (banked turns) through the trees. As a starter warm-up exercise it's not strenuous, and the downhill incline is still only gentle, as it is for all this trail. Continue through an airy glade of broadleaved trees, then cross an open area of bracken, with the path now rougher gravel. Turn right, back into the forest, and cross another road. Now we come to the Beater's most popular highlight – ❸ **The 39 Steps,** a sequence of tightly bermed bends around the tall, slender pines and slightly teeth-jangling caterpillar bumps over the undulating trail. It's great fun and never too tricky to enjoy at your own pace. As before, though, cycle considerately for others in front and behind you.

As you come out of The 39 Steps and back on to the level trail, it crosses the **Fir Trail**, an orange-marked footpath. Keep a look out here as many walkers, runners and dog owners also use the various other paths which criss-cross the forest. Soon after the Fir Trail, the Beater Trail splits into two, signposted either Long or Short Route: take the Long Route to the left – you'll be coming back this way later, on the way back to High Lodge.

Carry on downhill through the trees, eventually coming to a forest clearing on your left, signposted Military Firing Range. There's a red flag raised when firing is going on, with Do Not Enter signs on the high fence, but the trails around the outside are still safe and open at all times. Continue along the flat wide path alongside the clearing, then turn left back into the forest after around 200m, coming to the next MTB feature, ❹ **Duck and Cover**: this involves around 500m of gentle meandering under the trees, with a series of mild to moderate berms, bumps and tight bends to keep you busy. Again, there's nothing too challenging here even for beginner MTB riders. You need to keep focused on where you're going, though: there's no padding on the trees and the gnarly roots threading the path can be a challenge for bike wheels to keep a grip.

From here on, the trail continues happily through the trees, with occasional bumps and dips, but mostly staying quite level. Winding mostly to the left, eventually, after around 4km, we come back to the turning we made earlier on, descending again to The 39 Steps. Turn left here, giving us a second go at the fun challenge: a little faster now if you took it slowly the first time? Or vice versa!

At the Long/Short Route split in the Beater Trail that we passed previously, this time go straight ahead on the Short Route. This winds gently under the trees for around another 3km, rejoined by the Lime Burner Trail, and returning to High Lodge.

OPTIONAL DETOURS

If you're new to mountain biking and would like to combine a couple of the Beater Trail's technical sections with an easier ride, carry on ahead at the Firing Range clearing, where our main Beater Trail route turned left towards Duck and Cover. Instead, follow the green signs from here to join the return section of the **Shepherd's Trail**. This flat and easy route features a mostly level and wider trail with no other MTB technical features, continuing for around 5km back to High Lodge.

For wheelchair users and young children learning to ride a bike, there's also a short, multi-user path called the **Heritage Trail** (marked with orange

↑ Detours for all abilities abound in the forest (High Lodge/Forestry England)

signs). This loop route also starts from High Lodge, winding through the forest on a smooth level path for 4.2km, with a couple of shortcuts: 1km and 3km long. Along the way, there are benches and a couple of shelters, as well as information panels with audio recordings about the history of the forest.

Note too that there are also other off-road forest cycle trails nearby, including Brandon Country Park (Bury Rd, IP27 0SU), approximately 5km west of High Lodge, across the B1106 towards Elveden.

THE ESSENTIALS

GETTING THERE High Lodge is in the north corner of Thetford Forest (IP27 0AF). By **car**, it is 4.5km east of Brandon, via the B1107, Thetford Road, or approximately 58km southwest of Norwich, via the A11 and B1107. By **train**, the nearest station is Brandon, which has direct trains from Cambridge on greateranglia, taking around 40 minutes. There are no **bus** services to Thetford Forest.

THE BRECKS

One of the UK's warmest and driest regions, the Brecks are a little-known but fascinating area in the heart of East Anglia spanning more than 1,000km^2 between Norfolk, Suffolk and a corner of eastern Cambridgeshire. Besides their extensive forests, the Brecks are home to the only inland sand dunes in the country, as well as pingos, or glacial lakes, and meres – ponds fed by rivers and underground aquifers. Their shady forest trails and quiet back lanes make the Brecks ideal cycling territory. They are also rich in wildlife, with a wide range of plants thriving on the grasslands and dry heath, as well as breeding birds. Nightjars and woodlarks breed on the heaths and clearings in the pine plantations, including Thetford Forest, which has the largest area of conifers in England. Curlew too are abundant here, with some 60% of the UK's nesting population found in arable areas.

Although today the region is sparsely populated and mostly rural, its history of human settlement dates back thousands of years. Boudicca's Iceni tribe were based in the Brecks – it is thought that the ceremonial site of **Gallows Hill**, just to the north of Thetford, was used to launch their uprising against the Romans in AD60. Mining for flint, still a feature in local buildings, was the core industry of early settlers in the Brecks. Lying 12km northwest of Thetford is the major archaeological site of **Grime's Graves**. With some 400 pits pockmarking the heath like a lunar landscape, evidence has been found here of flint mining dating back 4,500 years.

↑ Nightjars breed on the heaths of the Brecks (CezaryKorkosz/S)

WHERE TO EAT Note that it gets extremely busy at Thetford during weekends and holiday periods, leading to long queues at the visitor centre café. Visitors are welcome to bring their own picnics, with plenty of benches and barbecues nearby.

✕ The Pantry High Lodge, Thetford Forest, Brandon IP27 0AF; ☏ 0300 067 4401; ⌂ forestryengland.uk/high-lodge. This café & take-away in the visitor centre has a range of hot & cold snacks, drinks & ice creams. Either eat inside the cavernous, timber-roofed building or at outdoor tables on the green. **£**

✕ The Mulberry 11 Raymond St, Thetford IP24 2EA; ☏ 01842 824122; ⌂ mulberrythetford.co.uk. This friendly & intimate gourmet restaurant in the centre of Thetford is the top choice for fine dining in the area (the walled garden is more suitable for muddy bikers & cleated shoes). The seasonal menu features contemporary English & Mediterranean cuisine, with 1 or 2 vegetarian options & a small but reasonably priced wine list. To top it all, just across the road, is the Dad's Army Museum (⌂ dadsarmythetford. org.uk), based on the vintage TV comedy series, for readers too young to remember Captain Mainwaring & Co. **£££**

✕ Tilly's Tearoom 15 Market Hill, Brandon IP27 0AA; ☏ 01842 339163; **f** Tillys Tearoom. With chintzy décor & tea served in proper china cups, this cosy local café in the centre of Brandon serves great homemade cakes, snacks, light lunches & cream teas. It also has a walled garden, handy for passing cyclists. **££**

FACILITIES AND FURTHER INFORMATION Although entry to Thetford Forest is free, there are parking charges: up to £12.50 all day, at the time of writing. Currently, no cash is accepted for payment anywhere in the park.

i Visitor Centre High Lodge, Thetford Forest, Brandon IP27 0AF; ☏ 0300 0674401; ⌂ forestryengland.uk/high-lodge. The information desk in the visitor centre has maps & leaflets about the forest activities & events, & staff will help with advice about the cycling trails & footpaths. There are also toilets, a café, bike hire (page 218) & an array of activities including table tennis, Go Ape high-wire adventure, archery & a climbing wall.

IXWORTH MILLERS' TRAIL | CHAPTER 11

START/FINISH	Ixworth
DISTANCE/TIME	23.9km/2½hrs
DIFFICULTY/TERRAIN	① All on road, mostly quiet back lanes, level or gently rolling terrain, with a couple of busy A-road crossings
SCENIC RATING	⑧ Peaceful countryside, historic windmills, a watermill, an Elizabethan manor and vineyard, and a wetland nature reserve
SUITABLE FOR	Hybrid, e-bike or road bike
NCN ROUTE	Partly on NCN13 and NCN51
MAPS	OS Explorer 230 (1:25 000)
KOMOOT REF	584135217

This rural route loops through traditional Suffolk agricultural countryside, where windmills and waterwheels have nurtured the land for centuries. We start from the ancient village of Ixworth, dating back to Roman days, with Tudor cottages lining its quiet streets. Heading north through sleepy villages and lush farmland, we pass an Elizabethan manor and vineyards, a watermill, a fen nature reserve and a handful of historic windmills.

THE ROUTE

Start in ❶ **Ixworth**, from the car park by the village hall and library opposite St Mary's church. Turn right and up through the High Street; this historic conservation area is lined with old timbered buildings leaning against each other, as if for support, and painted in subtle pastel shades. At the top of the road, we come to a T-junction with the A1088; turn right here and immediately left, signposted Bardwell, on to a quiet lane. It's only a very short dog-leg junction on the A-road, but the traffic can get really busy; if so, dismount and walk your bike along the verge. From here, the road winds downhill towards Bardwell, past the gated entrance to Bardwell Manor after a few hundred metres on the left.

After about 3km of gentle uphill between the fields, we come into ❷ **Bardwell**, passing a weathered old timbered manor house on the right. It's a quiet village with a pleasant mix of thatched cottages and tidy modern

← Built in 1831, five-storey Pakenham Windmill was restored in 2000 (SuperStock)

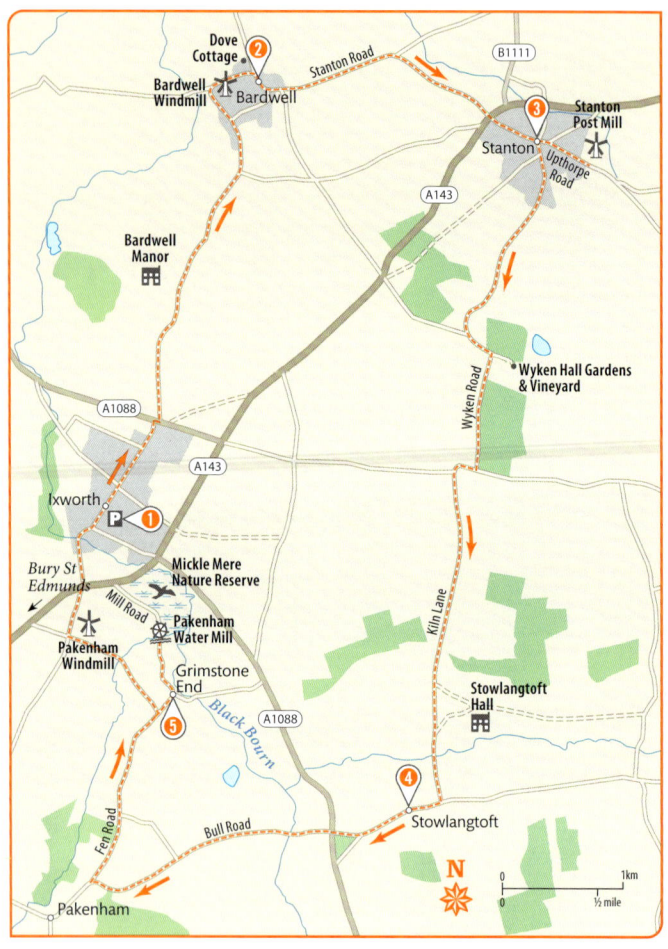

homes lining the main road. As we approach the village church and the road bears right, take the fork straight ahead, down Church Road. Coming to a triangle, wind right into School Lane and a couple of hundred metres on the right, tucked between the houses, is **Bardwell Windmill**. The stocky little black and white 19th-century mill still has its own sails and is still milling flour. Unlike some other mills in the area, it's not fenced in so you can have a look around. At the time of writing, the mill is not open to explore inside, but is fundraising for restoration work (**f** Bardwell Windmill), so hopefully will be soon. In the meantime, there's a little bakery and take-away café adjacent (page 118), which more than makes up for the lack of shops in the village.

Continue right along School Lane, coming to a T-junction after around 200m. Turn right here but first, have a quick peek at **Dove Cottage** on the left: it's a fine example of Suffolk's traditional 'pink-washing', one of about a dozen others along this trail to be painted pink, mostly in subtle shades but some less so (see box, page 116). The cottage also has a pair of doves hovering between their dovecot outlined in its front wall, a charming example of pargeting: decorative plasterwork, another popular Suffolk custom.

Take the left side of the road triangle on to Stanton Road, leading after a couple of kilometres to ❸ **Stanton**, a bustling modern village with a pub, chippy and a couple of convenience stores. Stanton has Roman roots, though, standing at the junction of two Roman roads (the Peddars Way and the Ixworth–Bildeston road). It also has two medieval churches: All Saints, which we're about to pass, and St John's, which is now roofless but still holds services once a year.

As you approach the village, first you have to cross the busy Bury Road (A143). It's another dog-leg junction, turning right then first left on to Old Bury Road. Again, it's better to dismount here and walk your bike across, via the footpath on the left, with a traffic island in the middle of the A-road. The path then leads through Jacobs Close, a residential side road, which joins the Old Bury Road a little further along.

Carry on up to the war memorial, on a triangle in front of All Saints Church on your right. Here, there's a short detour of a few hundred metres, to **Stanton Post Mill**. To get there, go straight on at the next triangle on to the Knowle/Upthorpe Road. The pretty, whitewashed windmill is just along the road here on the left, on the outskirts of the village. It's a Grade II-listed 18th-century mill; the post in its name refers to its construction,

in which the whole upper body, including sails and machinery, turn on a single post, one of only seven remaining in Suffolk. It's not open to the public at the time of writing, but is being restored, so it's one to keep an eye on (teamsmills.org/mills/Stanton).

Returning to the war memorial by All Saints Church, turn left along The Street, which winds out of the village and on to Wyken Road. Follow this flat road through open farmland for about 2km until we reach Wyken Hall. Just after the road into Wyken bends right, a driveway on the left leads to **Wyken Hall Gardens and Vineyard** (wykenvineyards.co.uk). Spread around the 16th-century manor house, Wyken's extensive estate has ornamental gardens, orchards and a woodland walk, which leads to its vineyard. There's also a restaurant, pizzeria (Moonshine Café, page 118), store and farmers' market every Saturday, so plenty of temptations for a break in the journey.

Continue left out of Wyken Hall and southwards towards Stowlangtoft. After about 1km, turn right at the T-junction, then as the main road veers sharp right some 200m later go straight ahead on to Kiln Lane. This narrow farm lane climbs gradually uphill, past a water tower on the left at the brow of the hill, followed by **Stowlangtoft Hall**. This grand country pile is

↑ Wyken Hall Gardens are centred around the 16th-century manor house (Stuart Aylmer/A)

a Grade II-listed mansion thought to date from the 1700s and is now run as a nursing home and with holiday cottages on the landscaped estate.

Carry on downhill now, along an avenue of tall conifers, and turn right after about 1km at another T-junction at the bottom of the hill. Go through the quiet residential hamlet of ❹ **Stowlangtoft**, then cross the A1088: there's no traffic island on this busy two-lane road, so dismount to walk across, continuing straight ahead on to Bull Road.

Stay on this long and winding country lane for around 2km, coming to another T-junction on the outskirts of Pakenham, a pretty village with a handful of the pink-washed cottages mentioned previously. Known as the Village of Two Mills, Pakenham is the last remaining parish in England to have both a working watermill and a windmill (proudly pictured on the village sign, which is left here and a short way along the road on the right, next to the post office).

Otherwise, to continue our route and see the actual mills, turn right at the T-junction on to Fen Road for about 1.5km, leading to ❺ **Grimstone End**. Just before we reach the village, a sign points left to Pakenham Mills. Before visiting these, there are a couple of other attractions, just up the road: Pakenham Water Mill and Mickle Mere Nature Reserve.

Continue straight ahead here, into Grimstone End. Turn left at the triangle, on to Mill Road, winding through the village. At the far end, standing by the roadside on the left, is the black and white timbered **Pakenham Water Mill** (⌘ pakenhamwatermill.co.uk), by the River Black Bourn. The current mill dates from around 1780, but it is thought that there has been a watermill here for more than 1,000 years. Today, it is owned by the Suffolk Building Preservation Society and is fully restored and once again milling flour. It's open to the public, with a tearoom and guided tours.

Around 100m or so further along Mill Road, is **Mickle Mere Nature Reserve**, with a bird hide at the end of the short path into the reserve, on the right. Mickle Mere was created by happy accident, when the sluice gates built for the Ixworth bypass failed and flooded, turning these former grazing meadows into a wetland haven for birds. Despite its small size, the reserve attracts an abundance of waterfowl, including teal, wigeon and shovelers, with an occasional sighting of the shy otter.

Returning to the main route, backtrack through Grimstone End, and take the turning on the right on to Broadway. This narrow farm lane leads, after around 2km, to **Pakenham Windmill** (pakenhamwindmill.co.uk) on the right, just before the crossroads. In fact, that should be mills plural, as there's a miniature, adult-sized model standing at the foot of the grown-up real thing. Built in 1831 and restored in 2000, the black-tarred, five-storey mill is open to the public, and there's a farmers' market here on Saturdays.

Exit the mill through the farm buildings, coming around to the right of the crossroads. Continue along the road leading right and coming shortly to the A143, on the outskirts of Ixworth. This is another very busy road, but thankfully there's a pathway crossing on the left. There's no traffic island here, though, so dismount and wait until it's safe to cross. The path continues on the other side and on to Bury Road, which

SUFFOLK'S OXBLOOD PINK-WASHING

Many of Suffolk's older, timbered buildings are painted in varying shades of pink. The origins of what has come to be known as Suffolk Pink are thought to date from the 14th century, when it was discovered that natural ingredients could be mixed with the limewash used to paint houses' outer walls, adding protection against the elements as well as creating the appealing colour. Berries, blackthorns and sloe juice were sometimes used, as well as pig or ox blood mixed with buttermilk.

Today, the tradition has been enthusiastically maintained. However, owners of listed buildings or in conservation areas can't just paint their homes any old pink. Neighbours, English Heritage and local planners have all been known to object to unsuitable tints, forcing hapless owners to redecorate, using the proper hue. In a widely reported case, councillors at Suffolk County Council derided the miscreant for what was described as 'Teletubby Land' or 'pantomime scenery'!

The original Suffolk Pink is described as a 'dusky terracotta', which is often darker than many shades seen today. There are some fine examples around the Ixworth Millers' Trail, including Dove Cottage near Bardwell, mentioned

THE ESSENTIALS

GETTING THERE By **car**, Ixworth is just under 13km northeast of Bury St Edmunds, off the A143. There is no **train** station here; the nearest is also Bury, with direct trains on greateranglia from London Liverpool Street taking just under 2 hours. The 304 **bus** connects Ixworth to Bury, with regular services throughout the day, taking around 25 minutes.

WHERE TO EAT

✖ **The Greyhound** 49 High St, Ixworth IP31 2HJ; ☏ 01359 230887; ￼ The Greyhound Ixworth. This traditional village inn on Ixworth's main street is noted for its above, and many others further afield across the county. There are no prizes on offer for spotting bubblegum horrors, but rest assured the pink police are on the prowl.

↑ Dove Cottage in Bardwell is a great example of Suffolk Pink (Huw Hennessy)

Sun roast lunches, as well as pub favourites including steaks, pasta & curries. Its little back courtyard garden is handy for propping up your bike while you sip one of its local ales (including Greene King, from Bury St Edmunds) – in moderation, of course. **£**

✖ **Wooster's Bakery** The Windmill, School Ln, Bardwell IP31 1AD; ✆ 01359 408409; ⌂ woostersbakery.co.uk. Next to Bardwell's windmill on the outskirts of the village, this little artisan bakery-deli sells a range of bread, rolls & cakes, as well as barista coffee & fruit juices to take away. **£**

✖ **Moonshine Café** Wyken Hall, Wyken Rd, Stanton IP31 2DW; ✆ 01359 250287; ⌂ wykenvineyards.co.uk. The more informal of 2 eateries at Wyken (**The Leaping Hare**, housed in its converted barn, is a regular entry in Good Food & Michelin Guides), this pizzeria serves sourdough pizzas baked in a wood-fired oven, with outdoor tables in the courtyard or take away to eat under the trees in its orchard. Drinks include Wyken Vineyard's own wines, as well as local beers & soft drinks. **££**

FACILITIES AND FURTHER INFORMATION There are public toilets behind the library in Ixworth's village hall car park; the car park is free and open 24/7.

ℹ **Bury St Edmunds Tourist Information Centre** Charter Sq St, Bury St Edmunds IP33 3FD; ✆ 01284 764667; ⌂ visit-burystedmunds. This, the nearest official tourist office to Ixworth, has maps, guidebooks & gifts for sale, as well as a booking service for guided local tours & events.

Ixworth Library ✆ 01359 231493; ⌂ suffolklibraries.co.uk. Situated by the village hall car park, the library staff may also be able to help with local information & directions.

The award-winning Slow Travel series from Bradt Guides

**Over 20 regional guides across Britain.
See the full list at bradtguides.com/slowtravel.**

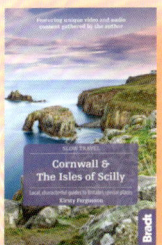 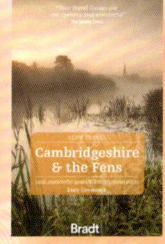 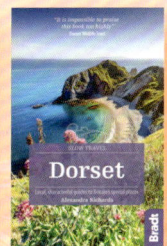

 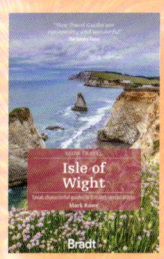 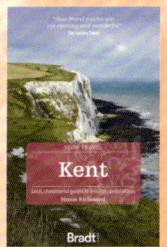

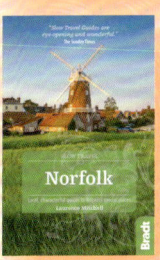  

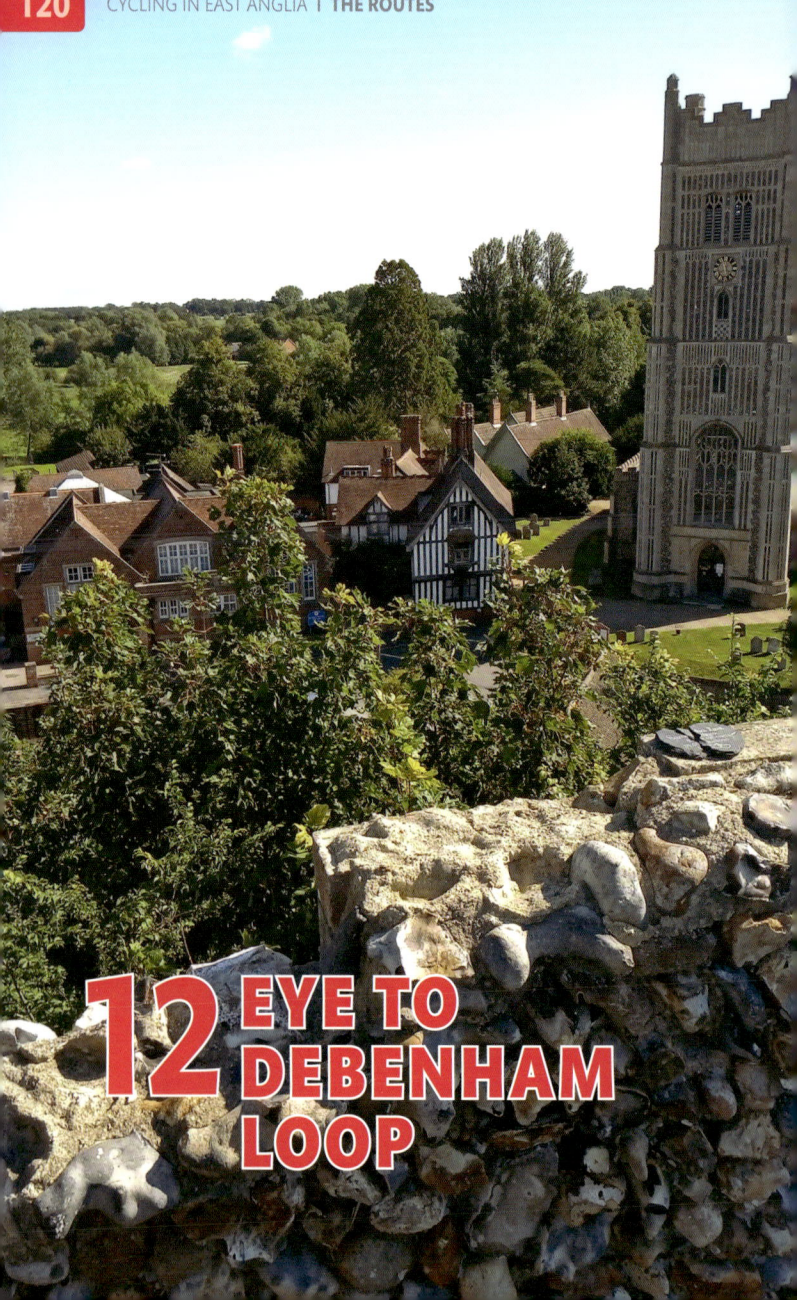

12 EYE TO DEBENHAM LOOP

EYE TO DEBENHAM LOOP | CHAPTER 12

START/FINISH	Eye
DISTANCE/TIME	34.4km/3½hrs
DIFFICULTY/TERRAIN	① All on road, mostly minor backroads and a short stretch on the B1077, with no major road crossings or tricky junctions; mostly level terrain, though slightly more rolling on the way back after Wetheringsett, but nothing strenuous
SCENIC RATING	Ⓐ From historic market town Eye to chic Debenham, via a vintage railway and a smattering of farming villages set in mid-Suffolk's rolling rural landscape
SUITABLE FOR	Road bike, hybrid or e-bike
NCN ROUTE	Partly on NCN40 (signposted as the Heart of Suffolk Route), between Debenham and Eye
MAPS	OS Explorer 230 (1:25 000)
KOMOOT REF	584204369

Between Eye, on the River Waveney, and Debenham, at the source of the River Deben, is an unspoilt region of golden wheat fields and simple farming villages often known as the Heart of Suffolk. From historic Eye, with its Norman castle and cobblestoned lanes, this loop heads southwards across the fields to well-heeled Debenham, enriched by the medieval wool trade. En route, we visit some medieval churches, which characterise much of Suffolk's historic countryside. On the way back to Eye, we make a short detour to the vintage railway at Wetheringsett.

THE ROUTE

Start at ❶ **Cross Street car park** in the centre of Eye, next to the library. Before you get going, you might notice a large carved wooden archway in the corner of the car park: *Michael's Gates*, by Ben Platts-Mills, inspired by the Ley Lines running across England from Cornwall to East Anglia. Coming out of the car park, turn right on to Cross Street, then left on to Magdalen Street, then in front of the Hexagon (gym club) and with the

← The historic market town of Eye (JamCor/WC)

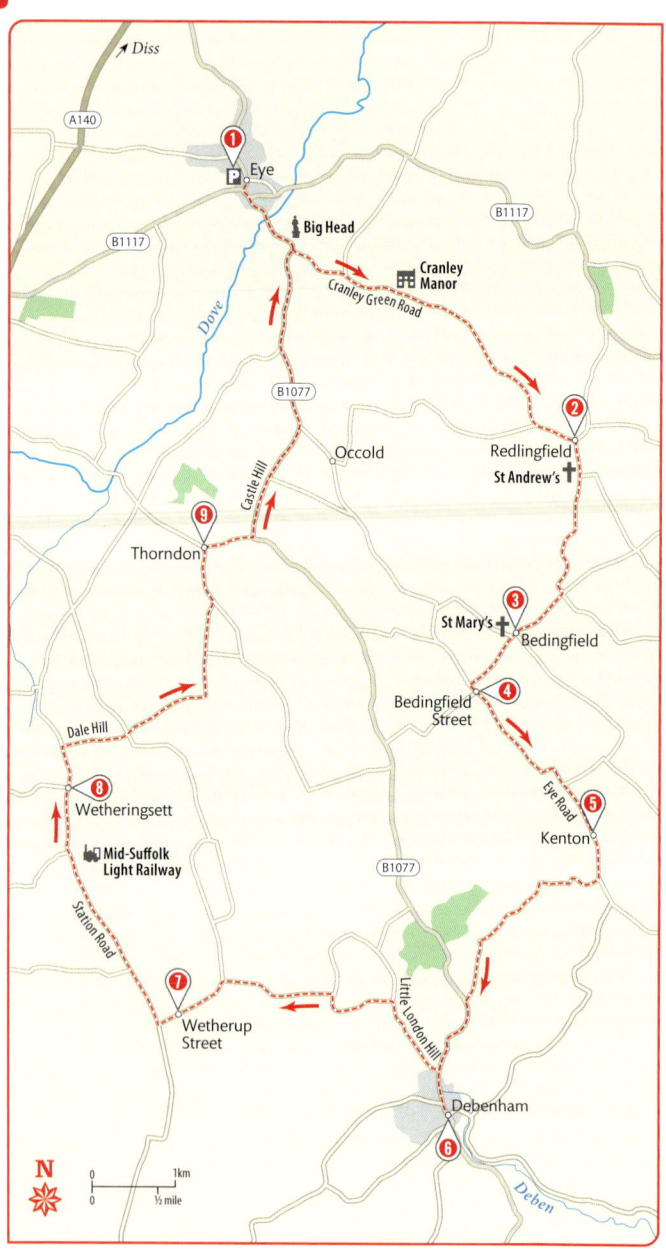

Bank Arts Centre on the corner, turn right onto Castle Street. This runs into Broad Street, Lowgate Street and finally Cranley Green Road. From here, we head gently downhill, south towards Redlingfield, out of town and into the countryside within a couple of minutes.

As the main road (B1077) winds around to the right, just after the *Big Head* sculpture on the left (more on that later), we go straight ahead, signposted Redlingfield and Worlingworth, the road narrowing and climbing gently uphill for a short stretch. Pass a water tower on your left, followed about 1km later by **Cranley Manor**, a rather austere-looking manor house, with adjoining farm, on the left.

Continue along this pleasant, tree-lined lane, through flat, arable fields, punctuated by a row of wind turbines on the horizon. Coming into ❷ **Redlingfield**, after about 3km, at a fork in the road, carry on ahead through the village. There's nothing particularly eye catching in this tidy, farming village, but its church – **St Andrew's** – is worth a peek. At a triangle on the outskirts, where Redlingfield Road winds around to the left, turn right on to Church Road, signposted Debenham, Worlingworth, Bedingfield and Southolt. Some 200m from here take the signposted path on the right; it's a squat little stone-and-brick building, easy to miss as its tower is no taller than the nave. Although much of what you'll see today was restored in the 19th century, the church still retains some fine architectural features from the 1300s, including the priest's doorway on the south side, the nave, porch and carved stonework around some of the windows. Another small detail I noticed as I took shelter from a sudden shower were wooden stocks under the bench in the entranceway.

Leaving the church, carry on to the right, passing a sign on the left to Wash Farm Barn, a luxurious swimming pool in a converted barn in the middle of the countryside. The road winds to and fro for a stretch after this, eventually coming to a crossroads, where we turn right, signposted Rishangles, Bedingfield and Debenham. After a further 200m, we reach the village of ❸ **Bedingfield**, not to be confused with Redlingfield, or the nearby hamlet of Bedingfield Street. In the middle of Bedingfield, by the triangle and opposite the village hall, is the handsome church of **St Mary's** on the right. It's equally attractive inside, with a high arch-braced nave roof. As in so many villages across the region today, only the church and village hall remain as the social hub of the community, with few shops and not as many pubs as in days gone by.

Carry on past the church, out of the village and straight ahead at the next crossroads, signposted Debenham and Rishangles. After just under 1km, at a T-junction, turn left, signposted Kenton, Debenham and Eye. Then after about another 100m, go straight ahead at the next junction, signposted Kenton and Earl Soham. Here, in the hamlet of ❹ **Bedingfield Street**, is a little roadside collection of antiquities: an old water pump and pockmarked antique AA road sign, in front of a thatched cottage and a pink-washed farmhouse. But just to bring us up to date, there's also a defibrillator here inside a phone box.

THE MIDDY

A short detour off our route, between Eye and Debenham, leads to the Mid-Suffolk Light Railway, or the 'Middy' to its devoted fans, offering a small but authentic taste of the Edwardian heyday of steam-train travel.

Inspired by the railway boom of the 1800s, the line had promising initial ambitions to cover the centre of the county, linking the Great Eastern Railway's main line between Halesworth and Haughley, with Needham Market and Westerfield to the west. However, years of financial setbacks left only a short section of the route between Haughley and Laxfield remaining in operation. Eventually, despite nationalisation, with fewer passengers and poor line maintenance, the line closed in 1952.

In 1990, however, the Mid-Suffolk Light Railway Museum formed as a registered charity, based at Brockford station, near Wetheringsett, with the aim of bringing at least some of the former line back to life. Original rolling stock that had been abandoned and scattered across Suffolk was hunted down and restored to working order, together with a workshop, locomotive shed, tearoom and the Kitchener Arms, the only pub in the area, based in a converted passenger coach. Today, the 'Middy' runs nostalgic train rides in Victorian passenger carriages, on a short demonstration line from Brockford

Follow the Bedingfield Road winding left and right on to Eye Road, coming into ❺ **Kenton** after around 3km. Kenton has a slightly smarter look and feel than its near neighbours. Several thatched and pink-washed cottages are dotted along the main road, as well as a thatch-roofed barn with black tarred walls, on the left as we come in, next to Potash Farm. Carry on through the village then turn right on to Church Lane, in front of All Saints Church.

From here, the road winds gently downhill to Debenham for another 4km or so, through meadows of wheat and barley. At a fork in the road, just before the River Deben (pronounced Dee-ben), carry on straight ahead and into the village. ❻ **Debenham** (pronounced Dee-benham) is definitely worth exploring: there's evidence of settlement here since

to Dovebrook. There are also driver experience days and seasonal events throughout the year, including the Santa Special and Steam Railway Days. To book tickets and for more information, including about the ongoing work to extend the line, visit ⊘ mslr.org.uk.

↑ After closing in 1952, the Mid-Suffolk Light Railway was reborn in 1990
(Peter R Foster IDMA/S)

the Iron Age, but Debenham rose to prosperity during the 14th and 15th centuries, as a centre for Suffolk's thriving wool trade. A close rival to the more famous Lavenham (page 156) as the most picturesque village in Suffolk, Debenham gets far fewer tourists and has a more relaxed feel as a result. Its humpbacked High Street is lined with stunning gabled medieval cottages, some of which now house antique shops, cafés and art galleries. Among its grander buildings, at the brow of the hill on the left, is the elegant **church of St Mary Magdalene**, with the imposing stone façade of the Order of Foresters opposite. Among its other 94 listed buildings are the gabled 16th-century **Ancient House**, on the corner of Gracechurch and High streets, and the 17th-century **Guildhall** opposite.

Continuing our route, go back to the turning towards Wetheringsett at the entrance to Debenham, now joining the NCN40 for a few short stretches on the way back to Eye. Leaving Debenham, turn left, then after about 100m take a right-hand turn at the crossroads, on to Little London Hill. The road climbs briefly then flattens out and winds sharp left, arriving after about 3km at ❼ **Wetherup Street**, a pretty little hamlet huddled around the T-junction. Turn right here, signposted Wetheringsett. A possibly useful landmark here is a tall, thin telecoms mast on the horizon, on your right as you come into Wetherup Street. Following the straight Station Road for just over 2km, notice a sign pointing right to the **Mid-Suffolk Light Railway** (see box, page 124). There's a pub and café here too, so you might fancy a short detour, as there aren't any other eateries en route until Eye. It's just a couple of hundred metres along the road, with the entrance on the right.

Continuing straight ahead, after another kilometre or so we come into ❽ **Wetheringsett**. Pass All Saints Church on your right and follow the road turning sharp right on to Dale Hill, past farm buildings on your left. At the staggered crossroads between the fields after another few kilometres, carry on straight ahead, signposted Thorndon (though confusingly it has five different fingers pointing to four roads). The one we want, to Thorndon, points to nowhere! Nevertheless, it is straight ahead to Thorndon – the same way as the sign to Eye and Stoke Ash.

Approaching Thorndon, the road turns left and passes **Shortts Farm** on your left, a stunning thatch-roofed, pink-washed farmhouse, behind an ornate brick wall (home to the Shortts Farm microbrewery; shorttsfarmbrewery.com). After about another kilometre, at a triangle with another lovely old thatched cottage on the left, turn left into ❾ **Thorndon** village itself. As we come to another triangle, notice Thorndon's particularly splendid **village sign**, in front of All Saints Church opposite. Turn right here, signposted Debenham, Eye, Occold and the delightfully named Rishangles, which sounds like it should be one of T S Eliot's Practical Cats…

At the bottom of the hill, after about 500m, turn left at the T-junction, on to Castle Hill (B1077 – look out for traffic), signposted Occold and Eye. Rejoining Cranley Green Road, turn left and continue downhill into Eye. By the roadside opposite is a giant wooden carving, labelled *Big Head*, a sculpture by Ray Brooks and Ben Platts-Mills, whose *Michael's Gates* we saw in the car park at the start. There's no explanation here about this

↑ The route passes through two quintessential English villages: Thorndon and Wetheringsett (Huw Hennessy)

↑ The giant wooden carving known as *Big Head* (geograph.org.uk/WC)

baggy-eyed, smiley face, but it was commissioned in 2003 by Mid-Suffolk District and the Arts Council, as part of a Hearts of Oak sculpture trail. Cross the river and uphill for the last short stretch into the town centre. Turn left by the Bank Arts Centre, then right down Cross Street to the car park.

THE ESSENTIALS

GETTING THERE By **car**, Eye is just under 9km south of Diss, via the A1066 and B1077. The nearest **train** station is also at Diss, with direct services to London Liverpool Street, taking from 2 hours 20 minutes, or to Norwich, taking just under 20 minutes. There are regular direct **buses** to Eye from Diss, taking about 15 minutes.

WHERE TO EAT

✖ **Cafeye** 14 Broad St, Eye IP23 7AF; ☏ 01379 87300. Just around the corner from Eye's Cross St car park, near the war memorial, this friendly little café serves great b/fast, lunches & snacks, specialising in English, Mediterranean & Italian cuisine, with a good range of veggie choices. Their coffee is excellent too, plus milkshakes & homemade desserts. **£**

✖ **River Green Café & Deli** Cross Green, Debenham IP14 6RW; 🖉 01728 860430; 🗗 River Green Café & Deli. This arty little corner café is just off the High St in delightful Debenham. They do b/fast, light lunches & afternoon tea, including scrumptious cream teas, tasty homemade snacks, sandwiches & soups, plus a tempting array of gourmet goodies in the deli; there's a few tables outside, with cycle racks in the small car park opposite. **£**

✖ **Kitchener Arms** Brockford Station, Wetheringsett IP14 5PW; 🖉 01449 766899; 🖉 mslr.org.uk. Housed in a former Great Eastern Railway compartment coach at Wetheringsett's heritage railway museum (see box, page 124), this cosy bar also doubles up as the only pub in the village, serving local real ales, cider from nearby Aspall, wines, spirits, soft drinks & cold snacks. On the museum's special Open Days, the adjacent Middy Tea Room offers a range of light lunches & afternoon teas, with outdoor tables in warmer weather. **£**

FACILITIES AND FURTHER INFORMATION There are public toilets in Eye, just outside the car park on Cross Street (free and open 24/7), and en route in Debenham and at Wetheringsett station.

🛈 **Diss Tourist Information Office** The Corn Hall, 10 St Nicholas St, Diss IP22 4LB; 🖉 01379 652241. This small information office in the nearest town to Eye has a selection of brochures, leaflets & listings of local accommodation.

Eye Library 🖉 01379 870515. The library also has a supply of brochures & staff will help with local information & directions.

13 WALBERSWICK TO SOUTHWOLD LOOP

START/FINISH	Walberswick
DISTANCE/TIME	31.3km/3½hrs
DIFFICULTY/TERRAIN	② Level or rolling terrain, mostly on quiet backroads or B-roads, including a couple of A-road crossings, plus a short off-road stretch through Dunwich Forest
SCENIC RATING	⑧ Between Walberswick and Southwold, traditional seaside resorts, across heath and countryside, through picturesque villages and a historic windmill
SUITABLE FOR	Gravel bike, hybrid or e-bike
NCN ROUTE	Partly on the NCN31, between Wangford and Southwold
MAPS	OS Explorer 231 (1:25 000)
KOMOOT REF	584265225

↑ Southwold Beach (Barnaby Thomas/Southwold Cycle Hire)

WALBERSWICK TO SOUTHWOLD LOOP | CHAPTER 13

Facing each other across the River Blyth estuary are the popular resorts of Walberswick and Southwold: the former an arty retreat and the latter a traditional bucket and spade seaside town. Starting from Walberswick, our route heads off-road through Dunwich Forest, then across country to the pretty village of Wenhaston and the historic windmill at Holton. Winding north and back towards the coast, we pass through more farming villages and fields, before reaching Southwold. You could stop here overnight, as there's plenty to see and a wide range of accommodation available. Or, to return to Walberswick, there's a footbridge across the river, and a little ferry (which takes bikes).

THE ROUTE

Start in ❶ **Walberswick**, at the harbourside ferry car park. This former fishing village has long been a favoured retreat for artists and is still today a popular, but quieter holiday destination than Southwold, its lively neighbour across the water. In midsummer though, Walberswick also

comes alive for its ever-popular crabbing season, the waterfront packed with families wielding whiffy buckets and fishing lines. Turn left out of the car park and go through the village, past the Bell Inn and the little green, lined with prettily painted cottages. Follow the road winding around to the right and, at the end of the village, take the left fork straight ahead on to Lodge Road. This soon narrows to a single lane, through residential suburbs and out into the countryside, between fields lined with high hedgerows.

After about 1km, Lodge Road comes to an end at a construction works. An unpaved, flint and sand track continues straight from here, through the fringes of **Dunwich Forest**, part of the Suffolk Coast and Heaths AONB protected area. The track climbs a little through clearings of heather and bracken; it's wild and peaceful here, though as ever be aware of others using this trail, including walkers and horseriders (and even husky training, which occasionally takes place before 10.30 and after 16.00). As the track descends through the trees, it gets a little rougher and sandier too. Take it slowly here as it's easy to skid on the loose sand: keeping one foot off the pedal after every few turns may help you keep steady. It can also help fend off the occasional protruding tree root and dangling bramble.

After about 3.5km of off-road fun, the track comes to a little parking area by the B1125/Dunwich Road. Go straight over on to the road opposite, signposted Hinton, and then turn right immediately, opposite a pig farm, signposted Wenhaston. The road starts climbing gradually, past another piggery on your right, and levelling out through shady trees. At the brow of the hill pass a little **lily pond** on your right, in front of wooden barns, a classic photogenic scene and perhaps a good place to catch your breath after the climb.

The road levels out now, through arable fields, and comes to the A12. It's quite a straight road, but the traffic can be fast, so cross carefully and dismount if necessary. Carry on straight ahead, with a nice downhill run through the trees, coming to a *careful* stop at the T-junction at the bottom, where we turn left, and into ❷ **Wenhaston** (pronounced Wenner-st'n). This attractive village is spread out along its long straight main road, running roughly parallel to the River Blyth in the valley below on the right. Pass the Star Inn on the left and then turn left at the fork just after **St Peter's Church** on the left. You might not guess from its rough, flint-clad exterior, but inside the church is a remarkable Doom painting. This early 16th-century depiction of the Last Judgement is one of only a few surviving in Suffolk. For its vividly coloured details, the painting is considered one of the finest in England, and is worth a peek even if only for another breather after the climb up through the village.

Continue along Back Road, through the houses and out of the village, heading north towards Holton. The road undulates through more woods and farmland and, about 2km from Wenhaston, we suddenly come across **Halesworth Golf Course** on the left: quite a surreal sight, of golfers clad in pastel pullovers and baseball caps, after the earthy pastures and pigs in muck. At a crossroads, alongside the golf course, turn right on to Wash Lane, which dips down over a little bridge across the River Blyth and up again, coming shortly to a T-junction. Turn left here on to the B1123, signposted Holton and Halesworth, coming into ❸ **Holton** after about 500m. Turn right at a fork down Mill Road, as we enter this lovely old riverside village. Just before the fork, a little footpath on the right leads to **Holton Post Mill**. The whitewashed 17th-century windmill has been closed to visitors since the pandemic, but is worth the short detour to see its ingenious design: it has a fantail attached to a turntable around the mill, allowing the whole building to rotate 360° with the prevailing wind.

Returning to the main route, turn right down Mill Road, passing a row of pretty cottages on the right and coming to a T-junction just after the Lord Nelson Inn on your right. Turn right here, signposted Brampton and Beccles, and out of the village on the B1124. The two-lane road is wide and flat, winding through tree-lined fields. There's not usually much traffic here, so it's not hard going. By way of contrast to the Holton windmill, look out for the tall wind turbines lining the horizon to the left.

About 3.5km from Holton, turn right on to the unmarked King's Lane, downhill over the river and up the other side, taking the first left, signposted Wangford and Southwold. This pleasant back lane cuts straight between open countryside, coming to a crossroads with the A145. Carry on straight ahead here, dismounting if it's busy, reaching a T-junction after another kilometre or so. Turn right here and after another kilometre you come to the A12. Luckily, there's a footpath on the right of this dual carriageway, with a safe crossing on to a traffic island in the middle, then another footpath on the other side, which winds left and into Wangford.

❹ **Wangford** is a no-frills working village (which incidentally gave its name to country singer Hank), mostly composed of modern housing estates. Go straight up the High Street, right at the crossroads, then left immediately on to Elms Lane, by a vet's clinic on the left-hand corner. Take the first right after a few hundred metres (joining the NCN31 now all the way to Southwold) towards Reydon, along quiet lanes winding gently downhill to the coast. Keep following the NCN31 signs, with Wood Farm Lane continuing into Rissemere Lane East winding right and left through open fields and past attractive farmhouses, barns and cottages. After around 3.5km, turn right on to School Lane, then left at the triangle on to Wangford Road, leading to Reydon. Then take the next left-hand turning, on to Green Lane, a small detour avoiding the busy main road straight ahead into Southwold.

Coming into ❺ **Reydon**, turn left at the T-junction continuing along Covert Road and passing a row of Victorian almshouses on the right. Go straight ahead/right at the next angled T-junction soon after the

SOUTHWOLD PIER

If you only do one thing when you're in Southwold, it absolutely must be to visit the pier. And go at the top of the hour so as to witness the chiming of its Water Clock, ingenious showpiece of 'Cabaret Mechanical Theatre' inventor Tim Hunkin.

Southwold Pier was built in 1900, as a docking station for steamships from London Bridge. It suffered adversities over the years since then, however, including being partly blown up as a defensive strategy against a potential German invasion during World War II. By the end of the century, it was on the verge of crumbling into the sea, after being hit by a mine in 1941 and suffering successive bouts of storm damage.

Happily, the pier was rebuilt in 2001, winning awards and becoming the only 21st-century pier in the UK. Today, it is one of Southwold's most popular attractions, the quintessence of the traditional British seaside resort. Soak up the sun with a bag of chips, slurp an ice cream and, uniquely, have a go at one of the wacky, alternative arcade games. As a blissful escape from high-tech virtual entertainment, Hunkin's witty creations offer real hands-on fun: take it out on the Whack a Banker, get a tickle from the Autofrisk and even let the Chiropodist get to work on your toes!

almshouses, signposted Southwold, joining the B1127/Lowestoft Road, past Reydon Village Hall on the right. This suburban village is practically contiguous with Southwold – there's more traffic here too, so leave space as you pass parked vehicles, in case of doors opening suddenly.

↑ Southwold Pier's charming Water Clock (Philip Bird LRPS CPAGB/S)

At the next T-junction turn left, with a short stretch of cycle path on the pavement on the left, and on to the main road into ❻ **Southwold**. There's a cycle path on both sides here, providing some escape from the traffic that flows in and out of this bustling resort, particularly during the summer. There's plenty to do and see here, not least the pier, with Tim Hunkin's gloriously wacky arcade games (see box, opposite).

The NCN31 carries on down the High Street to the seafront. If you're going straight back to Walberswick, though, there's a quieter route around the edge of town. Turn right at the fork in front of the Southwold Arts Festival building and on to York Road, passing the rugby club and golf course on your left. The road soon comes to the River Blyth. Turn left by the Harbour Inn and alongside the river, past the yacht marina and boatsheds to the ferry crossing. The small rowing boat ferry (⌀ walberswickferry. com) takes up to 12 passengers and a couple of bikes if space is available. There's no advance booking, so it's best to get in the queue to be sure of a place. There is also a footbridge across the river further upstream; take the right-hand turning before York Road, on to Blyth Road, which becomes a narrow, single-track footpath after the golf course on your left. Across the bridge, the path comes out on the outskirts of Walberswick, close to the fork where we turned off at the start of the ride, so turn left here and follow The Street back to the harbour.

THE ESSENTIALS

GETTING THERE By **car**, Walberswick is just under 55km north of Ipswich, via the A12 and B1387. The nearest **train** station with a direct

↑ A small rowing boat ferries passengers over the River Blyth between Walberswick and Southwold (I Wei Huang/S)

service to Ipswich is at Halesworth, 14km to the west, with trains to Ipswich taking just under 1 hour, and connections from there to London Liverpool Street station taking about 1 hour 10 minutes. By **bus**, Southwold has better onward connections to neighbouring towns, including the 99A to Halesworth, which takes about half an hour.

WHERE TO EAT

The Black Dog Deli The St, Walberswick IP18 6UG; 01502 723925; blackdogdeliwalberswick.com. Just a few minutes' walk or ride up the road from the harbour, this little take-away deli offers a range of delicious homemade gourmet snacks, soups, salads, filled baguettes, cakes & pastries, all made on the premises by the Anglo-Italian husband & wife team. They also sell locally made jams, pickles, preserves, Italian charcuterie & much more. Their barista coffee is also excellent & they do ready meals too, handy if you're staying self-catering nearby. **£**

The Star Inn Hall Rd, Wenhaston IP19 9HF; 01502 478240; wenhastonstar.co.uk. Right on our route through Wenhaston, this award-winning, traditional village inn is popular with local cycling groups, for its front garden overlooking the Blyth Valley. Its restaurant has a small but diverse menu, ranging from ham, egg & chips, to braised lamb ragu & stone-baked pizzas, plus filled baguettes at lunchtime. The bar stocks local ciders & cask ales, including Green Jack's Golden Best, & they usually run a twice-yearly beer festival. **££**

The Clockhouse Southwold Pier, Southwold IP18 6BN; 01502 722105; southwoldpier.co.uk. This little café halfway along the pier has a few indoor tables, or outside in semi-open cubicles, with stunning sea views. The menu covers b/fasts, light lunches & afternoon teas, with filled baguettes, scones, sausage rolls, cakes & pastries. There are hot & cold drinks, including beer & wine. **£**

FACILITIES AND FURTHER INFORMATION

There are public toilets in Walberswick on Ferry Road a few minutes from the car park, and in Southwold by the harbourside.

Visitor Information Point (VIP) Southwold Library, North Green, Southwold IP18 6AT; 0333 016 2000. The VIP within Southwold Library has a stock of leaflets, guides & maps of the area, including Walberswick. Library staff will also help with enquiries about local events, activities & directions.

14 ORFORD LOOP

START/FINISH	Orford
DISTANCE/TIME	33.9km/3½hrs
DIFFICULTY/TERRAIN	① All on road, quiet country lanes and B-roads, with mostly level or gentle inclines
SCENIC RATING	⑧ Historic Orford, arty Snape Maltings, a medieval church, a watermill, rolling, wooded valleys, plus an optional detour to a red-graded MTB forest trail
SUITABLE FOR	Hybrid, e-bike or road bike (mountain bike for the Viking Trail)
NCN ROUTE	Partly on NCN41
MAPS	OS Explorer 212 (1:25 000)
KOMOOT REF	584534379

↑ Attractive Orford is one of Suffolk's more upmarket seaside resorts (Martin Charles Hatch/S)

ORFORD LOOP | **CHAPTER 14**   **139**

Nautical Orford and musical Snape Maltings are two of the more refined retreats of this quiet corner of mid-Suffolk, between the busy port of Felixstowe to the south and the seaside-pier jollity of Southwold to the north. Starting and ending in Orford, this loop meanders inland across country, also taking in a medieval church at Iken, Butley Watermill and the dense woodlands of Tunstall Forest.

THE ROUTE

Start at Orford's ❶ **Quay Street car park**, opposite the Jolly Sailor Inn. This pleasantly secluded town at the mouth of the River Ore is one of the more select resorts along the Suffolk coast. From the 12th century onwards, it flourished under the watchful protection of Orford Castle, overlooking the safe harbour for naval and fishing fleets. Today, Orford attracts well-to-do weekenders and yachties, supporting an array of upmarket restaurants and

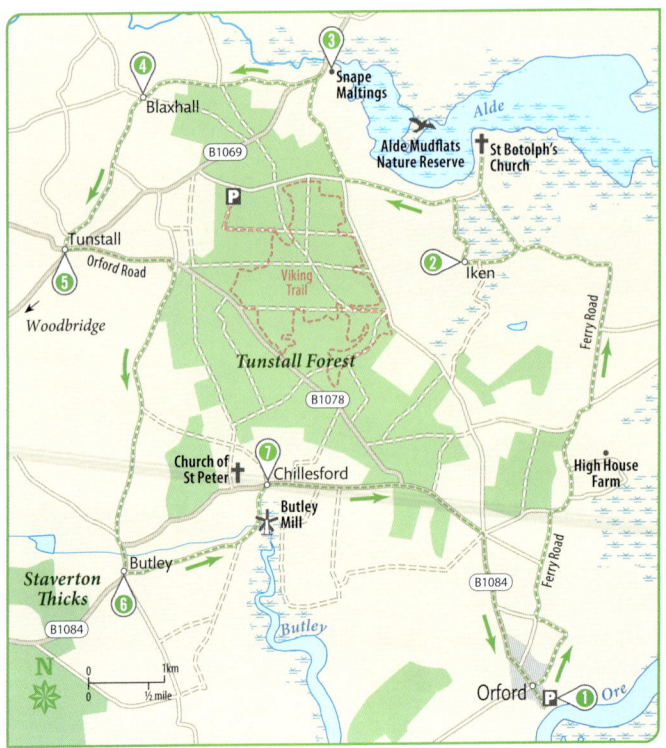

holiday cottages. There are boat cruises around RSPB Havergate Island and to Orford Ness, where top-secret nuclear research took place during the Cold War, but which is now a national nature reserve.

Turn right out of the car park on to Quay Street and take the next right on to Daphne Road, passing a row of pretty brick- and timber-gabled cottages on the left. We're soon out of the town and into the countryside, with the River Alde glimpsed between the trees on our right. Coming to a triangle after a few hundred metres at the end of Raydon Lane, turn left, signposted Suffolk Coastal Route/NCN41. Carry on along the tree-tunnel lane, going gently downhill between the fields. Turn right at the crossroads, after another few hundred metres, on to Ferry Road. Go straight ahead at the next crossroads, then right at the T-junction at the bottom of the hill. About another 500m beyond that, look out for a sign on the right to **High House Farm**, which has a tempting range of fruit and vegetables for sale, or pick-your-own. It's only a short way down the path so you might be tempted to stock up on healthy cycling snacks. Follow the road winding around to the left a short way after the turning to High House Farm, and turn left after around 2km, at the next T-junction, by a thatched cottage on your right, signposted Iken Common and Tunstall.

Coming to a left-hand fork before ⓘ Iken, go straight ahead through the village to visit the medieval, thatch-roofed **St Botolph's Church**, one of the finest and oldest in Suffolk. It is down a narrow cul-de-sac lane to the right as the road winds left at the end of the village, standing on a peaceful promontory overlooking the River Alde. It was founded by the missionary monk Saint Botolph in AD654, with some Norman features still surviving, including the nave and a tiny slit window in the north wall. Opposite the church is the Anchorage, a grand but well-hidden manor house, with its ornate chimneys towering above the tall hedgerows.

Return to the fork and turn right down Sandy Lane. In case you notice that we have now done effectively three sides of a square through Iken, instead of cutting straight across from the church, there is some method in my madness. This is a more scenic loop around the village, through meadows of grazing cattle and horses, with several immaculate thatched cottages by the roadside. Coming out into the open countryside again, with the broad expanse of the River Alde on your right, pass a sign to Iken Cliff on the right. The tidal marshes here must be the world's shortest cliffs, but they're part of Suffolk Wildlife Trust's **Alde Mudflats Nature Reserve** (⌀ suffolkwildlifetrust.org/aldemudflats). This is a great birdwatching spot, including sizeable numbers of avocets, curlews and oystercatchers, as well as the odd marsh harrier.

Turn right at the next crossroads, after around 1.5km, signposted Aldeburgh and Saxmundham, now crossing the edge of **Tunstall Forest**. As an optional detour for mountain biking, the forest has the red-graded **Viking Trail**. To get to the start of the trail, go straight ahead at the last

crossroads with the entrance about another 1.5km along the road, on the left. The 16km circuit is a bit too challenging for our more sedate ride, but for experienced MTB riders, it's one worth bookmarking for a return visit. For further information, see ⌀ trogmtb.com.

Next, turn right at the next fork after a few hundred metres (leaving the NCN41) to ❸ **Snape Maltings**, on your right. The former Victorian barley maltings are now home to Suffolk's foremost concert hall, with its annual Aldeburgh Festival, founded by composer Benjamin Britten. With its tranquil, riverside setting, the arty-industrial complex also houses galleries, shops and cafés. There's also a circular nature walk around the reed beds at Snape Warren, starting from the Tipi café (page 144).

Leaving Snape Maltings, turn left back to the fork. This time, turn right at a left-hand bend in the road, signposted Blaxhall (back on the NCN41). Take care at this tricky junction – dismount and walk across if unsure. Continue along this road, past the wooded heathland of Blaxhall Common on the left and fields on the right, then turn left at the next crossroads leading to the sleepy village of ❹ **Blaxhall** after a couple of kilometres.

↑ Snape Maltings is home to Suffolk's foremost concert hall (Jamesphotos/DT)

Coming into Blaxhall, go straight over the crossroads, with the YHA signposted to the left, and take the next left at a T-junction, passing the Ship Inn on your left. Carry on along this straight and level road through the fields, coming to Tunstall after about 2km.

Compared with somnolent Blaxhall, ❺ **Tunstall** is a bustling metropolis, with modern housing spread around the crossroads between the Woodbridge Road (B1069) and the Orford Road (B1078). Turn left here, with the Green Man Inn on your right, heading back now towards Orford, and cutting through the middle of Tunstall Forest. After about 500m, turn right, signposted Tunstall Baptist Church, and right again shortly after, at a T junction.

The road snakes smoothly downhill through the pine trees, with a small but dense broadleaved copse at the bottom of the hill on the right. The little-known but much-loved **Staverton Thicks** are ancient woods of gnarled oaks and giant holly trees, described by naturalist Oliver Rackham in *The Living Heart of the Countryside* as an '*awesome place of Tolkienesque wonder and beauty. The mighty and bizarre shapes of oaks of unknown age rise out of a sea of tall bracken, or else are mysteriously surrounded by rings of yet mightier hollies*'. In these still and shady woods, it may be easy to imagine elves and hobbits hiding in the roadside bracken.

Heading now towards ❻ **Butley**, turn right at the fork at the bottom of the hill, on to The Street, then first left down Mill Lane. The road winds alongside a tributary of the River Butley, hidden behind trees on your left, then passing **Butley Mill** itself on the left. Now housing artists' studios and holiday apartments, the 19th-century mill has been well preserved, complete with its loading dock overhanging the road.

Carry on along Mill Lane for another 500m or so, coming to a T-junction in the village of ❼ **Chillesford** (pronounced Chilluz-ford). The claim to fame of this little village is that its parish church, the 14th-century **Church of St Peter**, is one of only two in the whole of England whose tower is made of coralline crag. Apart from the fact that the rare geological deposits are quarried nearby, it also gives the tower a beautiful honey-toned glow, especially on sunny evenings. Inside, the church also has beautiful modern stained-glass windows, the work of Surinder Warboys, a Suffolk-based artist. If all this piques your ecclesiastical curiosity, the church is to the left at the T-junction, then up a footpath a few hundred metres along on the right.

Otherwise, turn right here and pass the Froize Inn on your right. Plunging back into dense trees after Chillesford, with the upmarket Chillesford Lodge Estate on your right at a fork with the B1078, continue right here and back into Orford along the flat, straight B-road for the last 2km or so. Coming into Orford, follow Munday's Lane straight ahead and downhill through the town centre, passing the King's Head Inn on your left, and back on to Quay Street with the car park on your left.

THE ESSENTIALS

GETTING THERE By **car**, Orford is just under 33km east of Ipswich, on the A12, A1152 and Orford Road, from Woodbridge. The nearest **train** station is at Melton, which has regular trains to Ipswich, taking around 20 minutes, and with direct trains from there to London Liverpool Street taking around 2½ hours. By **bus**, there's the 71 Village Links service from Melton, a milk-round route through neighbouring villages, taking around half an hour.

WHERE TO EAT

✕ Riverside Tearoom Orford IP12 2NU; ☎ 07708 632745; ⌂ riversidetearoomorford.co.uk. With an outdoor deck or indoor tables, this snug little waterfront café has unmatched views overlooking the River Ore estuary. They do delicious homemade cakes, snacks, sandwiches & pastries & hot & cold drinks, including what some claim to be the best coffee in town. Local artwork for sale adorns the walls. **£**

✕ Pizza in the Tipi Snape Maltings, Snape IP17 1SP; ⌂ snape-maltings-live.herokuapp.com/eat/the-tipi. Seated out on the lawn or under 2 traditional tipi-type tents overlooking the reed beds at Snape Maltings, you can feast here on traditional, hand-stretched, stone-baked pizzas. The take-away stall also offers a variety of fresh sandwiches, salads & desserts, Italian hot chocolates, tea, coffee, wines & local ales. **££**

✕ The Ship Inn School Rd, Blaxhall IP12 2DY; ☎ 01728 688316; ⌂ blaxhallshipinn.co.uk. This welcoming village pub midway around our route serves hearty traditional roasts, fish & seafood, pub-grub favourites & a couple of veggie dishes too, all from locally sourced produce. The bar keeps a good stock of local ales & ciders. **££**

ORFORD NESS

If you're looking out across Orford's waterfront, your eye might be caught by the strange, squat structures dotted along the horizon. These so-called pagodas were built by the Atomic Weapons Research Establishment at the height of the Cold War in the 1950s, for highly secretive testing of nuclear weapon components. No nuclear material was reported to have been used here in the end, but they were made to test the power of potential nuclear explosions, with the massive concrete lids designed to collapse on to the underground laboratories and absorb the impact. Today, the sinister-looking pagodas remain and are the only such test sites in the UK currently open to the public, on guided tours.

Alternatively, perhaps for those with more peace-loving interests, this tranquil and remote shingle spit – the largest in Europe – is also a national nature reserve. Access is via National Trust ferry from Orford, with trails along the dramatic, remote shingle spit, through reed marshes, mudflats and brackish lagoons. Besides owls, marsh harriers, hares and many waterbirds that frequent the reserve, Chinese water deer have also taken up home here, which probably escaped from private parks and swam across the estuary. For more details about visiting Orford Ness, see ⌀ nationaltrust.org.uk/orford-ness-national-nature-reserve.

FACILITIES AND FURTHER INFORMATION There are public toilets at Quay Street car park and at Snape Maltings, and customer toilets in pubs en route.

Woodbridge Tourist Information Point Woodbridge Library, New St, Woodbridge IP12 1DT; ⌀ 01394 330855; Woodbridge Library Suffolk. The nearest source of information to Sutton Hoo, this information point at the local library will help with advice & directions; they also have a supply of leaflets & guides available. Alternatively, the museum at **Orford Castle** (⌀ 01394 450472; free) may be able to help with local directions & tips.

15 SUTTON HOO & RENDLESHAM FOREST LOOP

START/FINISH	Sutton Hoo
DISTANCE/TIME	35.2km/4hrs
DIFFICULTY/TERRAIN	② Approximately half on road (B-roads or country lanes), half on forest trails; rough and bumpy in parts, but no tricky mountain bike technical features – best suited to experienced cyclists
SCENIC RATING	☺ Anglo-Saxon treasures at Sutton Hoo, Shingle Street's eerie coastline, and off-road mountain biking adventure in Rendlesham Forest
SUITABLE FOR	Sturdy hybrid, mountain bike, gravel bike or e-bike
NCN ROUTE	Briefly on NCN41 (Suffolk Coastal Route)
MAPS	OS Explorer 197 (1:25 000)
KOMOOT REF	584614388

↑ Rendlesham Forest (Alistair Macleod/DT)

SUTTON HOO & RENDLESHAM FOREST LOOP | CHAPTER 15 | 147

Take some dazzling Anglo-Saxon treasures, an end-of-the-world coastline, and shake them up with a generous measure of off-road mountain bike trails. This gloriously diverse loop offers a quirky mix of southern Suffolk's highlights. Starting at Sutton Hoo, we head across heathland to Shingle Street, then wind back through the pine forests and sandy trails of Rendlesham Forest, keeping alert for UFOs!

THE ROUTE

Start from the ❶ **Sutton Hoo NT car park**, just outside Woodbridge. It was here that amateur archaeologist Basil Brown found the decayed remains of an Anglo-Saxon longship in 1939, leading to the excavation of the most spectacular medieval burial chamber known in Europe. Although many of the original pieces, including the stunning helmet, are in the British Museum, many other artefacts are on display here in Sutton Hoo's own

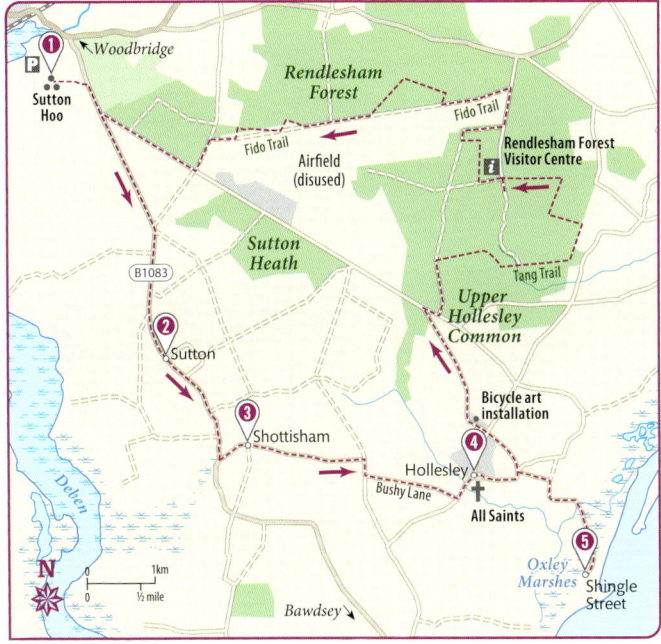

impressive museum. There is also a viewing tower, which looks over the burial mounds where the treasure was found. You could easily spend hours exploring the extensive grounds, so it might be wise to save these treats until after your ride, in case you run out of time and energy to do anything else!

So, to get started, turn right out of the main entrance and on to the B1083, signposted Bawdsey, looking out as you cross the traffic. It's a straight, undulating road lined with shady pine trees, arable fields and pig farms. There's usually some farm traffic too, including tractors, trucks and the like, but it's a two-lane road, with plenty of room for vehicles to overtake. Keep on the main road at the fork after about 700m, but make a mental note as we'll be coming back along the road on the left (signposted Hollesley and Sutton Heath), from Rendlesham Forest. Pass **Sutton Heath** on your left after another 800m, a popular spot for picnickers and dog walkers. About 1km after the heath, we come into ❷ **Sutton**, a quiet little village strung along either side of the road, with a handsome former schoolhouse on the left, a thatched cottage on the right, and the Plough Inn on the left on the way out.

A few kilometres later, turn left at a T-junction, signposted Shottisham and Hollesley (pronounced Hose-ley). To the right leads to the Bawdsey Radar Museum, about 9km south, by the mouth of the River Deben. The isolated stretch of coast from there up to Orford was used during World War II for highly secretive military research, prompting many conspiracy theories, but which led to the invention of radar (for more details, see box, page 145).

Shortly after the T-junction we come to ❸ **Shottisham**, a pretty little village on a tributary brook of the River Deben, with a colourful painted village sign on the left, in front of a pond filled with huge gunnera plants. As in many rural villages, the historic heart of Shottisham is focused around its pub and church. The lovely old thatch-roofed Sorrel Horse Inn stands on the corner of the road, in front of the medieval village church tower poking above the treetops behind. Continue through the village and just on the outskirts on the left is the Shottisham Campsite and the Blue Rabbit Café (worth noting as countryside cafés are rare anywhere inland in East Anglia, with only one or two others on this route).

As we head now towards Hollesley, the road is generally sloping down to the coast. About 0.5km after the campsite, after a right-hand bend, turn left opposite the Bailiff's Cottage on your right, on to Bushy Lane, signposted Hollesley, Butley, Orford and Shingle Street. After a further kilometre, at a T-junction turn left again, on to Alderton Road, now on the NCN41, briefly, just for this section through the village. Turn right in front of ❹ **Hollesley's** wrought-iron village sign and if you're as big a fan of churches as I am, take a short detour down a lane to the right to **All Saints Church**. Although much of the current church is Victorian restoration, it is thought to have been founded some 1,000 years ago, with an impressive flint-clad tower, carved wooden door and fine stained-glass windows.

Returning to the main road, School Lane, follow it around to the right, past the old schoolhouse on the left, and down towards the coast, with the wide, flat shoreline glimpsed between the trees on your right. Coming shortly to a crossroads, turn right, signposted Shingle Street. Now approaching the low-lying **Oxley Marshes**, there are noticeably fewer and shorter trees here, replaced by bullrushes, reeds and mudbanks. After a few hundred metres, across a bridge over a muddy stream and flanked by more reed beds, we reach ❺ **Shingle Street**: the end of the road!

↑ The beach at Shingle Street is made, unsurprisingly, of shingle (Huw Hennessy)

The seashore is hidden from the road behind the bank of shingle, so you'll have to wheel your bike through the car park to take it all in – a wide, flat expanse of shingle beach stretching far to left and right, with a few lonely-looking terraced houses behind. If you've already visited Southwold, for instance, just up the coast, what is striking about Shingle Street is what is *not* here: no café, shop or any other touristy paraphernalia. Instead – surprise surprise – lots of shingle, dotted with clumps of seagrass and sea cabbage, looking somewhat as if they're hanging on in quiet desperation, as the Pink Floyd song says. Shingle Street used to be a thriving fishing village with a reputation for its proudly independent community, but all that was wiped out during World War II, when the coast was lined with a defensive barrier of landmines, and the whole population was evacuated. Perhaps the echoes of its past might account for the faint sense of eeriness that still lingers today. On a more positive note, however, this area is part of the RSPB Boyton and Hollesley Marshes, a haven for birds including lapwings, barn owls and avocets. (For details of the nearby visitor centre, and the great little Marsh Barn Café, see page 154.)

Return to the crossroads, where we turned right down to Shingle Street. This time go straight ahead, signposted Melton and Woodbridge, cutting across the other side of Hollesley. At the next crossroads, a few hundred metres later, signposted Woodbridge, carry on straight ahead. Hoping it has survived through the winter, there's a **bicycle-art installation** (pictured) propped up by the roadside on the left next to Hollesley Village Hall and sports field, decorated with psychedelic-coloured wool.

Emerging from the suburbs of Hollesley, we're plunged instead into the heathland of **Upper Hollesley Common**, a lush contrast to the bleak coastline just left behind. Dense woods of oaks and pine trees line the road left and right, fringed with bracken, gorse and purple patches of heather. Soon after the common, we approach the pine plantations of **Rendlesham Forest**. Coming to the main road cutting through the forest, signposted Hollesley Bay Colony, Boyton and Butley, turn sharp right – it's a tight-angled junction, so take care. Then, after about 300m, look out for the forest path on the left: there's a sign saying 'Private Road: No vehicles or horses', and no sign announcing Rendlesham Forest – but, it *is*! We're

SUTTON HOO & RENDLESHAM FOREST LOOP | **CHAPTER 15**

going in through the back door, so to speak, as the main entrance is on the north side, off the B1084/Woodbridge Road.

So, trusting Komoot and me, let the off-road fun commence! Take the narrow path on the left, wriggle around a traffic barrier after 100m or so, and then join the cycle trail proper. Coming to a wide forest clearing, at the T-junction, follow the bluey-green arrows directing right along the **Tang Trail**: it's a rubbly-sandy track between the dense trees. It's blissful to be off the road and into the countryside for a while. This trail is shared with others, though, so be mindful of other trail users en route. Also, keep alert for the randomly changing trail, sometimes with sharp, rubbly flint, sometimes with loose, slippery sand, pine needles and tree roots. It's not so bad in dry weather – this being one of the driest parts of the UK after all. In the rain, though, you'll definitely need good grippy tyres, a reliable bike helmet and gloves. If you like to cycle like the proverbial bat out of hell, knee and elbow pads probably wouldn't hurt too. As for sand specifically, I've learned from many a slip and slide that the best/only way to get through it is – slowly! If in doubt, just get off and walk through the odd sandy patch – they're not very long. In general, this is a green-graded MTB trail, so it's suitable for beginners.

↑ It's hard to miss this colourful art installation in Hollesley (Huw Hennessy)

After a few hundred metres out in the clearing, turn right at a crossroads, still following the Tang Trail arrows. From here onwards, the trail sometimes narrows to single file under the trees, with the potential hazard of overhanging branches. Besides the trail route markers, there are also information signs on posts here and there too, with emergency contact phone numbers and grid references (including one at the far corner of the airfield, just before we leave the forest). Coming towards the main visitor

THE UFO MYSTERY OF RENDLESHAM FOREST

In late 1980, first-hand accounts of mysterious sightings in Rendlesham Forest hit news headlines across the world, in what is probably the UK's most compelling UFO mystery to date. On 27 December, at around 02.00, two United States Air Force servicemen, based at RAF Woodbridge East Gate, reported seeing unusual red lights in the forest. Joined by another patrolman, they approached the lights and saw a conical shape in a clearing, about the size of a car, floating about 30cm off the ground on projected beams of light. When they tried to get closer – and all three men claimed to have felt something 'dreamlike' slowing them down – the object shot up into the sky with a streak of light, and disappeared!

The following day, other military personnel checked the area and found broken treetops around the clearing, as well as three small triangular hollows in the ground below. Radiation readings taken in the area found background levels ten times higher than normal. On the next night, more unusual lights were seen in the area, amid reports of women screaming and agitated farm animals in a nearby field.

Subsequently, the RAF wrote a memo about the sightings, which was released by the US government and described as 'unexplained aerial phenomena' in the forest. Many more news reports and books have been published since those dramatic days but, to date, no definitive explanation has surfaced. If this piques your curiosity, Rendlesham Forest has created a walking trail, following the alleged sightings. For more information, visit ⌀ forestryengland.uk/rendlesham-forest/ufo-trail-rendlesham-forest.

centre and car park, the Tang Trail joins up with another cycle trail, the Fido Trail and, briefly, the UFO Trail, which relates to the forest's mysterious sightings from the 1980s (see box, opposite). Looking out for traffic, cross the main road just before the car park and carry on straight ahead. Turn left again shortly after the road on to a wide sandy path sloping downhill to the left to the main visitor centre. There's a take-away kiosk here, information board, playground, picnic benches, toilets and car park.

From here onwards, we continue on the **Fido Trail** (marked with brown arrows), winding through the trees, around an airfield and emerging out the other side of Rendlesham Forest, next to Sutton Hoo. Start by going along the paved road towards the exit, passing another small car park on the left. Turn left at the far corner of the military airfield, which is still in use, with razor-wire fencing and the occasional helicopter buzzing overhead, adding somehow to the forest's UFO mystique. The trail is signposted here and throughout the route, but they're sometimes quite well hidden by overhanging branches, so keep your eyes peeled. The going is bumpy here, narrow in parts too, so don't race too fast and be vigilant on the few short sandy stretches.

The trail sometimes veers away from the fence briefly, but generally keeps going alongside the airfield perimeter. Eventually, we approach the far corner, where the Fido Trail turns right and back towards the visitor centre. Carry on straight ahead here, on to a narrower trail. Coming shortly to a crossroads, turn left on to the wider track to rejoin the perimeter fence. Emerging finally from the forest, after around another 500m, we come to a small roadside parking area, by Heath Road. Turn right here, back on to the road, and after about 1.5km, at a sharp T-junction (the same fork we passed at the beginning of the route), turn right and back on to the B1083. Take care crossing the traffic; get off and walk across if it's too busy. Some 200m later, turn left at the entrance to Sutton Hoo and return to the car park. There are cycle racks by the Visitor Welcome building.

THE ESSENTIALS

GETTING THERE By **car**, Sutton Hoo is around 5km from Woodbridge, on the B1083 between Melton and Bawdsey. By **train**, the nearest station is

Melton, which has direct trains from Ipswich, taking around 25 minutes. The nearest **bus** stop is also at Melton, with the Ipswich to Framlingham bus 63 stopping en route in the town centre.

WHERE TO EAT

✘ **King's River Café** Sutton Hoo 1P12 3DJ; 01394 389720; nationaltrust.org.uk/sutton-hoo. In the visitor centre courtyard, by the ship sculpture, this little café does a good range of hot & cold snacks, sandwiches, soup of the day, ice creams, cakes & pastries. There are tables inside & out, or take-away, with benches around the grounds & at the picnic area next to the car park. **££**

✘ **Marsh Barn Café** Hollesley Marshes RSPB IP12 3JW; Marsh Barn Farm Shop. Down a rubbly road from Hollesley HMP, this great little café near Shingle St and next to the bird reserve is a wonderful find in such an isolated little spot. Run by former army vets training as baristas (combat2coffee.co.uk), the café has tables out in the yard or indoors, with thought-provoking artwork on the walls, a mix of wildlife paintings & war poetry. They serve a small selection of cakes, sandwiches & snacks, but above all, the fresh-brewed coffee is excellent. **£**

✘ **Bear Grills** Rendlesham Forest IP12 3NF; Bear Grills snack van. I'm not sure what

↑ Sutton Hoo is home to some dazzling Anglo-Saxon treasures (Wirestock Creators/S)

the famous scout leader would make of the cheeky namesake, but this mobile van parked at the main visitor centre in the middle of Rendlesham Forest comes in handy, with nowhere else nearby on the return leg of the route until Sutton Hoo. Serving take-away hot & cold snacks, tea, coffee & soft drinks, it's open mostly at weekends – check their Facebook page for updates. **£**

FACILITIES AND FURTHER INFORMATION There are public toilets at Sutton Hoo (⌂ nationaltrust.org.uk/sutton-hoo) and in Rendlesham Forest.

🛈 Woodbridge Tourist Information Point Woodbridge Library, New St, Woodbridge IP12 1DT; ✆ 01394 330855; **f** Woodbridge Library Suffolk. The nearest source of information to Sutton Hoo, this information point at the local library will help with advice & directions; they also have a supply of leaflets & guides available.

16 LAVENHAM LOOP

START/FINISH	Market Square, Lavenham
DISTANCE/TIME	20.7km/2½hrs
DIFFICULTY/TERRAIN	① Level or gently undulating, all on road, mostly quiet country lanes, with a few road crossings
SCENIC RATING	⑧ Lavenham, one of the best-preserved medieval towns in East Anglia, through sleepy villages and rolling agricultural countryside
SUITABLE FOR	Road bike, hybrid or e-bike
NCN ROUTE	Partly on NCN13 (from Lavenham N to Great Green)
MAPS	OS Explorer 196 and 211 (1:25 000)
KOMOOT REF	518873339

↑ Historic Lavenham is one of Suffolk's prettiest towns (Helen Hotson/S)

LAVENHAM LOOP | CHAPTER 16

istoric showpiece Lavenham is widely considered to be England's finest medieval wool town, crowned by its magnificent Guildhall on the cobblestoned market square. Escaping the crowds that flock to this picture-perfect scene, our easy-going route loops around the Stour Valley. We cross the trickling little River Brett several times, past arable fields dotted with poppies and hedgerows speckled with pink bindweed, primroses and foxgloves. Out here, the villages are tucked down narrow lanes, largely ignored by Lavenham's tour groups but many with their own ancient thatched cottages and neatly tended village greens.

THE ROUTE

Start from ❶ **Lavenham Market Place**, the historic heart of this ancient wool town, with the 16th-century Guildhall and other Tudor buildings propping each other up at implausible angles. Cross the market square to the right, with the Guildhall behind you – probably on foot here, because of the

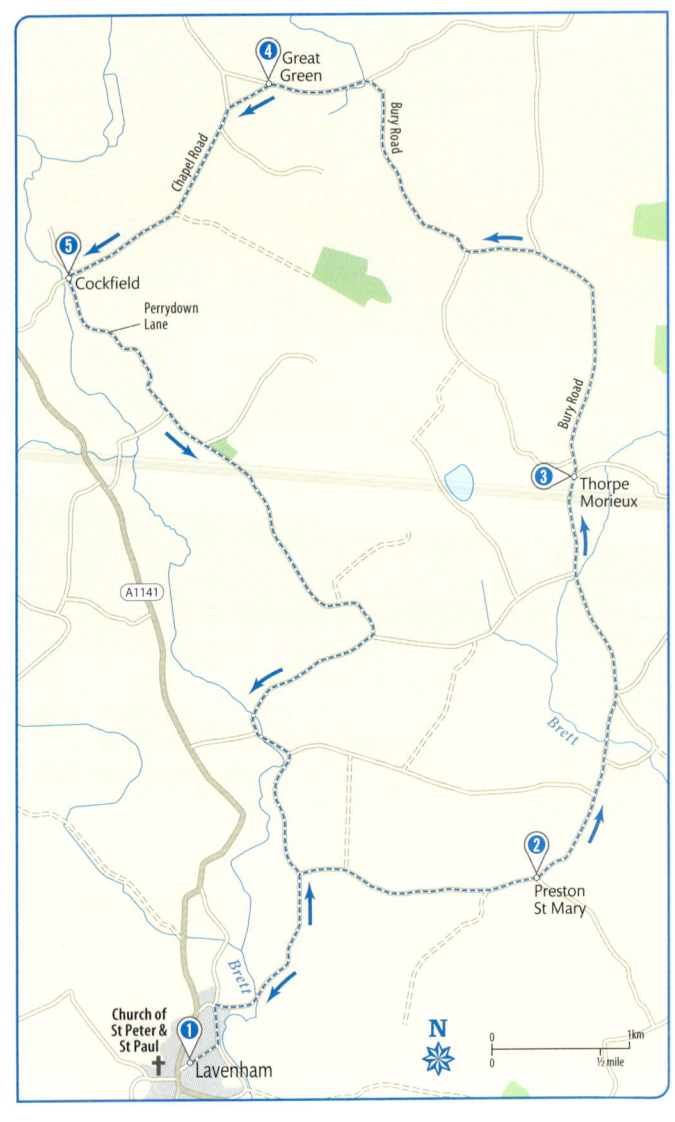

many sightseers that flock here, not to mention cars trying to squeeze into the limited parking spaces. Go down Prentice Street, leading to a T-junction with Lower Road. Turn left here then right at the crossroads, on to Preston Road.

Leaving the town centre and going downhill briefly here, note that Lavenham is perched on a hill – not that high, but the tower of its **Church of St Peter and St Paul** stands out proudly on the horizon for miles around, serving as a useful landmark on the way back. So, after a short dip down and across the River Brett, we head uphill now, turning right at the top of the hill, signposted Preston (Preston St Mary). There's also a signpost here for the South Suffolk Route, the NCN13, which you may have spotted elsewhere on other routes. This is the main cycle route going up through the middle of the county, from Sudbury northwards through the Brecks and on into Norfolk.

Coming in to ❷ **Preston St Mary** after about 1.5km, our route winds left at a fork before the village, just past the brightly ochre-washed Priory Barn on the left. It's quite a pretty village if you wanted to detour for a quick look, with one or two thatched cottages lining The Street, no shops but one pub: the red-brick Six Bells (page 163), at the end on the right.

Otherwise turn left and continue straight ahead for around 2km, down across the River Brett again and up the other side, taking the left fork shortly after that, signposted ❸ **Thorpe Morieux** (pronounced Moroo, as a local corrected my clunky effort at what I assumed was a French connection). Coming into the village, turn left at the painted village sign at the road triangle on to Bury Road. It's a peaceful little place, with no shop or pub, but its phone box, on the left after a couple of hundred metres or so, has been repurposed as a miniature tourist office, with a handy local map stuck inside.

Follow the road around to the left at the triangle, about 1.5km out of Thorpe Morieux, signposted Lavenham, Cockfield and Bury St Edmunds. From here, we go gently downhill through the fields and up again, turning left at the T-junction after another 2km and coming to the aptly named ❹ **Great Green**. This is another tidy little village, centred around a broad

green, with a playground at the near end and a cricket field at the other. Follow along the left side of the green, coming to a small lily pond just to the right at the far end. Looking as if they might have escaped from a nearby pet shop, goldfish can be seen swimming around beneath the lily pads – slightly nervously too, under the watchful eye of moorhens bobbing on the surface.

Turn left at this corner of the green, on to Chapel Road, and signposted Cockfield. Carry on along this level road and, no sooner have we left Great Green, we come into ❺ **Cockfield**. Not to make too much fanfare about it, but for once, there's a shop in the village! The Cockfield Stores & Post Office are at the end on the left, so, as we're about halfway, this might make a good time for a break.

Refreshed here or not, hopefully you'll enjoy the nice downhill run out of the village now, turning left at the war memorial (signposted NCN13) on to Perrydown Lane. This soon levels out, and gently climbs through a shady tunnel of trees at the brow of the hill. About 500m after that, turn

↑ The pretty village of Cockfield (Adrian Turner)

right at the T-junction at the bottom of the hill, then follow the rolling road between fields and hedgerows. As promised earlier, you should catch sight of Lavenham again now, on the horizon to the right, with the church tower standing tall over the rooftops.

Pass a beautiful pink-washed farmhouse on your right: Apple Mount Retreat (page 213). Soon after that, at the T-junction, turn left, signposted Preston – not right to Lavenham, as that leads to the busy A1141. About 800m later, we come to another T-junction, signposted Lavenham, which you might recognise from the start, en route to Preston St Mary. Turn right here, and on to the last stretch back into the town, nicely downhill most of the way. After crossing the river one last time, and going up to the residential suburbs, take the left turn on to Lower Road (signposted Local Traffic, NCN13). Continue up here, then take the fourth turning on the right up Prentice Street, and returning finally to Market Square.

THE ESSENTIALS

GETTING THERE By **car**, Lavenham is just over 11km northeast of the nearest town, Sudbury, either via the A134 and Lavenham road after 3km, or on the B1115 and B1071. By **train**, Sudbury is also the nearest station, with services from London Liverpool Street, changing at Marks Tey, near Colchester, taking around 1½ hours. By **bus**, there's the 753 Boomerang from Sudbury, which as its name might suggest, bounces around the countryside, taking just over half an hour.

WHERE TO EAT

✘ **Lavenham Blue Vintage Tea Rooms** Market Pl, Lavenham CO10 9QZ; ✆ 01787 248295; ⌖ lavenhambluetearooms.com. Just off Market Pl in the centre of town, this pretty little tearoom in a Grade II-listed Tudor cottage sums itself up accurately in its name, with tea served in real china cups, lacy tablecloths, chintzy knick-knacks adorning the walls & retro jazz played on the gramophone. Besides afternoon tea, the menu also offers ploughman's lunches, homemade cakes & scones. Their take-away tea-boxes are handy if it's full inside, or the back garden is a sunny nook on warm summer days. **££**

✘ **Lavenham Guildhall Tea Room** Market Ln, Lavenham CO10 9QZ; ✆ 01787 247646. With outdoor tables in its shady courtyard

LAVENHAM GUILDHALL

There are more than 320 listed historic buildings in Lavenham, but the most prestigious is the magnificent Guildhall of Corpus Christi. The building, with timber frame and plaster infill, is one of the finest of its kind in England. Its prominent role in the development of the town over 500 years reflects Lavenham's own important position in the heart of Suffolk's medieval wool trade. The town gained a market charter in 1259 and soon grew to be England's major centre for wool traders. The high-quality local broadcloth, known as Lavenham Blue, was woven across eastern and southern England, then dyed in Lavenham. The Guild of Corpus Christi was a religious group of merchants, who set tightly controlled trade rules and principles, giving them immense power in the important wool trade. With booming exports as far afield as North Africa and Russia, Lavenham became one of the wealthiest towns in England.

By the time the Guildhall was built in 1529, however, Lavenham was already beginning to decline, after cheaper cloth began to be produced in Colchester. The Guild was abolished, and the hall used for a sequence of roles, including a prison, wool store, workhouse, home for World War II evacuees and a restaurant. Finally, in 1951 it was taken over by the National Trust. They run lively events here to help bring the building's rich history alive, including family-friendly quiz trails and traditional spinning demonstrations. For more details, visit ⌀ nationaltrust.org.uk/Lavenham-guildhall.

↑ The Guildhall is arguably Lavenham's most impressive listed building (Paul Wishart/S)

garden, this café is a real find & surprisingly wasn't too packed on our visit last summer, perhaps because of its location, tucked inside the Guildhall. Its small menu offers hot & cold snacks, soup, sandwiches & delicious, freshly made cakes & scones (including Scone of the Month), & all at reasonable prices in what is quite a pricey town. **£**

✖ **The Six Bells** The St, Preston St Mary CO10 9NG, ✆ 01787 247440; 🌐 thesixbellspreston.com. This beautiful old country inn – a Grade II-listed building – in the quiet village just off our route, has a warm local feel & welcoming ambience. Its traditional pub menu features favourites such as beer-battered fish & chips, bangers & mash, with a few newcomers, including mac & cheese, & chilli with guacamole & nachos. The bar stocks local ales on tap as well as a decent selection of wines. In warm weather, its west-facing back garden is an added attraction: watch the sun go down with a pint of Adnams in hand (other refreshments are also available). **££**

FACILITIES AND FURTHER INFORMATION There are public toilets in the Prentice Street car park in Lavenham. There is parking space on the market square itself but it can be busy.

ℹ️ **Lavenham Village Information Point** 2 Lady St, Lavenham CO10 9RA; ✆ 01787 249939. This small information point in the post office building will help with local directions, what's on & local attractions; they also sell guides & maps.

17 MOULTON LOOP

START/FINISH	Moulton
DISTANCE/TIME	13.1km/1½ hrs
DIFFICULTY/TERRAIN	① On minor backroads and a couple of B-roads; mostly flat but with a few moderate climbs
SCENIC RATING	Ⓐ Rolling meadows and woods, pretty villages, a stud farm, a medieval bridge and three great country pubs
SUITABLE FOR	Road bike, hybrid or e-bike
NCN ROUTE	Partly on NCN51
MAPS	OS Explorer 10 (1:25 000)
KOMOOT REF	585336179

↑ Moulton's Packhorse Bridge dates from the 15th century (Peter Moulton/S)

This short loop around the River Kennett takes us through the picturesque villages of Moulton, Dalham and Gazeley, with a clutch of traditional country pubs en route. The valley is gently undulating, with sprawling fields and shady woods – it's a slightly more demanding ride than the pancake-flat Fens nearby, but nothing that steep or strenuous. It stands on its own merit, but if you've got energy to spare, you could combine it with the Jockey Trail (Route 18), which also starts in Moulton but which visits Newmarket too. Or, you could stop overnight in this pretty riverside village and do both rides on consecutive days.

THE ROUTE

Start from ❶ **Moulton**, by the hilltop Church of St Peter, just across the River Kennett in the southeast corner of the village. There are a few

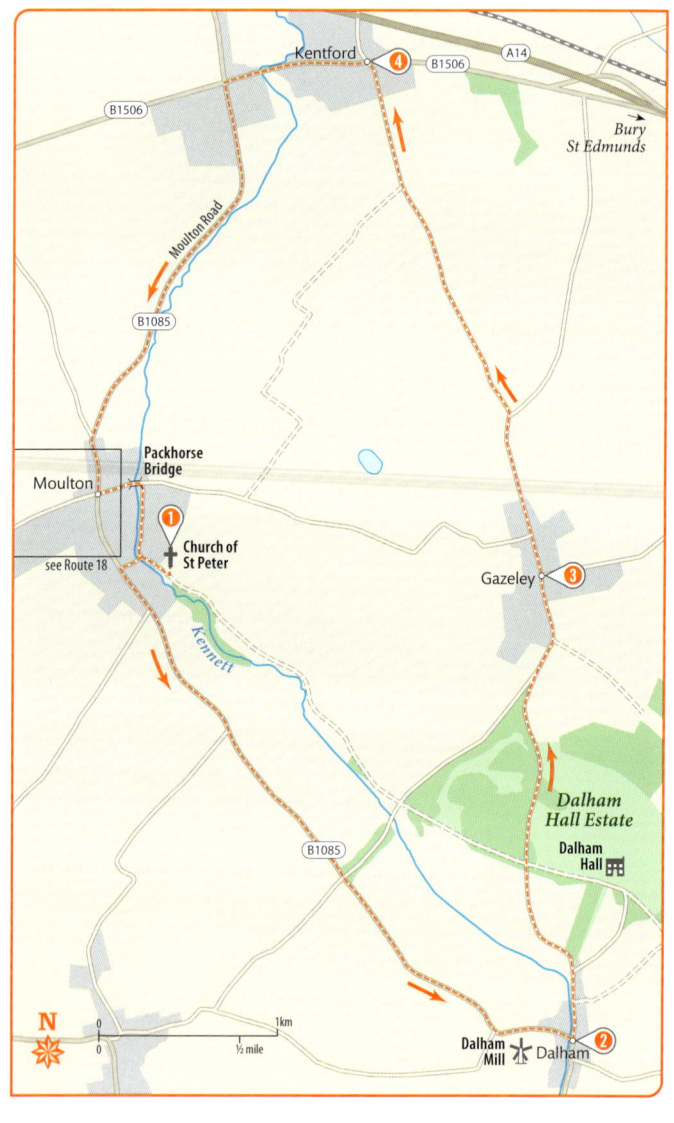

parking spaces in front of the church. The ancient village is thought to pre-date the Domesday Book, and lies on the ancient Icknield Way from Cambridge to Bury St Edmunds. Now the B1506, it also serves as the county border between Suffolk and Cambridgeshire.

With the church behind you, turn right along Brookside, then left across the ford or the bridge on to Church Road, and up to a T-junction. Turn left through the village and along the B1085, the road winding downhill between fields and woods. As you come around a bend to the left, after about 3km, note **Dalham Mill** on your right. The late 18th-century smock mill has been shorn of its sails, but it's being restored and is now a gin distillery (⌀ millgincompany.com). At the bottom of the hill, cross over the River Kennett again and come to a T-junction, with the thatch-roofed Affleck Arms on your right. ❷ **Dalham** is a pretty village, with several other thatch-roofed cottages lining the riverbank that runs alongside The Street, its main road. Turn left here and continue through the village, climbing towards woods, with a glimpse of **Dalham Hall** on your right. The private estate, with a Queen Anne-style 18th-century house and stud farm, is currently owned by Sheikh Mohammed, ruler of Dubai.

As we come into the small woods on the brow of the hill, take the narrow right fork ahead into ❸ **Gazeley**. This is another picturesque village, with a large church and a handful of thatch-roofed cottages and Georgian townhouses spread along its straight main road. Pass All Saints Church on the left and keep going for another 3km or so, along the straight and flat road through fields up to the crossroads. Turn left here and through ❹ **Kentford**, a neat and tidy modern village, though the B1506 can be busy at peak times, so cycle carefully. Coming soon to the first crossroads, with the ivy-clad Bell Inn on the right, turn left onto the B1085, back towards Moulton. Follow this quieter and level road, with the Kennett on your left, for another 2km or so.

Coming into the village, turn left on to Bridge Street, past the Packhorse Inn and coming to the adjacent **Packhorse Bridge**. This listed historic monument dates from the 15th century; its four broad arches and wide span reflect the fact that the River Kennett was once wider. This also allowed a gentler slope over the bridge, which was wide enough for carts

LOCAL HAUNTS

The Bell Inn, Kennett, which we pass by on this cycle route, claims to be haunted, with mediums testifying to the presence of otherworldly beings in recent years. True or not, there are many tales told of ghosts throughout this region full of ancient folklore – none more chilling, perhaps, than that of Newmarket race jockey Fred Archer. Considered the best champion jockey of all time, Archer (1857–86) won 2,747 out of his 8,084 rides. When his wife Helen died in childbirth, however, Fred was heartbroken. The couple had also lost their first child William, two years previously. Stricken with grief, Fred shot himself dead on 8 November 1886, two years after Helen's passing. In tragic irony, his short-barrelled pistol had been given to him as a prize for one of his many race victories.

Archer was buried in Newmarket, aged only 29. Stories have been told since, however, of his ghost roaming the nearby heath – still today the jockeys' training grounds – mounted on Scotch Pearl, his grey phantom racehorse. Ghostly sightings have also been reported at Pegasus Stables, which Archer built for himself (as Falmouth Lodge).

So, if you do our adjoining Route 18 (page 170), which runs across Newmarket Heath, be sure to keep an eye out for ghostly horseriders on dim and misty mornings.

to cross. Today, however, it is only a footbridge alongside the ford over the River Kennett, which in summer months at least is virtually a trickle here. Turn right immediately after the bridge back on to Brookside, returning shortly to St Peter's Church.

THE ESSENTIALS

GETTING THERE By **car**, Moulton is just over 5km east of Newmarket, on the Moulton Road, or 18km west of Bury St Edmunds, via the A14 and B1085. There's no direct **bus** to Moulton from either Newmarket or Bury; the best route is from Newmarket, changing buses at Kentford and taking about half an hour.

WHERE TO EAT If you're in need of a snack on the go in Moulton, the village store has a take-away counter, with freshly made rolls and snacks. It's a couple of hundred metres down the main road to the right.

✖ **Packhorse Inn** Bridge St, Moulton CB8 8SP; ✆ 01638 751818; 🌐 thepackhorseinn. com. Standing proud alongside the eponymous historic bridge, this upmarket country inn serves modern gastro-pub cuisine, with a menu strong on local produce from across East Anglia, supported by a sizeable wine list. Besides several eating areas inside, there's a back garden & a tipi with a log burner for cosy fireside dining in colder weather. **£££**

✖ **Affleck Arms** Brookside, Dalham CB8 8TG; ✆ 01638 500306. This snug thatched pub overlooks the River Kennett in the pretty village of Dalham, with a reputation for its welcoming landlords. The bar stocks local real ales & cider, as well as a selection of wines & spirits. There are no regular meals on offer, but they usually set up a barbecue in the back garden during summer weekends. **£**

✖ **Bell Inn** Newmarket Rd, Kennett CB8 7PP; ✆ 01638 750333; 🌐 thebellkennett. co.uk. This gabled 16th-century coaching inn stands on the outskirts of Kentford, with a colourful history of ghosts & visits from highwayman Dick Turpin. Today, refurbished but still retaining its original character, it offers a warmer welcome, livened up with occasional live music tribute nights. The restaurant menu features classic pub steaks, fish & burgers, or blow out sharing platters, served in its cosy lounge or covered back garden. **£**

FACILITIES AND FURTHER INFORMATION There are no public toilets en route, but the pubs listed here may allow you to use their facilities – especially if you stop for a drink!

ℹ **Discover Newmarket** Palace St, Newmarket CB8 8EP; ✆ 01638 501122; 🌐 discovernewmarket.co.uk. The official tourist centre for Newmarket & the area, the online-only service is a good source of local information. They also do guided walks – & not only about horses – also including literary & food tours.

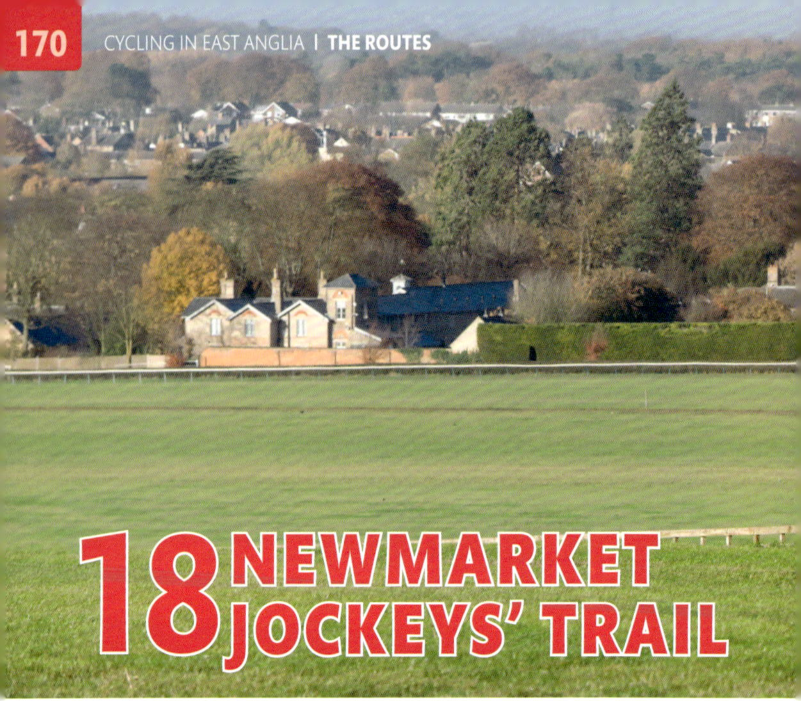

18 NEWMARKET JOCKEYS' TRAIL

START/FINISH	Moulton
DISTANCE/TIME	45.7km/4½hrs
DIFFICULTY/TERRAIN	② On roads and cycle paths, level or gently rolling terrain. There are a few straight stretches which can attract speeding traffic, plus, several busy A-road crossings. It's also the longest ride in this book, so, overall, it's best suited for experienced cyclists.
SCENIC RATING	⑧ Mix of sleepy villages, rolling meadows, horsey Newmarket and pristine stud farms
SUITABLE FOR	Road bike, hybrid or e-bike
NCN ROUTE	Partly on NCN51
MAPS	OS Explorer 10 (1:25 000)
KOMOOT REF	585668391

↑ Newmarket is East Anglia's horse-racing hub (cornfield/S)

This diverse route combines manicured racing paddocks with wild, windswept Fens and a rolling river valley. As with Route 17 (page 164), we start from Moulton, a historic village on the banks of the River Kennett. Crossing Newmarket's training grounds, past elegant stud farms, we get a glimpse of the affluent world of professional horse racing. Returning to Moulton, we cross this farming county's fertile grasslands, through isolated Fen-edge villages, like islands floating in the vast meadows.

THE ROUTE

Start from ❶ **Moulton**, by the hilltop Church of St Peter. Follow Brookside, running along the right bank of the river, and coming to a crossroads with the 15th-century Packhorse Bridge on your left. Turn left here, passing the bridge and the Packhorse Inn on your right (signposted NCN51, which we follow all the way through Newmarket and into the Fens). Go straight ahead at the staggered crossroads on to Moulton/Newmarket Road, signposted Newmarket.

Carry on up this wide road, going gently uphill past Fleet Cottages on your right, then coming to a string of stud farms, with their grand gateways, clipped hedgerows and tidy verges. First up is **Ashley Heath Stud** on your left, with the adjacent stately home, at the end of a long, gated driveway. Beyond that is **Warren Hill Stud** on the left, followed by **Newmarket Heath Stud** and **Warren Towers**. In fact, there are lots of smart properties around here, ostensibly connected to Newmarket's historic horse racing heritage. As you soak in all this wealth, look out for horseriders coming in and out of the stud farms. Fortunately, most come clad in gaudy jerseys, and keep to a restrained walk, presumably saving energy for race day. We're approaching Newmarket now, the town at the bottom of the hill, as the road runs down through **Warren Hill exercise grounds**. These meticulously groomed fields have been used for horse training since the time of Charles II, 350 years ago, so don't be surprised if you're held up briefly by orderly lines of jockeys, waiting for their trainer to call instructions from the back of the queue.

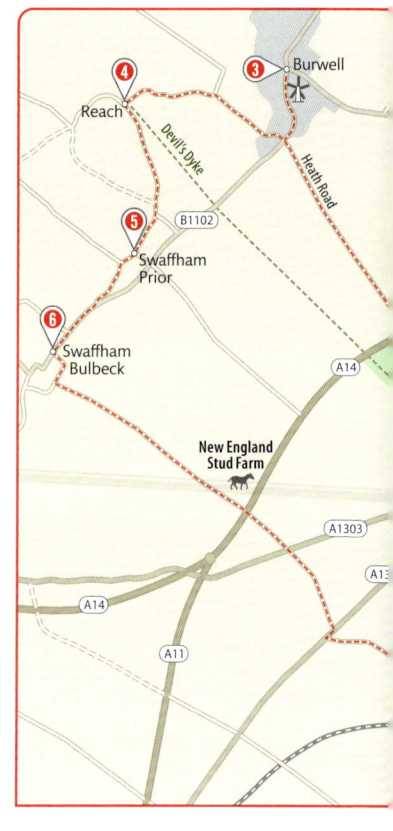

Coming out of the heath and into ❷ **Newmarket**, turn right on to Old Station Road. At the roundabout, take the shortcut on the left – a cycle lane crossing the pavement in front of the clock tower. This leads to Palace Street, a small side road that forks off the main High Street,

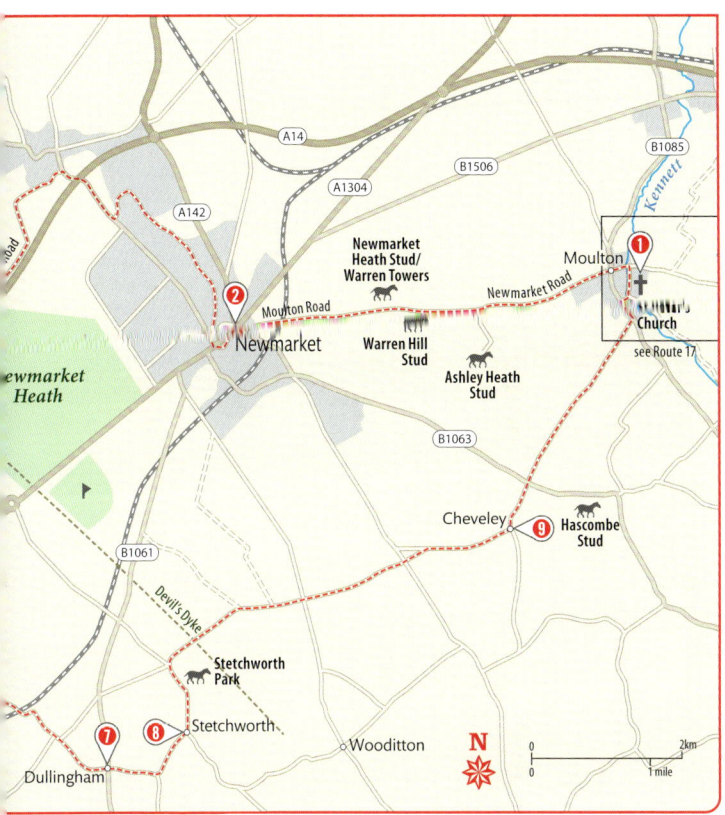

between the old Rutland Arms hotel on the right, and TK Maxx on your left. Newmarket's main town centre is bustling and well-to-do. It's not as affluent as the stud farms, but everything revolves around horses in this self-proclaimed 'headquarters of horse racing'. There's even a network of horse walks through the town, allowing jockeys to ride from their training grounds on one side to the other on special matted tracks, all of which adds a splash of colour to the high street, as well as wafting a horsey aroma into the air.

There are a couple of historical sites in the town worth a look, both conveniently on our route, on Palace Street. Firstly, we pass **Nell Gwynne House** on our left; the black and white shuttered late 17th-century building is now a private property but it is thought that Charles II bought it for his mistress to accompany him to the horse races. Adjacent, appropriately, is the king's former palace, now housing the **National Horse Racing Museum** (see box, opposite), which charts the history of the sport and the global spread of horse racing. It's also got a rather nice open-air café in the courtyard.

Passing the museum and coming to the crossroads with All Saints Church on your left, turn right down the pedestrianised Sun Lane, leading to the High Street. This walkway is lined with cafés and shops and buzzy with shoppers; it's only about 100m up to the road, so it's better to walk here. Cross over at the pedestrian crossing, and into Wellington Street, the first part of which is also pedestrianised. Continue past Market Place on your right and walk your bike across Fred Archer Way/B1103, around railings and a potentially tricky bend in the road, leading to The Watercourse. This is a shared footpath, running alongside one of the aforementioned horse walks and a stream. So, take it slowly, giving way to pedestrians – and horses. Follow this path winding between the houses and across Exeter Road, under the (Yellow Brick Road) wrought-iron archway. The path continues through a modern housing estate; you might notice a red and gold **statue** of a horse peering over the fence on the left – horses are everywhere here! Carry on straight ahead, crossing Noel Murless Drive, a minor residential road.

All this weaving through Newmarket suburbs and industrial estates may not be picturesque, but it is on a good cycle path (still clearly marked NCN51, by the way), and maybe it gives us a more balanced view of the 'headquarters of racing' to contrast the elite stud farms ringing the town. Please bear with it – we'll be back out in the countryside again soon. When you finally come out of the industrial complex, cross Willie Snaith Road at pedestrian lights and turn left, passing more factories on your left. If you're not a racing expert and wondering about Noel Murless and Willie Snaith, it's perhaps no surprise that they were both in the horse racing business.

HORSE RACING AT NEWMARKET

The first recorded horse race at Newmarket took place 400 years ago. Lord Salisbury's horses won a race on the heath against George Villiers, Marquess of Buckingham and the King's Master of the Horse. The prize was £100, which would be inflated to around £13,000 today. Not to be sniffed at, of course, but this is small change compared with the biggest winnings on offer at Newmarket now: the 2022 QIPCO Guineas Festival is currently worth £1.7 million.

Newmarket's worldwide status is about much more than the money, of course. Its tradition and heritage may date back in time as far as the Iron Age, more than 1,500 years ago. When the Romans settled the area, they reported that the Iceni tribe bred, sold and even exported fine horses. In medieval times, Newmarket developed as a major market town, with a plethora of inns and breweries opening up to cater for the growing influx of travellers. Landholdings spread too, with the heaths around the town providing the ideal land for grazing livestock and building stables.

It was royal patronage, however, that really galvanised the bloodstock breeding industry and made horse racing the hugely popular sport it is today. King James I (1556-1625) counted horse racing as one of his favourite pastimes. And today, of course, Queen Elizabeth is famous for her lifelong love of horseriding, not to mention as one of its most prestigious racehorse owners.

Willie Snaith (1946–2019) was one of the most garlanded jockeys of Her Majesty the Queen, a lifelong racing fan; Noel Murless (1910–89) was a horse trainer and father-in-law of Sir Henry Cecil (1943–2013), who was one of the most successful trainers in flat racing history.

It's all a bit wiggly along here, but there are plenty of NCN51 signs to guide you between the houses. At the fork in the path, in front of a convenience store, turn left, down Brickfields Avenue, signposted Exning, Burning, Burwell and Cambridge. Eventually, this comes out on to the Exning Road/Cemetery Hill (B1103), leading to the village of Exning. It's quite a busy stretch but the cycle path runs off-road along the pavement to the right; keep alert here for vehicles coming out unexpectedly from obscured driveways.

The cycle path continues under a bridge (for the A14), but soon afterwards comes to an end. Dismount and cross over here, with the cycle lane continuing on the left. After around 100m, turn left on to Ducks Lane, passing St Martin's Church, Exning, on your right. Carry on straight ahead on Laceys Lane, past a cemetery on your left and winding left on to Heath Road, a nice, broad farm lane. We're back into the countryside at last, through fields and hedgerows which try to muffle the traffic roaring along the A14 on your left. Thankfully, before the traffic noise becomes a distraction, the road veers to the right, and towards the village of Burwell. We're approaching the Cambridgeshire Fens, the broad, flat stretching northwards beyond Ely to the market town of Wisbech. These fertile, drained lowlands are also rich in wildlife, with a superb national nature reserve at Wicken Fen (see Route 19, page 188).

After continuing straight through the fields for around 3km, turn right at the T-junction on Swaffham Road, coming into ❸ **Burwell**. Our main route turns immediately left here, up Reach Road, but if you fancy a short detour, Burwell has a classic 19th-century **windmill**, with sails intact, that today houses a museum and tearoom (⌁burwellmuseum.org.uk); continue along Swaffham Road, up the village high street, then sharp right on to Mill Lane.

Back on the main route, turn left off Swaffham Road (or right if you went to the windmill) and up Reach Road, which winds behind the outskirts of Burwell. Note that the NCN51 cycle path divides just around the corner here: one branch forks off to the right, alongside Mandeville Hall, northwards to Wicken Fen, mentioned above, but we carry straight ahead on Reach Road. About 1km further on, at a triangle, continue around to the left, signposted Reach, after a small industrial estate (and ignoring another NCN51 side route up to Wicken). Finally, after about another kilometre, we reach ❹ **Reach**! This beautiful historic village is one of the oldest in the Fens. In 1201, King John granted a charter for Reach to hold a fair on its long village green, Fair Green, and the custom has been kept up ever since (apart from 2020 and 2021). Today, hundreds of stalls

and fairground rides attract visitors from far across the region, including sometimes in excess of 1,000 cyclists, on a group tour led by the Cambridge Cycling Campaign (⌘ camcycle.org.uk).

There's no shop in the village, but there is one pub, the Dyke's End Inn, next to the tiny church of St Etheldreda, overlooking Fair Green. The pub is aptly named, as Reach does indeed mark the western end of the **Devil's Dyke**, an Anglo-Saxon earthwork considered the finest of its kind in the UK, running southeast in an almost perfect straight line for 12km from the edge of Reach. Originally built as a defensive barrier across the wide, open fens, the dyke is now a protected monument and Site of Special Scientific Interest (SSSI), for its chalk grassland and rare plants.

From Reach, we head southwest: follow the NCN51 sign across the green from the Dyke's End pub, next to a particularly impressive painted village sign, directing us left towards Swaffham Prior. Follow the Swaffham Road, which runs close to the Devil's Dyke for about 1km, the overgrown earth mound just visible over the hedgerow on your left. The road then veers away to the right and into ❺ **Swaffham Prior**. Carry on through this sleepy village, past the Red Lion pub and the twin churches of St Mary

↑ The Devil's Dyke stretches for 12km in an almost perfect straight line from Reach
(Stephen McKay/WC)

↑ Swaffham Prior's Church of St Mary boasts a beautiful octagonal tower (Peter Moulton/S)

and St Cyriac, both sharing the same churchyard. The two parishes were merged and St Cyriac's Church abandoned (though now restored by the Churches Conservation Trust), but St Mary's still has some surviving Norman features, including its rare octagonal tower.

Leaving Swaffham Prior, the High Street comes to a T-junction with the busy B1102. Luckily, there's a cycle/footpath on the right, passing the gated entrance to Swaffham House, so you can avoid the traffic. Carry on along the path, between flat, prairie-sized fields more evocative of midwestern Oklahoma than East Anglia. After about 1km, we come to a crossroads, just outside ❻ **Swaffham Bulbeck**. Cross over the road and turn left, signposted Dullingham and Stetchworth. (Note that we're finally leaving the NCN51, which heads through the village and on to Cambridge.) Carry on along Heath Road, which winds right and then left on to Swaffham Heath Road, continuing straight ahead.

After this stretch of several kilometres of empty countryside, we've got three road crossings coming up, so time to switch on again. Firstly, cross the A14 over a bridge, passing **New England Stud Farm** on the left, then at the crossroads soon after, cross the A1303. It's a straight road so it's easy to see oncoming traffic, but take care. Finally, after a further 1km we come to a staggered crossroads over the A1304 – it's only 100m right then left off the A-road, but if you're not a confident cyclist and it's busy, there's a wide verge so you could walk up to the turning.

After a long, slow 1km climb, we're rewarded with a nice downhill stretch (taking care over the railway crossing) into ❼ **Dullingham**. At first, it seems to suit its name but, at the far end of the village, we pass two or three thatched cottages, including the magnificent thatched and timber-gabled Guildhall on the left, by the crossroads. Carry on straight ahead here, over the B1601, past the King's Head pub on the left and on to the Stetchworth Road. Turn left at the T-junction a few hundred metres later, winding around to the left and left again at another T-junction, coming into ❽ **Stetchworth,** past the Marquis of Granby pub on the left.

Carry on through this quiet little village and, at a left-hand bend in the road on the way out, turn right on an unmarked road, just past the gated entrance to **Stetchworth Park**, another distinguished stud farm. The road climbs gently uphill now and into woods. At the brow of the hill, we come to the **Devil's Dyke** again, with a marked pathway running left and right through the trees. The historic site ends around 2km to the southeast, at Woodditton (cycling along the dyke is strictly prohibited). Coming out of the trees it's another straight and gently undulating stretch for around 2km, through fields and stud farms. Go straight ahead over a couple of crossroads, the first a dog-leg crossing on the Woodditton Road. Neither is on major roads, but take care as always.

After a further 2km or so, we come into ❾ **Cheveley**, another well-to-do village among the stud farms. At the T-junction, with Cheveley primary school on your right, turn left on to the High Street. Go straight on at the crossroads over the B1063 and on to the Moulton Road. Keep an eye out for horses at **Hascombe Stud** on the right, crossing the road from the training paddock opposite. There's another nice long downhill stretch now, leading all the way to the T-junction on the Dalham Road. Turn left here, approaching Moulton (though it's only signposted Chippenham and Islenham). Finally, after about 100m, we're back in Moulton. Carry on a short way along The Street, then right on to Church Road. Cross the bridge or ford over the River Kennett (usually only a trickle here) and turn right, back to St Peter's Church.

THE ESSENTIALS

GETTING THERE By **car**, Moulton is just over 5km east of Newmarket, on the Moulton Road, or 18km west of Bury St Edmunds, via the A14 and B1085. There's no direct **bus** to Moulton from either Newmarket or Bury – the best route is from Newmarket, changing buses at Kentford and taking about half an hour.

WHERE TO EAT See also The Packhorse Inn & Moulton Stores take-away café on Route 17 (page 164).

✖ **The Tack Room** National Racing Museum, Palace St, Newmarket CB8 8EP; ☏ 01638 667314; ⌘ nhrm.co.uk/the-tack-room. With indoor seating during the winter, or at outdoor tables in its cobbled courtyard, this café-restaurant offers a choice of formal meals & light snacks. With main dishes including steak & frites, salads & halloumi veggie burgers, it's open to non-museum visitors too, so it's handy for our route passing the main entrance en route through the town. **££**

Dyke's End Inn 8 Fair Green, Reach CB25 0JD; 01638 743816; dykesendreach. co.uk. This lovely old inn has a great location by the village green in Reach, with its locally famous May Fair. The well-stocked bar has a good range of cask ales, including Adnams, from Southwold. The menu has a limited choice but offers classic pub grub including burgers, fish pie & lasagne & Sun lunch take-aways, if you want to sit out on the spacious village green. **£**

Black Horse Inn 35 High St, Swaffham Bulbeck CB25 0HP; 01223 811366. This friendly village local, a former 18th-century coaching inn, is just off our route in the pretty Fen-edge village of Swaffham Bulbeck. The bar stocks a good range of local ales & the menu covers reliable pub classics, including steaks, burgers & fish & chips. **£**

FACILITIES AND FURTHER INFORMATION There are public toilets in Newmarket (inside the Guineas Shopping Centre, between the High Street and the B1103). In Moulton, there are a few parking spaces in front of the church by the river.

Discover Newmarket Palace St, Newmarket CB8 8EP; 01638 501122; discovernewmarket.co.uk. The official tourist centre for Newmarket & the area, the online-only service is a good source of local information. They also do guided walks, not only about horses but also literary & food.

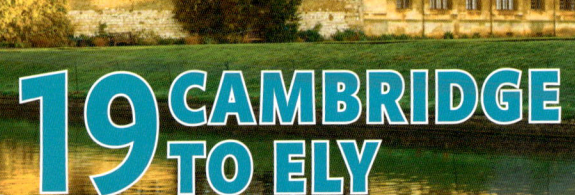

19 CAMBRIDGE TO ELY

START/FINISH	King's College, Cambridge to Ely Cathedral
DISTANCE/TIME	39.1km/4hrs
DIFFICULTY/TERRAIN	② Level terrain, mostly on road – some cycle paths, gravel tracks and sandy trails
SCENIC RATING	☺ Historic Cambridge University colleges, Anglesey Abbey, Ely Cathedral, Cam riverside path and wild Wicken Fen
SUITABLE FOR	Hybrid, e-bike or road bike
NCN ROUTE	NCN51 and NCN11
MAPS	OS Explorer 226 and OS Explorer 209 (1:25 000)
KOMOOT REF	586480067

↑ King's College Chapel is one of Cambridge's most iconic sights (Pajor Pawel/S)

This ride links two of East Anglia's most distinguished, historical cities across the broad expanses of the Fens. Cambridge is one of the country's most popular tourist destinations, with ivy-clad colleges, world-famous museums and dreamy riverbank. From iconic King's College chapel, we wind through the back streets, across Jesus Green, and along the banks of the River Cam. Within minutes we're out in the countryside, past Anglesey Abbey, across marshes and meadows, and on to Ely Cathedral – 'The Ship of the Fens'.

THE ROUTE

Start from in front of ❶ **King's College Chapel**, one of Cambridge's most recognisable landmarks, founded by Henry VI in 1446. Its stunning Gothic façade attracts most sightseers' attention on King's Parade, but an eccentric newcomer on the block is also eye-catching: the gold **Corpus Clock** in a

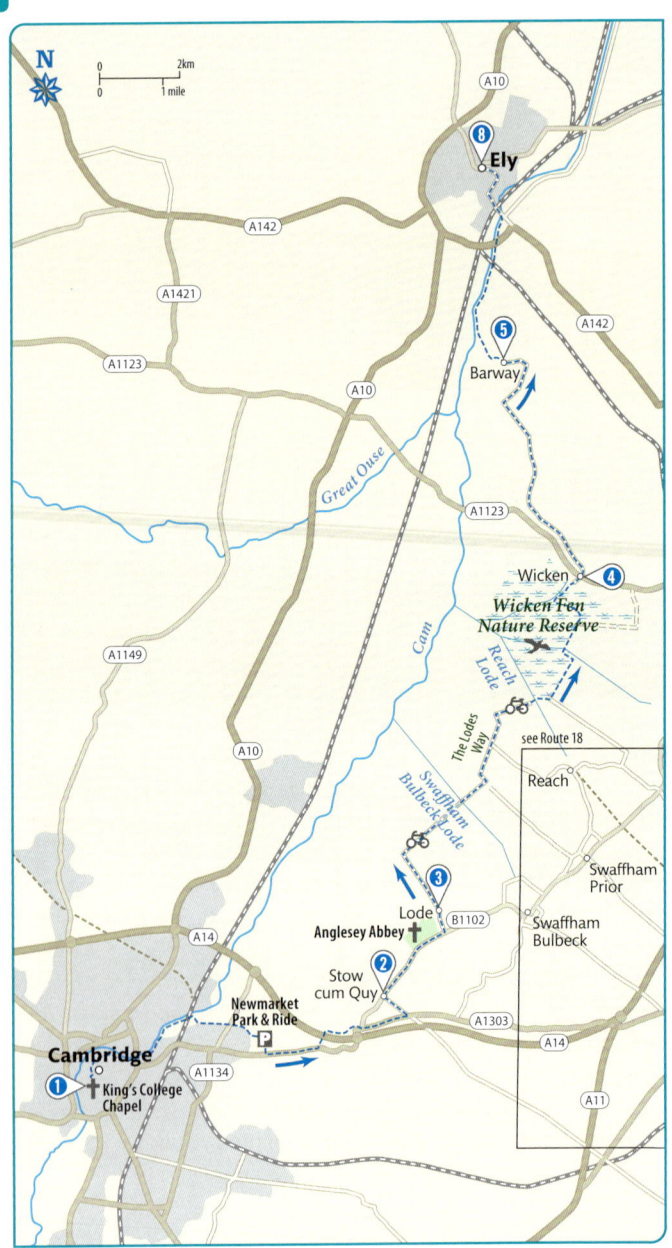

glass case on the corner of Bene't and Trumpington streets, opposite. This intriguing, slightly blingy Corpus Chronophage clock was created in 2008 by inventor John C Taylor, complete with blinking LED lights and a locust-like insect perched on top.

From King's Parade, turn left and wind through the back streets (signposted NCN11): right along St Mary's Street, left on Sidney Street, right on Jesus Lane, left on Park Street and following it around to the right finally to Jesus Green. The city centre streets are frequently packed so you might spend more time wheeling your bike rather than cycling, but there are plenty of cityscape features to spot here, so there's no need to rush. You might notice, for instance, curious little street installations dotted here and there, usually at ground level, such as **TOM**, a 'Teleport-O-Matic' transporter, tucked between two phone boxes on St Mary's Street, or **DFO**, a 'Dinky Flying Object' on the wall in front of the riverside Museum of Technology, both of which we pass shortly. These are a couple of the **Dinky Doors**, a gloriously quirky collection of mini-creations hidden around the city, particularly aimed at children or anyone with a keen eye for hidden treasures. There's a trail map on their website, with news of their latest creations: ⌀ dinkydoors.co.uk.

Emerging at last from the busy streets and on to **Jesus Green**, you might spot cows grazing this grassy common. This slightly surreal sight is a long-standing Cambridge tradition as a city which, despite all its students and visitors, is also still an important agricultural market, and still surrounded by farmland. Cross the green and turn right on to the riverside path, following it under the A1134 on to Riverside, and carrying on past pubs, cafés and the **Museum of Technology** on the right. Note that branches of the NCN11 and NCN51 cross the river just after the museum, but we stay on the right bank all the way.

Continuing along the riverfront, cross Stourbridge Common on the right and go under the railway bridge. Follow the NCN51 winding right now, away from the river and skirting around the edge of Ditton Meadows, across the B1047/Ditton Lane, and continuing down Fison Road opposite. This leads through modern housing, coming shortly to the **Newmarket Road Park & Ride**, under a giant bicycle sculpture spanning the path. The

car park on the eastern outskirts could be an alternative start to the ride if you're not interested in the hubbub of Cambridge city centre. Parking is free here; it's easier for loading and offloading bikes too.

Cross the Park & Ride and continue left on the cycle path alongside the A1303. Pass the Darwin Farm Shop on your left, then turn left by a signpost to ❷ **Stow cum Quy** (pronounced Kwai, like the river); go through a tunnel under the A14, and then turn sharp right as the cycle path continues to the church of St Mary, on the edge of the village. Go to the right of the church, along the NCN51 running parallel to the A1303, as far as the Missing Sock pub. Turn left here along Albert Road, then right through Stow cum Quy and along the cycle lane on Colliers Lane (B1102) until you reach **Anglesey Abbey**, on your left. The former 13th-century priory was restored in the 1930s as a stylish country house for Lord Fairhaven. Now owned by the National Trust, it's filled with opulent art treasures and set in landscaped gardens, also with a historic watermill. Its restaurant and take-away kiosk are open to non-members.

After the abbey, turn left at the crossroads on to Lode Road, then wind left and right to the attractive old village of ❸ **Lode**, on the fringes of

↑ The pretty village of Lode (Dmytro Kurko/S)

the Fen. Several thatched houses line Lode High Street, including an impressive hall on the left opposite the chic-looking Shed pub. The name Lode refers to the waterways that were built through the Fens before medieval times, for carrying supplies via the River Cam and for protecting the low-lying lands from frequent flooding. From here onwards, the road becomes increasingly peaceful and traffic-free as we head into the Fens, alongside one such lode channel through reed beds on the left.

A couple of kilometres after Lode, turn right on to White Fen Drove, now on NCN11 and part of **Lodes Way**, which connects Fen villages with the Wicken Fen Nature Reserve, which we pass through shortly. At the T-junction, after crossing Swaffham Bulbeck Lode, turn left and then follow the path to the right, carrying straight on at the next crossroads, on to a potholed, roughly paved lane (Headlake Drove). A right turn here leads to Reach, another traditional Fen village, which is on Route 18 (page 170). In very wet weather this short lane can become a bit of a quagmire, in which case, you could take a detour left here on to a paved road, passing the Five Miles from Anywhere Inn, and then winding around to rejoin our route at Wicken Fen.

Otherwise, follow the lane to Reach Lode. At the footbridge here, cyclists have to dismount and carry bikes up a dozen or so steps over the waterway, with a metal channel alongside the steps to make it easier. Some people might wonder why a raised bridge at road level just to the right doesn't obligingly lower to let traffic cross instead. According to locals, this so-called 'Cock-up Bridge' hasn't been lowered for years, though there have also been plans to build a permanent crossing here. The other, more polite, explanation is that horses are sometimes also known in the Fens as cocks. So the bridge was built for their benefit rather than for cyclists, who were then in the minority. Choose whichever version you prefer!

After crossing the bridge, we approach **Wicken Fen Nature Reserve** (see box, page 188). The path narrows here virtually to single file, and it's a popular trail with dog walkers and birdwatchers (pink binocular signs mark bird lookouts and hides along this stretch), so take it slowly. Passing the main entrance to the reserve on the left, there's also the Docky Hut Café (page 191) – this may be a good spot for a break, with no other eateries en route before we get to Ely (13km from here). From Wicken Fen, continue left up Lode Lane and zigzag right, left and left again through the village of ❹ **Wicken**, following the NCN11 signs towards Barway and Ely.

As we draw near to Ely, on a clear day you'll catch your first glimpse of the tall cathedral towers. Its poetic nickname, 'The Ship of the Fens', seems apt from out here, more so perhaps on a summer's day, when it seems to float on the shimmering sea of reeds. More down to earth, however, are the agricultural warehouses we pass in the farming hamlet of ❺ **Barway**. Multilingual roadside signs here are in Russian, Polish and Spanish for the international workforce who pick and pack vegetables grown in the Fens' fertile soil. In fact, it's common to see some of these workers on their days off, trudging along the path from Ely to their purpose-built accommodation blocks, laden down with shopping bags.

WICKEN FEN

Wicken Fen National Nature Reserve lies at the heart of a huge area of fenlands which stretch across eastern England, from Lincolnshire across Cambridgeshire and into Norfolk and Suffolk, much of it lying several metres below sea level. Comprising some 400,000ha, nearly three times the size of Greater London, the fertile wetlands have been exploited for thousands of years for peat digging and farming. They are also rich natural habitats for an abundance of wildlife, none more so than at Wicken Fen, one of the most important wetland habitats in Europe.

The oldest national nature reserve run by the National Trust, Wicken was acquired in 1899 for the princely sum of £10. Today, it is home to more than 9,600 species of plants and animals. Its birdlife is particularly impressive, including kingfishers, golden plovers and the rare marsh harriers, distinctive for their V-shaped wing formation when in flight. Cycling through Wicken Fen, you may well also spot the stocky, dusky-coated Konik ponies. These hardy, feral ponies were introduced to Wicken from their native eastern Europe. Together with the placid Highland cattle, they help stimulate new plant growth by grazing and trimming the vegetation: in other words, they're the

After winding through Barway, the cycle path runs along the right bank of the River Great Ouse before reaching the outskirts of ❻ **Ely**. Cross over the busy Stuntney Causeway – it's safer to walk your bike across – to the cycle path continuing on the other side of the road. Cross the bridge to the left then take the path immediately to the right running steeply back down to the riverbank. The lively riverfront is one of the nicest areas of Ely, with the tree-lined promenade crossing the marina, with cruise boats, terraced pubs, and open-air cafés. The cycle path passes right along the waterfront, with occasional narrow stretches, so go slowly here and give way to pedestrians and other users.

Continue along the riverside, until it winds around to the left on Waterside Road and up Fore Hill to Market Place. This open square is filled with an array of food stalls and delis, and flanked by cafés, bars and

Fen Gardeners! There are bird hides and walking trails through the reserve as well as boat trips, giving great opportunities to observe the wildlife or simply to soak up its special natural tranquillity.

↑ Wicken Fen is known for its Konik ponies (Andy333/S)

tearooms. It's also a handy place to lock up your bike and duck through an archway across the road leading to magnificent **Ely Cathedral**; alternatively, there are also bike racks in front of the cathedral and in its south car park. Its oldest parts dating back to Norman times, the cathedral extends from its soaring 52m octagon tower, with a painted carving of the resurrected Christ. Besides its ceiling friezes, stained-glass windows and many sculptures, the cathedral also has a stained-glass museum in its southwest transept. Off the north transept is the Lady Chapel, which has occasional art exhibitions and cultural displays. Guided tours include the opportunity to climb up the 170 steps to the roof tower, from where you may even be able to see the route you have just done, across the Fens far below.

To return to Cambridge, you can either cycle back the same way or catch a train. To get to **Ely station**, it's only about 1km from here. Go down Fore Hill, which winds right on to Broad Street, turn left on to Station Road, then take the second exit off the roundabout.

THE ESSENTIALS

GETTING THERE By **car**, Cambridge is just off the M11, 103km from London, or 103km from Norwich to the northeast, via the A11. Its mainline **train** station has regular services to London (taking just under

↑ 'The Ship of the Fens' – Ely Cathedral (Steve Cymro/S)

an hour to King's Cross), to Peterborough (approx 45 mins), connecting to the north, and to Norwich (approx 1½hrs). There are frequent trains all day from Ely to Cambridge, taking about 20 minutes. Bikes are allowed on board, but there are three different train operators, four types of train and the rules are changing, so it's best to ask at the station or check online.

WHERE TO EAT

✖ OtherSyde The Engineer's House, Riverside, Cambridge CB5 8HN; ✆ 07761 049353; ⌂ othersyde.co.uk. Next to the Museum of Technology, this hip café has a spacious terraced garden great for people-watching along the riverfront. They serve stone-baked pizzas, burgers, veggie dishes, coffee & cakes, & the bar stocks wines, cocktails, & craft beers, including their in-house lager, The Guv'nor. **£**

✖ The Docky Hut Café Lode Ln, Wicken Fen Nature Reserve CB7 5XP; ✆ 01353 720274; ⌂ nationaltrust.org.uk/wicken-fen-nature-reserve/features/cafe. Right by the cycle route & with a hanging bike rack out front, this is a handy little café for a bite en route. They serve freshly made hot & cold snacks, sandwiches & cakes, as well as veggie options, including tasty vegan curry pasties. **£**

✖ The Cutter Inn 42 Annesdale, Ely CB7 4BN; ✆ 01353 662713; ⌂ thecutterinn.co.uk. This smart riverside inn has a traditional menu featuring pub classics, including steaks, burgers, fish & chips, plus salads & 1 or 2 veggie options. There are outdoor terrace tables handy for propping up your bike by the adjacent railings. **££**

FACILITIES AND FURTHER INFORMATION Cambridge and Ely have plenty of public toilets.

ℹ Visit Cambridge e info@visitcambridge.org; ⌂ visitcambridge.org. Startling perhaps for a world-class city & tourist hotspot, but Cambridge has no walk-in visitor information centre; fortunately, the official website compensates, with comprehensive listings of places to stay, eat, shop, tours & how to visit its many cultural & historic attractions.

ℹ Visit Ely Oliver Cromwell's House, 29 St Mary's St, Ely CB7 4HF; ✆ 01353 662062; ⌂ visitely.org.uk. Housed in the historic former home of Oliver Cromwell, Ely's tourist information centre has expert staff offering advice, information & booking for a range of tours in & around the city. There's also the full panoply of books & souvenirs for sale, & also free Wi-Fi.

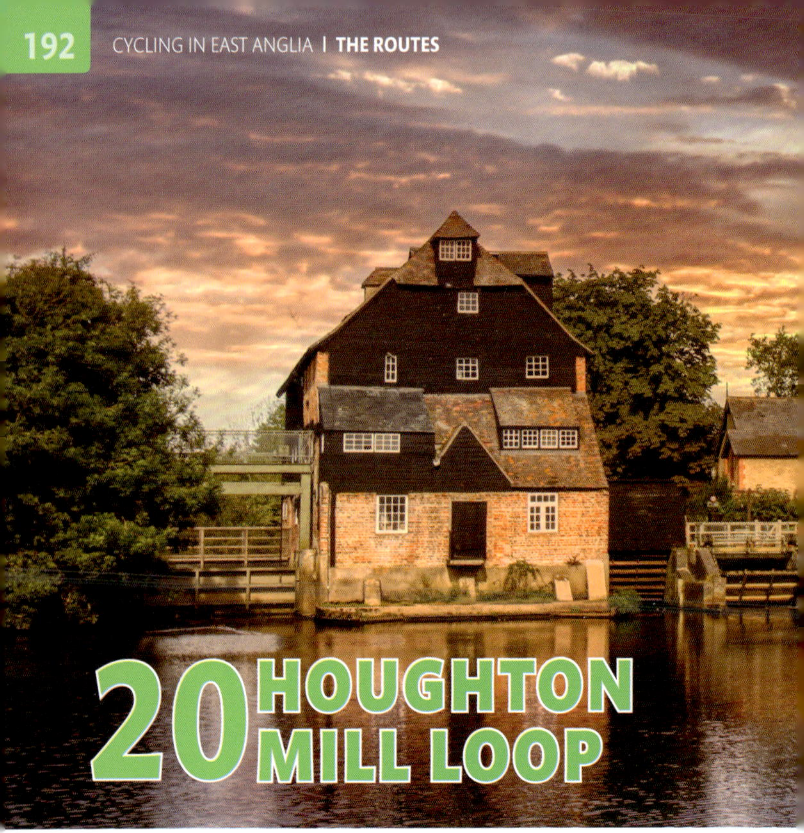

20 HOUGHTON MILL LOOP

START/FINISH	Houghton Mill
DISTANCE/TIME	28.3km/3hrs
DIFFICULTY/TERRAIN	① Level going on quiet country roads, cycle paths and gravel tracks
SCENIC RATING	⑧ Historic watermill, riverside villages and the Busway–Cycleway eco-route through Fen Drayton Lakes RSPB Nature Reserve
SUITABLE FOR	Hybrid, e-bike and road bike
NCN ROUTE	NCN51 and NCN24
MAPS	OS Explorer 225 (1:25 000)
KOMOOT REF	586551892

↑ Houghton Mill sits on the banks of the Ouse (robert f cooke/S)

This riverside route loops around the peaceful Ouse Valley, only a short hop from cosmopolitan Cambridge. Starting from the historic watermill at Houghton, we pass through pretty waterside villages, then join the Busway–Cycleway, a pioneering eco-route crossing Fen Drayton Lakes to St Ives, a picturesque old market town with outdoor cafés and narrowboat river cruises. It's a relaxing and largely off-road ride, giving a snapshot of the Cambridgeshire Fens, past and present.

THE ROUTE

Start from ❶ **The Green**, Houghton's village square. Turn right along Mill Street, following NCN51 signs to **Houghton Mill**, 200m from here. This huge, five-storey watermill on the Ouse was the driving force for the local economy in the 18th century, producing industrial quantities of flour sold across the region. The mill is now run by the National Trust; it has been immaculately restored and still produces stone-ground flour, which you can buy here, or sample at the café in their home-baked cakes, sandwiches and scones. It's open to visitors, but you can also get a good view from the outside as the route runs under an archway through the wood-panelled building and across the canal lock (though cyclists must dismount here). Go straight ahead at the lock gate, across Hemingford Meadow. There are footpaths to the left and right here too, so take care and give way to other users.

Coming out of the meadow and over a river tributary, follow NCN51 signs left through ❷ **Hemingford Abbots**, on the south bank of the River Great Ouse, a beautiful old village lined with thatched cottages, manicured village greens and flower-filled hanging baskets. Continue along the High Street, which becomes Manor Road, then take a left at the T-junction into ❸ **Hemingford Grey**, rated as one of the most attractive villages in Cambridgeshire. Go straight ahead at the staggered crossroads, then right

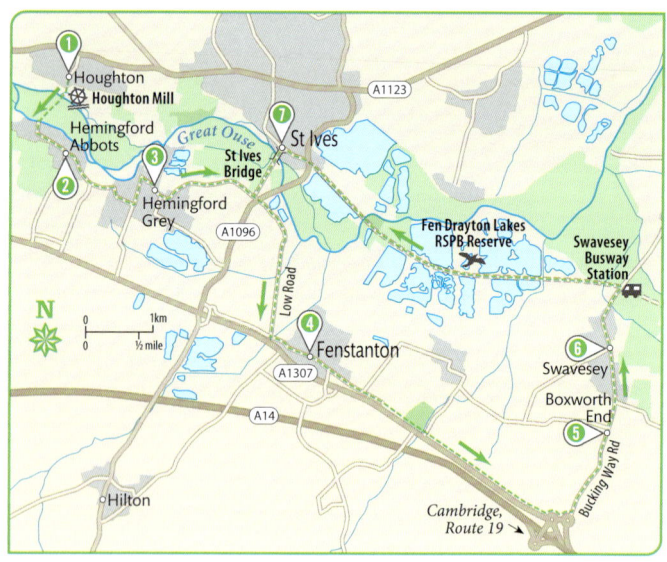

HOUGHTON MILL

Houghton Mill is the last working survivor of the Ouse Valley watermills' industrial heyday, which brought considerable prosperity to the area in the 18th century. The earliest record of a watermill at Houghton was in AD947, when the newly built Ramsey Abbey acquired a mill along with the manor house. It was taken over by the Crown following the Dissolution of the Monasteries in the 1530s, then sold and developed as a commercial enterprise. Boosted by the technological advances in the 18th century, Houghton increased its output. By 1850, the mill was producing one tonne of high-grade flour per hour, which was transported by barge and sold across the south and east of England, as far as Leicester and London.

As steam power developed and cheaper imported flour became available, however, Houghton Mill's fortunes waned. Its output fell drastically, eventually only making flour for animal feed, and it closed in 1928, with the retirement of Arthur Chopping, its last miller. The National Trust reopened the mill in 1983 and began restoration work, leading to the reintroduction of a new waterwheel in 1999. Now, on special milling days, visitors can witness the massive workings brought back to life once again.

at the next crossroads, winding around the village and avoiding the busier section of the High Street. Just left off the High Street, at the crossroads where our main route goes up Church Lane, is one of the oldest continually inhabited houses in England: the **Manor House** (greenknowe.co.uk/the-house), built in about 1130. Two of its more notable owners were Richard Cromwell, Oliver Cromwell's grandfather, and Edmund Dudley, one of Henry VII's closest ministers.

Leaving Hemingford Grey, follow the road meandering alongside the River Great Ouse, behind the houses on the left. Coming to a couple of busy junctions, follow the cycle route across the London Road, then over a footbridge at the roundabout. Note that the cycle route divides here – the NCN51 goes left up to St Ives, our return route, but we carry on straight ahead here along Low Road, signposted NCN24. Low Road

winds right, southwards now, leaving the river and crossing fields to
❹ **Fenstanton**, a modern dormitory town. Turn left at the end of Low Road, as the NCN24 joins the road briefly, past the shops, then rejoins the cycle path on the way out.

Carry on straight along this flat stretch, running parallel to the A14, thankfully with some embankments, fences and trees to shelter us from the traffic on this major arterial road. Take the first exit at each of two successive roundabouts, signposted towards Swavesey Nature Reserve (part of the Fen Drayton Nature Reserve). Finally we leave the traffic behind and head back towards the river and the peace of the Fens. Spare a glance, though, for the gleaming modern suspension bridge over the A14 on your right, recently built as part of the ongoing construction of cycle trails, bridleways and footpaths ringing Cambridge and linking it to the Fens.

↑ Fen Drayton Nature Reserve is made up of a series of lakes and lagoons (David1968M/S)

After the second roundabout on to Bucking Way Road, cross over as the cycle path continues along the right side of the road. After about 1km, we reach ❺ **Boxworth End**, where we rejoin the road. Carry on through the village and the contiguous ❻ **Swavesey**, past the White Horse Inn on your right and up Station Road to the modern Swavesey Busway Station on your right, with a park and ride car park and bike racks. The impressively futuristic Busway Cycleway Service links Cambridge to St Ives along a former railway line through the Fens (page 199).

Once you have got used to the sight of a double-decker bus floating quietly through the Fens (on specially made sideways wheels running along the concrete rails), turn left here and join the path. Shortly after Swavesey station, we enter **Fen Drayton Lakes RSPB Reserve**. A series of three footpaths has been set up around the reed-lined ponds dotting both sides of the route: Ferry Lagoon, Holywell Lake and Elney Lake, each

with bird hides, cycle racks and information boards. Huge numbers of waterbirds frequent the reserve all year round, including swans, geese and ducks, such as mallards, wigeons and teals. Buzzards, egrets, terns, oystercatchers, herons and even a seal has been spotted here, so it is well worth stopping here to explore its waterways.

Continuing along the Cycleway, pass Elney Lake on the left and Drayton Lagoon on your right. After about another 3km, we come to ❼ **St Ives**. Follow the NCN51 signs into the town, past the park and ride car park on your right, and up Station Road to Market Hill, the main square. To get to the riverside, cross the square and turn right on to the cycle lane on The Pavement, then left on to Bridge Street, leading to The Quay. There are market stalls (Mon & Fri) and open-air cafés on Market Hill, as well as riverside pubs and restaurants in the alleyways around The Quay.

From The Quay, cross the river over the **St Ives Bridge** and on to London Road. The medieval bridge is one of the town's oldest monuments, completed in 1425. It's also one of the few bridges in England to incorporate a chapel, still occasionally open for services. Continue straight ahead after the bridge, back to the crossroads with Hemingford Road, which we passed through earlier on. Turn right here and follow the NCN51/NCN24 signs through the Hemingfords, retracing our route to Houghton Mill.

↑ The handsome riverside town of St Ives (SuperStock)

THE ESSENTIALS

GETTING THERE By **car**, Houghton is off the A1123, between Huntingdon (5km west) and St Ives (3km east), or 29km from Cambridge, via the A14. By **bus**, the excellent Busway (thebusway.info) has a regular daily service from Cambridge to St Ives, then take the 904 to Houghton, around an hour in total. Fold-up bikes, inside carry bags, are allowed on the buses, when space is available.

WHERE TO EAT

The Cock Inn 47 High St, Hemingford Grey PE28 9BJ; 01480 463609; thecockhemingford.co.uk. This cosy little gastro-pub in the beautiful village of Hemingford Grey has a spacious back garden, with private pods providing a snug setting in all weathers. Its modern British menu features steaks, fish, local sausages & 1 or 2 veggie dishes; gluten-free & dairy-free menus are available too, plus daily specials & Sun roasts. Meals are served in the garden & the formal restaurant, also in the pub bar at lunchtimes except Sun. **££–£££**

The Nook 5 Market St, Swavesey CB24 4QG; The Nook – Swavesey. A great little café, just around the corner from the cycle route, by the White Horse Inn, The Nook makes delicious homemade cakes, pastries, bacon baps & filled flatbreads. Their freshly brewed coffee, tea & smoothies are excellent too. **£**

Tom's Cakes 19 Market Hill, St Ives PE27 5AL; 01487 842200; tomscakes.co.uk. The St Ives outlet of this small local chain is in the heart of St Ives's main square, with outdoor tables ideal for cyclists. The menu is regularly updated, but offers a great selection of cakes & biscuits from its Cambridge bakery, plus snacks, paninis & savoury dishes, with hot & cold drinks. **£**

FACILITIES AND FURTHER INFORMATION There are customer toilets in cafés and pubs in Houghton, St Ives and other villages en route. There is free parking on the roadside in Houghton's village square.

Cambridgeshire Fens 7 York Row, Wisbech PE13 1EB; 01945 232456; visitcambridgeshirefens.org. This is the nearest information centre in the area, based in Wisbech in northern Cambridgeshire, but it has plenty of online tips about what's on, where to go, places to stay & eat out, in and around the Fens.

CYCLING IN EAST ANGLIA | **THE ROUTES**

21 GRAFHAM WATER LOOP

START/FINISH	Marlow Park, Grafham Water
DISTANCE/TIME	14.5km/1½hrs
DIFFICULTY/TERRAIN	① Level, with a few short ups and downs (around Savage Spinney), mostly off-road and mostly gravel track, with short road sections through Grafham and Perry
SCENIC RATING	Ⓐ Lakeside trail fringed by wooded countryside, with nature reserves and watersports facilities
SUITABLE FOR	Hybrid, e-bike or mountain bike
NCN ROUTE	A short stretch on the NCN12, down the east side of the lake
MAPS	OS Explorer 225 (1:25 000)
KOMOOT REF	410779691

Grafham Water is a broad reservoir lake set in tranquil countryside, northwest of Cambridge. This lakeside trail is fringed with woods and side creeks; it's a short and mostly off-road route, so it's an ideal ride for young families and beginners. As an SSSI (Site of Special Scientific Interest) Grafham is renowned as one of the best birdwatching sites in the county, but its meadows and reed banks are also rich habitats for dragonflies, butterflies and wildflowers. There are play areas, watersports and a laser game centre too, so there's plenty here to make a day of it. It gets busy during holidays and weekends, so if you're planning to hire a bike here (page 221), check ahead and book, if necessary. Most of the route is gentle and undemanding, but MTB riders will have fun on the bumpier sections through the woods.

THE ROUTE

Start at the ❶ **Grafham Water Visitor Centre**, at Marlow Park, on the southeast side of the lake. Follow the cycle signs (NCN12) from the car park, going to the right, anticlockwise around the lake. As one of Grafham's main visitor hubs there may be lots of other people around, so take it slowly and be alert, particularly for children and dogs; the path around the lake is shared with walkers and other users too. The gravel trail soon winds right, away from the lake, and through meadows.

← Grafham Water's tranquil lakeside trail is ideal for families (Christopher Chuter/A)

It then bends back to the left and heads gently downhill through woods: on the left under the trees is **Rumble** (⌕ rumblelive.co.uk) – a fun laser adventure circuit.

Coming out of the woods, the path takes a sharp right on to a straight road, leading through the trees to ❷ **Grafham**. Turn left at the T-junction here, past All Saints Church on your left. The path joins the main road through the small and quiet village, but look out for traffic as you turn left. We leave the NCN12 here – it continues to the right and north up to Huntingdon, or also to the south of the lake to St Neots.

Otherwise, continue along Church Road, which carries on straight for about 1km, through arable fields and then left downhill back to the lake shore. Follow the signs behind the car park here, leading to the right, through **Savages Spinney**. Much of this western side of the lake is protected as a nature reserve (see box, page 204), with information boards and marked footpaths leading to bird hides at the various side creeks. The trail is bumpier here, with a few short ups and downs and warning signs before some of the steeper sections and sharp bends – good fun if you're an avid mountain biker. You might also notice Highland cattle grazing under the trees on the left, apparently nonplussed by careering mountain bikers.

After the bumpy gravel, the trail then goes through **Littless Wood**, where it can be muddy and slippery in wet weather. As we come out of the woods along a downhill stretch, there are a few more ups and downs for a further 2km or so, winding around Dudney and Valley creeks, but none are very long or steep. The path levels out as we come to **Mander Park** on the south shore of the lake, by the village of ❸ **Perry**. This is Grafham's other main visitor centre, so you could alternatively start the ride from here.

Continue winding left around the lakeshore. There's a short stretch alongside the road after Mander Park, but on a separate cycle path. Pass **Plummer Park** on the southeast corner of the lake (another parking spot), then cross the **reservoir dam**. There are great views from here across the lake. It's also a favoured spot for waterbirds, with large numbers of swans, geese and ducks sheltering in the shallows beneath the dam wall. From here, it's just another couple of minutes along the flat lakeside path back to the visitor centre.

THE ESSENTIALS

GETTING THERE By **car**, Grafham Water is around 38km from Cambridge, via the A14 and A1. The nearest **train** stations are at St Neots, 10.5km south, or Huntingdon, around 12km north, both with direct trains to London St Pancras with journey times around 50 minutes and 1 hour respectively. The nearest **bus** service is the 400, operated by Whippet Coaches, which goes from Huntingdon to Perry and Grafham village twice daily Monday to Friday. Only fold-up bikes are allowed on board, and only if there is space available.

WHERE TO EAT

✕ **Grafham Water Visitor Centre Café** Marlow Car Park, Grafham PE28 0BH; ✆ 01480 812154; ⌂ anglianwaterparks. co.uk. Next to the visitor centre, this little café with a lakeside outdoor terrace & adjacent playground serves a good range of hot & cold food, with family favourites focusing on burgers, paninis & chips, plus hot & cold drinks, cakes & perhaps best of all, 24 flavours of ice cream. **£**

GRAFHAM WILDLIFE

The western shores of Grafham Water are a nature reserve, comprising 113ha of scrub and wetland habitats, protected as an SSSI (Site of Special Scientific Interest) since 1986. There are seven bird hides dotted around the western and southern shorelines, which give the best opportunity to view some of the many birds that frequent the site (there's no cycling allowed, but it's OK to walk your bike to the hides, or lock it up by the path side). Some 170 species of birds have been recorded here, including rarer visitors such as ospreys and Slavonian grebes, together with mallard ducks, greylag geese and swans. Besides the waterside bird hides, the reserve's hedgerows and coppiced woodlands are also good sites for spotting wildlife. In springtime, the forest floor is a blaze of colourful wildflowers, particularly bluebells and primroses, as well as the pale blue bugle and purple clusters of self-heal. Several species of bats also roost in the trees here, and there's a Dragonfly Pond in the far southwestern corner of the lake, which is home to many water-loving invertebrates. The reserve is managed in partnership with the Wildlife Trust, so if you'd like more information about the wildlife, they have an office in the angling centre at Mander Park on the south side of the lake.

↑ Grafham Water is home to a variety of birdlife, including rare visitors like Slavonian grebes (Wolfgang Kruck/S)

✖ **Market Café** 48 Market Sq, St Neots; 01480 216116; ▮ Market Cafe. Around 11km south of Grafham Water in the village of St Neots, this Turkish-run café serves full English & Turkish b/fasts (a tower of feta & halloumi cheese, Turkish sausage, boiled eggs, filo pastry & more). Their huge menu also includes everything from liver & bacon to club sandwiches – eat indoors or outdoors on the square. **£**

✖ **The Falcon** 10 Market Hill, Huntingdon PE29 3NE; 01480 457416; falconhuntingdon.co.uk. A 10km hop northeast of Grafham Water in Huntingdon, this terrific pub with 2 floors & a walled back garden has been carefully restored to reflect its origins as a 16th-century coaching inn. It overlooks Market Sq, one of the oldest parts of Oliver Cromwell's home town (a museum to the Civil War leader is just across the square). The menu is big on hearty meat dishes, including an extensive choice of pies & speciality sausages, & the bar offers a huge range of real ales, ciders, fruit wine & mead. **££**

FACILITIES AND FURTHER INFORMATION As well as Grafham Water Visitor Centre, the visitor centre at Mander Park also has a car park, toilets, café and a sailing club and angling centre.

▮ **Grafham Water Visitor Centre** Marlow Park car park, Grafham Water PE28 0BH; 01480 812154; anglianwaterparks.co.uk/grafham-water-park/visitor-information. The information desk inside the café will help with local information, & there's a selection of leaflets in the entrance lobby. There's also a pay-and-display car park here, toilets, café, visitor information centre, play area & cycle hire (page 221).

ACCOMMODATION

These hotels, B&Bs, self-catering cottages, holiday parks and campsites have been chosen for their character, value for money and location close to the cycle routes (the numbered circles in each listing shows which route/s they are close to). Accommodation is ordered by county, in descending price order. Price codes are based on room rates per night during the summer high season, although most places also have cheaper off-season rates:

£ up to £50   **££** £50–90   **£££** £90+

NORFOLK

Appleton Water Tower West Newton, Sandringham PE31 6AY; 01628 825925; landmarktrust.org.uk; ❶ & ❷. This Victorian water tower has been magnificently converted into a luxurious holiday apt complete with period furnishings & fittings & offering amazing views from the tower terrace – though bear in mind that this also means lots of climbing up & down steep stairs. It sleeps up to 4, in a dbl & twin room. There are reception rooms & a fully equipped kitchen. Min stay 4 nights. **£££**

Black Boys Hotel Market Pl, Aylsham NR11 6EH; 01263 732122; blackboyshotel.co.uk; ❻. This Grade II-listed 17th-century coaching inn is in the heart of Aylsham, only about 5 mins' bike ride from the station at the end of Marriott's Way. They have 8 en-suite rooms, traditionally furnished, with TV, Wi-Fi & tea- & coffee-making facilities. The restaurant has an extensive menu, including pub classics as well as light bites & a good selection of veggie dishes. It also has a private car park, with cycle storage available. **£££**

Cley Windmill Cley-next-the-Sea NR25 7RP; 01263 740209; cleywindmill.co.uk; ❹. This 18th-century, Grade II-listed windmill in the centre of Cley has been converted into a luxurious guesthouse with 11 rooms on 5 floors, giving stunning views over Cley marshes to the coast. 9 rooms are B&B, plus 2 self-catering cottages in adjacent outhouses. **£££**

Foxes Croft Sandy Ln, Ingoldisthorpe PE31 6NN; 01485 520216, 07905 965153; christines-norfolk-cottages.co.uk; ❶ & ❷. This cute little self-catering bungalow, a few kilometres north of Sandringham, sleeps up to 3 people in a dbl & sgl room. It also has a large garden & off-road parking on a private drive. 3–4 nights off-season short breaks, or weekly only in high season. **£££**

George & Dragon Cley-next-the-Sea NR25 7RP; 01263 740209;

georgeanddragoncley.co.uk; ❹. This distinguished 18th-century hotel has a prime location in the heart of Cley & overlooking the coast. With 10 en-suite rooms (7 with views over the marshes) individually decorated with fine period furniture and stripped floorboards, all have free Wi-Fi, tea- & coffee-making equipment, flatscreen TV & other little extras. A full b/fast is included, & there is on-site parking. **£££**

Heacham Manor Hunstanton Rd, Heacham PE31 7JX; 01485 579800; onghou-manor.co.uk; ❷ & ❸. One of the smartest hotels in west Norfolk, between Hunstanton & Snettisham, this 16th-century manor is set in extensive grounds, with an 18-hole golf course & spa (closed at time of writing, Sep 2021). It has 52 rooms, distributed between the main house & converted barn cottages, including self-catering rooms & suites. Despite its grandeur, the hotel is informal & welcoming, with 2 restaurants, bar & ample free parking, including a locked bike enclosure. There's also a bike shop nearby in Heacham (A E Wallis) & local Wheel Travel bike hire will drop off & pick up bikes at the hotel. **£££**

Holkham Lodges Wells-next-the-Sea, NR23 1AB; 01263 715779; norfolkcottages.co.uk; ❸. Pamper yourself in one of these boutique lodges on the Holkham Estate. The 4 period properties include the Gatehouse & the sumptuous Grade I-listed Triumphal Arch, with 4-poster bed. Each lodge sleeps 2, with kitchen, sitting room, garden & private parking. Available per night or weekly rates. **£££**

Briars Cottage 10 Riverside, Reedham NR13 3TF; 07836 569661, 01795 872594 (eve); reedhamholidaylets.co.uk; ❼ & ❽. This large holiday home on Reedham waterfront is ideal for large families or groups of friends, sleeping up to 10 guests in 5 bedrooms. The 200-year-old cottage is fully equipped & well furnished, with accessible facilities, including adapted downstairs bedroom & wet room. There's also Wi-Fi, a private garden, sun room, games room & parking for 2 cars. **££**

The Cockatrice B&B Ferry Rd, Norton Subcourse NR14 6SF; 01508 548901; Cockatrice B&B; ❼ & ❽. This former pub is just down the road from Reedham Ferry, in a tranquil setting overlooking the River Yare. With dbl & twin bedrooms sharing a bathroom, it's very quiet, cosy & friendly, with a decent continental b/fast. There's also Wi-Fi & off-road parking. **££**

Horsey Barns Horsey NR29 4AD; 0344 800 2070; nationaltrust.org.uk/holidays; ❺. This immaculate granary barn conversion, with typical National Trust high standards, is just off the route on the outskirts of Horsey, conveniently next door to the Nelson Head pub & only 10 mins' walk from the coast. The 3 barns overlook a traditional courtyard – each sleep from 3 to 6 people, with shared bathroom. There's also a downstairs lounge & open-plan kitchen. Min stay 3 nights. **££**

🏠 **The King's Head Hotel** Great Bircham, King's Lynn PE31 6RJ; ☎ 01485 578265; 🖱 thekingsheadcountryhotel.co.uk; ❷. This restored Edwardian country house boutique hotel in the centre of the rural village has 12 spacious, plush & stylish rooms, plus an à la carte restaurant or bar meals. **££**

🏠 **Shepherd's Hut** Bircham Windmill, Great Bircham, King's Lynn PE31 6SJ; ☎ 01485 578393; 🖱 birchamwindmill.co.uk; ❷. These traditional wooden huts on wheels will give you the complete rural experience (exchanging 2 wheels for 4). Each hut sleeps 2 & is well kitted out, with pull-out dbl bed, plus kitchen equipment, tables, chairs & candle lamps for cosy nights. There's a shared shower in the separate shepherd's hut & camping in the windmill grounds is also available. **££**

🏠 **Ling House** Anmer, King's Lynn PE31 6RR; ☎ 07964 692444; 🖱 onghouse.co.uk; ❶ & ❷. This luxurious B&B in a charming old red-brick cottage in Anmer on the Sandringham Estate has 6 tastefully decorated bedrooms, including 2 en suite. There is ample off-road parking & access to its pretty garden, with barbecue & games. **£**

🏠 **The Station** Attlebridge NR9 5AA; ☎ 01603 261510; 🖱 caravanclub.co.uk; ❻. This simple but tranquil & spotless Caravan & Motorhome Club site is ideally located right next to Marriott's Way, in a meadow behind the restored old railway station, with 5 electric hook-up pitches for caravans & motorhomes. Open to members only. **£**

🏠 **YHA Wells Next the Sea** Church Plain, Wells-next-the-Sea NR23 1EQ; ☎ 0345 371 9544; 🖱 yha.org.uk/hostel/yha-wells-next-the-sea; ❸. This rather grand red-brick hostel is well located right in the centre of Wells. It has 31 beds in dorms & private rooms, plus a TV lounge & large kitchen (self-catering only). There's also a cycle store & a drying room. **£**

⛺ **The Old Vicarage Campsite** Moulton St Mary NR13 3NH; 🖱 oldvicaragecamping.co.uk; ❼. This quiet & basic tents-only campsite is well located between Reedham & Halvergate, just off our route, with some 20 pitches in a spacious field, with composting toilets & open-air showers, a marquee for eating out & barbecue braziers (for hire). Glamping in bell tents & pods is also available, sleeping up to 4, & with brazier included. **£–££** *bell tent & pod*

⛺ **Top Farm Camping & Glamping Site** Kittles Ln, Marsham NR10 5QF; ☎ 01263 733962; 🖱 top-farm.info; ❻. This tranquil campsite is just a few kilometres from Aylsham at the end of Marriott's Way, set in a big open meadow fringed by woods & heath. There are 18 tent pitches, as well as various glamping options, including bell tents, shepherds' huts & cabins; at the other end of the luxury scale they also offer 'wild camping' in your own private meadow (with toilet, shower & water tap, so not totally jungle survival). There are covered areas for locking up bikes & they also have lists of other local bike routes. **£** *camping*, **££** *glamping*

⛺ Walnut Farm Touring Park Waxham NR12 0EG; ✆ 01692 598217; ⌖ walnutfarmwaxham.co.uk; ❺. On the outskirts of Waxham & with a direct footpath to the beach, this family-run campsite has 32 grass pitches for tents, hook-ups for caravans, static caravans, cottages & fully kitted-out glamping yurts, sleeping 4/6 people. **£** *tents*, **££** *others*

⛺ Amber's Bell Tent Camping Wiveton Hall, Holt NR25 7TE; ✆ 07580 072861; ⌖ ambersbelltents.co.uk; ❹. Next to the coast path between Cley & Blakeney, this family-friendly glamping site in the grounds of the 17th-century Wiveton Hall & Farm has 6 bell tents ready set up with beds, log burners & eco-lighting, plus campfire, children's play area, nearby shop & café. The local bike-hire shop will drop off & pick up hire bikes. **£**

⛺ Hickling Campsite Heath Rd, Hickling NR12 0AX; ⌖ coolcamping.com/campsites/uk/england/east-anglia/norfolk/north-walsham/405-hickling-campsite; 🅵 Cool Camping; 🕐 May–Sep; ❺. With 30 tent pitches, 3 shepherds' huts & a glamping pod, this is a small & quiet campsite, with shower block, fire pits & on-site 'Hickling Hut' food store, in a grassy meadow sheltered by hedgerows a few hundred metres from Hickling Broads NWT close to our route. **£**

⛺ Pine Cones Caravan & Camping Site Dersingham PE31 6WL; ✆ 01485 544224; ⌖ pineconescc.co.uk; ❶ & ❷. This spacious campsite is set among pleasant woods just off the A149 3km northwest of Sandringham. There are around 100 pitches for tents & caravan hook-ups, & glamping pods, with a kids' outdoor adventure area & nearby Sprinqside Lake for anglers. It's about 20 mins to the nearest pubs & 10 mins to a supermarket in Dersingham. **£**

⛺ Pinewoods Caravan Park & Campsite Beach Rd, Wells-next-the-Sea NR23 1DR; ✆ 01328 710439 ⌖ pinewoods.co.uk; ❸. Next to Wells Beach Car Park, right at the start of the route is this family-friendly site with static caravans, lodges & pitches for mobile caravans. There's an on-site shop, café & playground, & even its own miniature railway. **£**

⛺ Potters Farm Campsite Wighton, Wells-next-the-Sea NR23 1AB; ✆ 01328 713002; ⌖ pottersfarmwighton.co.uk; ❸. At the start of the off-road track from Wighton to Wells, this cosy little farm campsite has a grassy paddock with 15 pitches for tents & motorhomes, as well as a tipi & glamping bell tent, along with a washroom, covered veranda, welcome food packs & locally cooked ready meals available. They also run workshops, including fleece-rugmaking, & have a few adult bikes for guests' use (there's also a barn for locking up bikes, as well as a workshop & repairs if needed). **£**

⚑ **Reedham Ferry & The Archers Touring Park** Ferry Rd, Reedham NR13 3HA; ☏ 01493 700999; ⌕ reedhamferry.co.uk; ❼ & ❽. This motorhome, caravan & camping site by the Reedham Ferry on the north bank of the River Yare has 90 pitches on a spacious tree-lined meadow, with hook-ups, washroom & barbecue area. It also has its own fishing lakes, slipway to the river & adjacent riverside pub (page 80). **£**

⚑ **Sandringham Camping and Caravanning Club** Coach Rd, The Sandringham Estate PE35 6EA; ☏ 01485 542555; ⌕ campingandcaravanningclub.co.uk; ❶ & ❷. Set in the shady pine forest on the Royal Estate just 5 mins by bike from Sandringham House, this peaceful site is ideally located for cycling around the area. With plenty of pitches (270) for tents, motorhomes & caravans, they also have 9 glamping 'Ready Camp' tents, comfortably kitted out, with beds for up to 6 people in 2 separate rooms, plus kitchen, electricity & covered balcony. There are no fancy amenities on site, but there's a small playground, shop, washroom & a fish & chips take-away van visits several times a week. **£**

SUFFOLK

🏠 **The Bell Inn** Ferry Rd, Walberswick IP18 6TN; ☏ 01502 723109; ⌕ bellinnwalberswick.co.uk; ⑬. Overlooking the green in the heart of Walberswick, this 15th-century inn has 6 en-suite bedrooms, including 1 larger family room sleeping 4. Most rooms have views of the beach, garden or the harbour, Wi-Fi is included (though the signal around here is notoriously weak), as is b/fast, including locally smoked kippers on request. There's limited private parking space behind the pub. **£££**

🏠 **The Dairy** Walberswick ☏ 01502 722717; ⌕ suffolk-secrets.co.uk (cottage ref: TDAIR); ⑬. Conveniently located in the centre of Walberswick, this converted former dairy self-catering cottage has a dbl & twin room, sleeping up to 4. With living room, TV, kitchen, washing machine & Wi-Fi, it also has a private rear garden, ideal for locking up bikes, a heated swimming pool & private off-road parking. **£££**

🏠 **Deben View** Tranmer House, Sutton Hoo IP12 3DJ; ☏ 01394 389700; ⌕ nationaltrust.org.uk/sutton-hoo; ⑮. One of 3 converted flats in Tranmer House, where owner Edith Pretty lived when the famous burial ship was uncovered. What is special about this 2-bedroom apt is that its living area was her bedroom, where she hid some of the treasures under her bed. Apparently, Edith & archaeologist Basil Brown would bring the daily finds from the burial site, escorted by gamekeeper William Spooner, armed with his shotgun! The 1st-floor apt comes with period furniture, fully equipped kitchen, washing machine, TV & DVD player; it also has a veranda with lovely views over the grounds to the River Deben. Wi-Fi signal only in the downstairs lobby & parking space behind the house. Min stay 4 nights. **£££**

🏠 **Stowlangtoft Estate** Kiln Farm, Stowlangtoft, Bury St Edmunds IP31 3JZ; ✆ 01359 230210; 🌐 stowlangtoftestate.co.uk; ⓫. This country estate near Ixworth has 6 holiday cottages dotted around its peaceful, secluded grounds, with a range of sizes sleeping from 2 up to 24 for large groups. Accommodation is comfortably furnished, with flatscreen TV, Wi-Fi & with garden or patio for storing bikes; available for 1-night short breaks or longer stays. **£££**

🏠 **The White Horse Inn** Stoke Ash, nr Eye IP23 7ET; ✆ 01379 678222; 🌐 whitehorse-suffolk.co.uk; ⓬. Conveniently located by the A140 between Eye & Debenham, this 17th-century former coaching inn has 11 bedrooms in an adjacent modern annex. Rooms are simply furnished but quiet & comfortable, with TV & Wi-Fi, the hotel restaurant serves reliably good pub cuisine & off-road parking & storage space for bikes are a useful plus. Cheaper room rates may be available through online booking agencies. **£££**

🏠 **Cowpasture Barn B&B** The Common, Mellis IP23 8EE; ✆ 01379 788196; 🌐 cowpasture-barn-bb.suffolk-hotels.co.uk/en; ⓬. Peacefully located in Mellis 5km west of Eye, by one of the biggest village commons in England, this luxurious B&B has 2 en-suite dbl bedrooms in a beautiful converted barn, each with king-size beds & well kitted out with tea- & coffee-making facilities, great full English b/fasts & even a daily cake treat, flatscreen TV & Wi-Fi. There's also cycle storage under cover & off-road parking. **££**

🏠 **The Crown Hotel** Crown Rd, Mundford, Thetford IP26 5HQ; ✆ 01842 878233; 🌐 the-crown-hotel.co.uk; ❿. This 17th-century former hunting inn overlooks the village green in Muntford, in the Brecks forests between Thetford & Swaffham. It has 40 en-suite bedrooms, simply but comfortably furnished, with free Wi-Fi, & TV. It also has 2 bars & restaurants & storage space for bicycles. **££**

🏠 **Gate Cottage** Long Melford; ✆ 03332 020899; 🌐 originalcottages.co.uk (cottage ref: 9WS); ⓰. On the outskirts of the pretty village of Long Melford about 7km south of Lavenham, this cosy, 2-bedroom (dbl & sgl beds) holiday cottage is comfortably furnished, with TV, Wi-Fi & back patio garden with storage space for bikes & private off-road parking for 2 cars. **££**

🏠 **Grove Barn Bed & Breakfast** Middle Rd, Denton IP20 0AH; ✆ 01986 788015; 🌐 grovebarnbedandbreakfast.com; ❾. This peaceful B&B (adults only, no pets) has 3 en-suite bedrooms in a luxuriously converted barn in a quiet village between Flixton & Bungay, just over the Norfolk border. Wi-Fi, TV, courtyard garden & off-road parking, with bike storage. **££**

🏠 **The Jolly Sailor** Quay St, Orford IP12 2NU; ☎ 01394 450243; 🌐 jollysailororford.co.uk; ⑭. In the centre of Orford, right by the start & end of our route, this gorgeous old family-run inn has 4 en-suite dbl rooms: 3 on the 2nd floor & the private Garden Room downstairs with its own courtyard garden & private entrance. A hearty b/fast is included, with vegetarian alternatives available. **££**

🏠 **Lynford Hall Hotel** Mundford IP26 5HW; ☎ 01842 878351; 🌐 lynfordhallhotel.co.uk; ⑩. Set in rolling landscaped grounds a couple of kilometres north of Thetford Forest, this 19th-century country mansion hotel has 38 rooms, with a range of options from good-value simple rooms to opulent suites, with prices to match – all have LCD TV, Wi-Fi & tea- & coffee-making facilities. **££**

🏠 **Maglia Rosso** Metcalfe Arms, Hawstead IP29 5NR; ☎ 01284 386884; 🌐 wigwamholidays.com; ⑪, ⑮ & ⑯. Part of a vibrant local cycling centre, with bike hire & sales shop on site, café & group rides, these 6 comfortable pods overlook a 2ha meadow in quiet countryside near Bury St Edmunds. Each sleeps up to 4 people, with en-suite bathroom, kitchen, TV & Wi-Fi. 1 pod is low-level, adapted for accessibility, & 2 are dog-friendly, with covered deck in front (space for 2 bikes) & off-road parking behind. **££**

🏠 **Mallards Cottage** Plovers, Chedburgh Rd, Whepstead IP29 4UB; ☎ 0333 202 0899; 🌐 originalcottages.co.uk (cottage ref: MAL); ⑪ ⑯ ⑰. This delightful holiday cottage is set in tranquil countryside south of Bury St Edmunds, midway between 3 of our cycle routes. With 1 king-size bedroom, sitting room & airy kitchen, it's all very comfy & tastefully decorated, with TV & Wi-Fi. There's also a rotating pod in the field behind, where you can sit & watch the resident ostriches! Pigs, hens, ducks & other assorted pets also roam around to make you feel welcome. With private parking space & indoor storage for bikes. **££**

🏠 **The Old Stable** Church Ln, Iken IP12 2ES; ☎ 01728 688263; 🌐 farmstay.co.uk; ⑭. This self-catering accommodation in a converted stable has a quiet setting adjacent to Iken's historic church with views of the nearby River Alde. It sleeps up to 6 people with 2 bedrooms, plus a futon bed. There's a log burner in the lounge, TV/DVD & music system, along with cycle storage space. **££**

🏠 **The Six Bells Inn** Daveys Ln, Bardwell IP31 1AW; ☎ 01359 250820; 🌐 sixbellsbardwell.co.uk; ⑪. This late 16th-century country inn is in the little village of Bardwell, near the start of the Ixworth Millers' Trail. There are 10 en-suite bedrooms set around the courtyard in the adjacent converted barn & stables, with TV, radio & tea- & coffee-making facilities. A full English b/fast is included & the pub restaurant menu features locally sourced meat & vegetables, plus several vegetarian dishes. **££**

🏠 **Little Lodge Farm** Santon Downham, Brandon IP27 0TX; ☎ 01842 813438;

forestlodgeholidays.co.uk; ❿. This farm in idyllic woodlands bordering the River Little Ouse & Thetford Forest (approx 7km northeast of High Lodge) has a range of accommodation, from fully kitted-out log cabins to tent camping site, static caravans & hook-ups. They also offer transport to & from High Lodge on its live concert nights. **£**

🏠 **YHA Blaxhall** Blaxhall IP12 2FA; 01728 688206; yha.org.uk/hostel/yha-blaxhall; ⓮. Housed in the former village school, this comfortable 43-bed hostel has dorms & private rooms, as well as excellent amenities including spacious lounge, garden & fully equipped kitchen. Note that at the time of going to press, this hostel is available for booking only the whole place; check the website for updates. There's also a cycle storage room. **£**

🛖 **Kenton Hall Estate Glamping** Debenham Rd, Kenton IP14 6JU; 01728 862062; kentonhallestate.co.uk; ⓬. Set in peaceful woodland on this historic Tudor hall's estate just outside Kenton, & close to our route, this campsite offers some truly luxurious glamping treats. Its traditional Mongolian yurt comes furnished with rugs & electric lanterns. There's also a shepherd's hut & lodge tents, each sleeping 2 people, with outdoor seating areas & fire pits. Bedding & towels are included, plus kitchen & cooking facilities & a wood-burning stove in the shepherd's hut. **£££**

🛖 **Apple Mount Retreat** Apple Mount Farmhouse, Thorpe Morieux IP30 0NQ; 07823 772138; applemountretreat.co.uk; ⓰. Right on the route, about 7km outside Lavenham, this idyllic glamping site has 4 luxurious wooden pods in a tree-lined meadow set back from the road, each sleeping 3 people, with en-suite bathroom, compact kitchen, complimentary welcome pack (tea, coffee, washing-up kit & toiletries) & Wi-Fi. There's a deck in front, barbecue & fire pit & the site has tennis courts & an open-air swimming pool. The main house also offers holistic meditation retreats & workshops. **££**

🛖 **Barn Owl Glade** Low Farm, Locks Rd, Brampton NR34 8DX; 01502 575840; barnowlglade.co.uk; ❽ & ❾. With its self-catering cottages, rustic wooden pods & indoor swimming pool, this comfortable campsite near Beccles, in the heart of Suffolk, truly lives up to the glamping tag. The grounds are lush, green & peaceful, also including a Wi-Fi lounge & games room, children's play area & country store. The co-owner Ruth also runs a special educational therapy centre on the site, while husband Nick runs the campsite. **£**

🛖 **Haw Wood Farm Caravans and Camping** Hinton IP17 3QT; 01502 359550; hawwoodfarm.co.uk; ⓭. Inland from Walberswick, about 7km from Wenhaston on our cycle route, this well-equipped farm campsite has 100 pitches for tents & caravans/motorhomes, with a large shower & washing-up block, farm shop & café, with room in the barn if needed to lock up bikes indoors. They also have a small campsite on the beach at Walberswick, with 16 pitches, but no facilities apart from a freshwater tap. **£**

⚠ Ling's Meadow Stanton Row Farm, North Common, Hepworth IP22 2PR; ☎ 01359 250594; ⌘ lingsmeadow.co.uk; ⓫. This family-run farm & eco-campsite lies to the north of Stanton, close to the Ixworth Millers' Trail. It has 5 spacious tent pitches in a grassy meadow, as well as glamping options, including shepherds' huts, bell tents & something called a StarDome, which apparently is like a cross between a yurt & a geodesic dome. Facilities include solar-powered showers, composting toilets & washing-up area. There's a footpath around the farm, so you can meet the sheep, alpacas, ducks & chickens. They also have a few bicycles available for guests to borrow during their stay & a safe, under-cover bike storage space. **£**

⚠ Outney Meadow Campsite Outney Meadow, Bungay NR35 1HG; ☎ 01986 892338; ⌘ outneymeadow.co.uk; ⓽. Just a short walk from the centre of Bungay, this spacious campsite has a level, tree-lined riverside field with 45 tent pitches & hook-ups for caravans & with toilet/shower block & laundry. They also hire out canoes & fishing equipment. **£** *2-person tent/caravan high season*

⚠ Shottisham Campsite Hollesley Rd, Shottisham IP12 3HD; ☎ 01394 411247; ⌘ shottishamcampsite.com; ⓯. On the outskirts of the pretty village of Shottisham, this family-run campsite has 50 tent pitches well spaced out over 5 fields sheltered by mature trees. There are also electric hook-ups, toilets, shower block & fire pits. The on-site Blue Rabbit Café serves b/fasts & brunches & sells home-grown produce, plus Pete's wood-fired pizzas on Fri. **£**

⚠ Tangham Campsite Woodbridge IP12 3NF; ☎ 01394 450707; ⌘ www.forestcamping.co.uk; ⓯. In the heart of Rendlesham Forest close to the off-road trails on our route, this large campsite includes 90 tent pitches in a spacious open meadow between the trees. It's well set up with toilet & wash-block, kitchen, laundry, freezer hut & children's play area – there are also electric hook-ups for caravans & motorhomes. **£**

CAMBRIDGESHIRE

🏠 The George 39 High St, Buckden PE19 5XA; ☎ 01480 812300; ⌘ thegeorgebuckden.com; ㉑. This chic boutique hotel & former coaching inn is in the historic village of Buckden, a few kilometres east of Grafham Water. Its 10 individually furnished rooms have a tastefully mixed contemporary-classic style. Its gourmet restaurant offers a tasting menu or à la carte, with a 'colonial-inspired' menu offering a good range of traditional local dishes & imaginative global cuisine, including several vegetarian & vegan options. **£££**

🏠 **The Old Bridge** 1 High St, Huntingdon PE29 3TQ; 📞 01480 424300; 🖱 oldbridgehuntingdon.co.uk; ⑳ & ㉑. Housed in an elegant, ivy-clad 18th-century townhouse by the River Ouse in the centre of Huntingdon, this 3-star hotel has 33 romantically decorated rooms, some with garden & riverside views. All have free Wi-Fi, flatscreen TV & audio centre & AC, & some have views over the garden & river. Its restaurant looks out over the patio garden, serving British cuisine & it also has a wine shop with 'Enomatic' wine-tasting machines. Free on-site parking. **£££**

🏠 **The Packhorse Inn** Bridge St, Moulton CB8 8SP; 📞 01638 751818; 🖱 thepackhorseinn.com; ⑰ & ⑱. This upmarket village inn has 8 dbl rooms, either in the main pub or adjacent converted coach house. Each are individually styled & luxuriously furnished, some with self-standing bath & underfloor heating & several adapted for accessibility. The downstairs restaurant serves award-winning gastro cuisine. **£££**

🏠 **The Bell Inn** Newmarket Rd, Kennett CB8 7PP; 📞 01638 750333; 🖱 thebellkennett.co.uk; ⑰ & ⑱. This ivy-clad, gabled 16th-century coaching inn on the outskirts of Kentford, near Newmarket, has 10 rooms above the pub, all with free Wi-Fi. Rates are for room only, though they offer brunch boxes at £8.95, kept in the room's fridge. It also has a secure storage space for bikes. **££**

🏠 **The Golden Lion** Market Hill, St Ives PE27 5AL; 📞 01480 492100; 🖱 thegoldenlionhotel.co.uk; ⑳ & ㉑. Overlooking Market Hill, the main square in St Ives, this 18th-century former coaching inn has 27 comfortable modern rooms, with free Wi-Fi, Freeview TV, tea- & coffee-making facilities. The downstairs restaurant offers a good mix of British pub classics & international dishes, as well as afternoon cream teas. There's no car park but guests can leave bikes in the function room. **££**

🏠 **Grafham Water Lodge** 16 Westwood Lodge, Grafham PE28 0BB; 📞 07740 776404; 🖱 cambridgeshireholidaycottages.com; ㉑. This rustic, Scandinavian-style wooden lodge has a great location in Grafham, just a few minutes by bike from the north lakeshore of Grafham Water. With 3 bedrooms sleeping up to 6, there's a fully equipped kitchen, lounge, TV, DVD player & games, & an outside front terrace with space for bikes & a parking area for 2–3 cars. **££**

🏠 **Cambridge City East Premier Inn** Newmarket Rd, Cambridge CB1 3EP; 📞 0333 321 9289; 🖱 premierinn.com; ⑲. What it may lack in individual style, Cambridge's City East Premier Inn more than makes up for with good-value accommodation, plus guests can take bikes – with clean tyres – into the room. This branch of the budget chain is only about 5 mins' ride from the riverside path on our route. Comfortably furnished rooms have TV, free Wi-Fi, tea- & coffee-making facilities, & the unlimited buffet b/fast will set you up well for the ride. **£**

⌂ Riverside Inn 8 Annesdale, Ely CB7 4BN; ☏ 01353 661677; ⌘ riversideinn-ely.co.uk; ⑲. This elegant 19th-century townhouse overlooks Ely's riverside marina, right by our route into the city. With comfortable, traditionally furnished rooms, tea- & coffee-making facilities, LCD TV, free Wi-Fi & a private car park with safe space to lock up bikes. **£**

▲ Church View Campsite Church Rd, Barrow IP29 5AX; ☏ 07852 101598; ⌘ churchviewcampsite.co.uk; ⑰ & ⑱. In a level field between Bury St Edmunds & Newmarket only 10 mins' walk from the village pub & shops nearby, this small & peaceful family-run campsite is well located for several of our bike rides in the area. It has 26 pitches for tents, caravans & motorhomes, with hook-ups, & also a glamping pod sleeping up to 5 people. There are 2 wash-blocks, fire pit & barbecue, a children's play area & eggs on sale from the campsite hens. **£–££**

▲ Back to Basics Campsite Wicken Fen National Nature Reserve, Lode Ln, Wicken CB7 5XP; e wickenwildcamping@nationaltrust.org.uk; ⌘ nationaltrust.org.uk/holidays/wicken-fen-back-to-basics-campsite-east-anglia; ⑰, ⑱ & ⑲. With open-fronted log shelters, no water supply & only accessible on foot or by bicycle, this truly wild campsite does what it says on the tin, to quote the catchphrase, with only compost toilets & campfires for your creature comforts. You'll be in the heart of the countryside & it's ideally located for spotting some of the Fens' wildlife, including badgers, bats & owls. **£**

▲ Grafham Water Caravan & Motor Home Club Site Grafham, Huntingdon PE28 0BB; ☏ 01480 810264; ⌘ caravanclub.co.uk; ㉑. Only 5 mins by bike from Grafham Water Visitor Centre & right on the cycle route, this club site (non-members welcome) has 61 hook-up pitches for caravans & motorhomes (no tents) on a tree-lined & level grassy field with shower room, including accessible facilities, playground & dishwashing area, plus nearby sports amenities (including tennis, golf & horseriding). A 17th-century cottage on the site was formerly owned by Oliver Cromwell's family & the remains of the moat now serve as a home for their resident ducks. **£**

▲ Waterclose Meadows Campsite Houghton Mill PE28 2AZ; ☏ 01480 499996; ⌘ nationaltrust.org.uk/holidays/waterclose-meadows-campsite; ⊙ mid-May–end Oct; ⑳ & ㉑. With 65 pitches for tents, caravans & motorhomes on a level grassy field next to Houghton Mill, this campsite is ideally located for our route through the Fens to St Ives. They also have fully equipped camping pods, toilet & shower block, with shops a few minutes' walk in Houghton village. **£**

PITCH UP, RIDE OUT.

With 30 quality assured campsites across East Anglia, we're the perfect partner for every adventure.

Find out more and join today
campingandcaravanningclub.co.uk

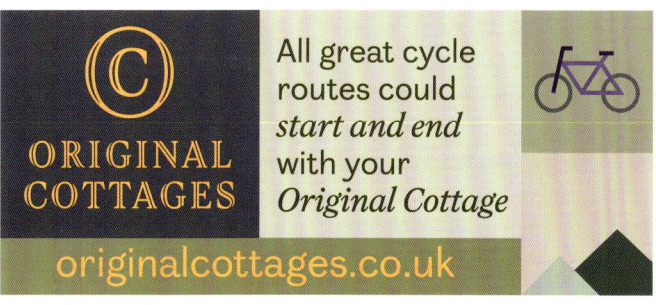

ORIGINAL COTTAGES

All great cycle routes could *start and end* with your *Original Cottage*

originalcottages.co.uk

BIKE HIRE

NORFOLK

A E Wallis 30–40 High St, Heacham PE31 7EP; 01485 571683; aewallis.co.uk; ❶ & ❷. This classic Norfolk multi-purpose emporium has a good range of bikes for hire, including e-bikes, fold-up bikes, tricycles & children's bikes. Competitive rates & reductions for 2+ days' hire.

Bike Art High Lodge, Thetford Forest, Brandon IP27 0AF; 01482 810090; bikearthire.cc; ❿. Based at the visitor centre in Thetford Forest, with its 60km+ of off-road trails, this hire shop has mountain bikes & e-bikes for adults, children's mountain bikes & child-trailers, with hourly rates or cheaper full-day hire.

Black Bikes 28 Beeston Rd, Sheringham NR26 8EH; 01263 822255; black-bikes.co.uk; ❹. This independent shop run by former racing cyclists is currently only doing sales & repairs, but could be useful if in need and you're in the vicinity of the north coast.

Broadlands Cycle Hire BeWILDerwood, Horning Rd, Hoveton NR12 8JW; 07747 483154; norfolkbroadscycling.co.uk; ❺ & ❻. Based at the outdoor family adventure centre near Wroxham, this large, well-established company has a range of adults' bikes, including hybrids, e-bikes & tandems, also children's bikes, tagalongs, baby/child seats & trailers. They also have masses of useful information about cycle routes across the Norfolk Broads & will deliver hire bikes up to a 16km radius from BeWILDerwood.

Clippesby Hall Cycle Hire Hall Rd, Clippesby NR29 3BL; 01493 367800; clippesbyhall.com/portfolio-items/cyclehire; ❺ ❻ & ❼. Bike-hire office in the Clippesby Hall caravan & camping holiday park between Norwich & Great Yarmouth. With standard bikes for adults & children, with toddler seats, tagalongs & buggies. Hire charge also includes helmet, lock & repair kit.

Cockle Bay E-bike Hire Blenheim House, 26 Theatre Rd, Wells-next-the-Sea NR23 1DJ; 07958 327622 (Nicky), 07913 187251 (Marie); ebikehirenorfolk.com; ❸. Hire specialised rugged RADPower e-bikes, which are versatile on road as well as along the sandy trails around the coastal AONB.

Holkham Cycle Hire Holkham Hall, Wells-next-the-Sea NR23 1AB; 01328 713071; holkham.co.uk/visiting/cycle-hire; ❸. Based at Holkham Hall, on our route, with standard hybrid bikes & e-bikes for adults, plus children's bikes, trailers, kids' seats & tagalongs. No advance booking required; it's first come first served.

Huff and Puff Cycles Kelling Heath Holiday Park, Weybourne, Holt NR25 7HW; 07500 865095; huffandpuffcycles.co.uk; ❹. Good range of bikes to fit all sizes, adults & kids, plus tandems, tricycles & buggies for tots/

pets & tagalongs. From 3hrs' hire to multi-day with discount.

On Yer Bike The Laurels, Nutwood Farm, Binham Rd, Wighton NR23 1NX; ☎ 07584 308120; ⌖ norfolkcyclehire.co.uk; ❹. This handy hire shop to the east of Wighton, just off our route, has a great range of bikes, including hybrids, mountain bikes, tandems & e-bikes, & also kids' & dog trailers & tagalongs.

Overland Cycles 34 Norwich Rd, Holt NR25 6SQ; ☎ 07733 445511; ⌖ sites.google.com/site/overlandcycles; ❹. This cycle shop in the village of Holt stocks a wide range of hire bikes for adults & children. They also do repairs & sales.

Torque-ebikes Thursford Castle, Great Snoring NR21 0PE; ☎ 07377 185474; ⌖ torque-ebikes.co.uk/hire-fleet; ❸ & ❹. Based near Thursford Castle, midway between Wells-next-the-Sea & Fakenham, Torque stock an impressive fleet of e-bikes for hire (& occasionally ex-demo for sale), including mountain bikes & even a 'cargo' e-tricycle with a roomy front basket (holding up to 4 toddlers). It's not cheap (£55–80/day), but with discounts for 2–5 days & weekly hire, they will also pick up & drop off bikes locally for longer hire periods, & they run their own guided cycling tours.

Wells Bike Hire 7 Southgate Close, Wells-next-the-Sea NR23 1HG; ☎ 07920 016405, 07766 258064; ⌖ wellsbikehire.co.uk; ❸. Family-run company with mountain bikes, trail bikes & e-bikes, & a good range of kids' add-ons, trailers, tagalongs, baby seats, dog trailers even. Repairs & servicing also available.

Wheel-Travel ☎ 07940 497093; ⌖ wheel-travel.co.uk/daily-adult-cycle-hire; ❶ & ❷. Based in Heacham, north of Sandringham, this online hire company will pick up & drop off bikes within a wide range of northwest Norfolk, from King's Lynn up to Burnham Market, with hybrid bikes, kids' bikes in a range of sizes, child seats, tagalongs & trailers.

SUFFOLK

Hippersons Boatyard Gillingham Dam, Beccles NR34 0EB; ☎ 01502 712166; ⌖ hippersons.co.uk/bike-hire; ❾. This multi-purpose, all-singing all-dancing outfit on the Suffolk Broads has a few adults' & children's bikes for hire; besides its boat tours, houseboats & glamping campsite.

Maglia Rosso Metcalfe Arms, Lawshall Rd, Hawstead IP29 5NR; ☎ 07487 566475; ⌖ magliarosso.co.uk; ⓫ ⓰ ⓱ & ⓲. With cycle hire, sales, repairs, guided local rides, cyclo-cross training course & adjacent glamping site, this excellent outfit is virtually a one-stop cycling portal. Their hire fleet includes road bikes, hybrids, mountain bikes, e-bikes, a tandem, children's bikes & trailer, & their on-site café also does scrumptious b/fasts & fresh roasted coffee.

Outdoor Hire Centre Unit 3D, The Gattinetts, Hadleigh Rd, East Bergholt CO7 6QT; 🕿 01206 700707; 🖰 outdoorhirecentres.com; ⑭, ⑮ & ⑯. This multi-activity adventure centre with several sites across Suffolk & Essex has an extensive fleet of hire bikes, including hybrids, road bikes, mountain bikes, tandems, children's bikes, tagalongs & trailers available from their Bergholt base, where they also run their own themed cycle routes.

Somerleyton Cycles The Street, Somerleyton NR32 5PS; 🕿 01502 732004; 🖰 somerleytoncycles.com; ⑧. This versatile cycle shop and ice cream parlour are based in the Suffolk Broads, between Great Yarmouth and Lowestoft. They have classic Raleigh hybrid bikes for hire, with adults and children's bikes available, as well as child seats and tagalongs.

Southwold Cycle Hire Old Hall Farm, Halesworth Rd, Reydon IP18 6SG; 🕿 07946 338097; 🖰 southwoldcyclehire.co.uk; ⑬. Based outside Southwold, just off the A1095, this long-standing, family-run business has a fleet of high-quality Dawes road & hybrid adults' bikes, as well as a range of children's bikes, trailers & tagalongs either to pick up or be delivered, up to 8km from Southwold.

Suffolk Cycle Hire Yoxford; 🕿 07851 402587; 🖰 suffolkcyclehire.co.uk; ⑫–⑯. This long-established, online cycle-hire company is based on the Suffolk coast. There's no physical shop but they will deliver & collect bikes up to around a 25km radius, from as far north as Southwold, inland to Framlingham, Rendlesham & south to Orford. Their extensive fleet includes hybrids, mountain bikes, e-bikes, children's bikes & seats for toddlers & infants.

CAMBRIDGESHIRE

Circe Cycles 37 High St, Longstanton CB24 3BP; 🕿 01954 782020; 🖰 circecycles.com/hire; ⑲ ⑳ & ㉑. Specialists in tandem bikes, Circe hires a range of models including Helios, Eos & reclining Morpheus bikes. Price includes lock, lights & toolkit. In a handy location between Cambridge & St Ives, convenient for several of our rides.

City Cycle Hire 61 Newnham Rd, Cambridge CB3 9EY; 🕿 01223 3654629; 🖰 citycyclehire.com; ⑲ & ⑳. With a long-standing reputation for their knowledge of local cycle routes & helpful with safe cycling tips, this is a good city-centre outfit. Their bikes are standard hybrids, including smaller sizes & children's bikes, with good rates for longer hire periods. Lock & lights included.

Grounds Cycle Centre (Milton) Milton Country Park, Cambridge Rd, CB24 6AZ; 🕿 07869 469960; 🖰 groundscyclecentres.uk; ⑲. This cycle centre is in a leisure park north of Cambridge with mountain bike trails. It has MTBs, hybrids & children's bikes for hire at competitive prices, particularly for longer periods. It's also quite close to the Newmarket Rd Park & Ride, handy for our route.

Rutland Cycling Cambridge Station 156 Great Northern Rd, Cambridge CB1 2FX; ✆ 01223 352728; ⓲. Extensive fleet of bikes as well as sales & repairs.

Rutland Cycling Grafham Water Marlow Car Park, Grafham Water PE28 0BH; ✆ 01480 812500, 0330 555 0080; ⌕ rutlandcycling.com; ㉑. Based next to the car park at the Grafham Water Visitor Centre, this has a fleet of hybrid bikes, as well as mountain bikes, e-bikes, tandems, children's bikes, tagalongs & trailers.

FURTHER INFORMATION

CYCLING ORGANISATIONS

Cycling UK ⌔ cyclinguk.org. One of the largest & oldest cycling membership organisations in the UK, founded in 1878 & formerly the Cyclists' Touring Club, with lots of members' activities & cycling tips. Local groups & campaigns, including the broad-based EXPERIENCE project, an ambitious scheme to promote cycling in southern England & northern France.

Euro Velo ⌔ en.eurovelo.com. A Europe-wide cycle network run by the European Cyclists' Federation, with more than 90,000km of cycle routes covering 36 countries, including the UK. The site has maps, apps & masses of other useful information.

Sustrans ⌔ sustrans.org.uk. The nationwide charity that set up & manages the National Cycle Network, with paths for cyclists & other users in towns, cities & the countryside around the whole of the UK. The website has detailed maps & recommended routes with helpful tips, plus printable maps for sale.

APPS

These are a few of the best-known navigation apps (with offline maps to use where internet signal is unavailable). Useful in conjunction with this book, of course!

Gmap Pedometer ⌔ gmap-pedometer.com. Useful for planning routes in advance, for cyclists & walkers. Covers footpaths & gives details of overall ascent/descent.

komoot ⌔ komoot.com. Ready-made routes worldwide for cyclists, runners & walkers, with downloadable route maps & handy offline. Its well-involved membership add community feel, with useful tips & feedback. As used in this book, so unsurprisingly it's my favourite.

Strava ⌔ strava.com. One of the big worldwide route trackers for runners & cyclists, with lots of buttons & bells for competitive athletes (or those who want to be one).

USEFUL WEBSITES

Cambridge Cycling Campaign ⌔ camcycle.org.uk. This large & lively cycling charity runs group cycle rides in & around Cambridge, including an annual outing to the historic Fen village of Reach (see Route 19, page 182).

Forestry England ⌔ forestryengland.uk. The UK's forestry management service, which includes Rendlesham, Thetford & Tunstall among its forest parks in East Anglia, with details of local activities & facilities. It's worth checking in advance if you're planning to visit one of their forests, for updates on seasonal forestry work, during which time some routes may be closed.

Norfolk Churches Trust ⌀ norfolkchurches trust.org.uk. This church preservation charity has information about Norfolk's many historic churches, & runs an annual fundraising bike ride.

Norfolk County Council ⌀ norfolk.gov.uk. The county council website contains masses of cycling news & information, including several cycle routes that are also covered in this book: search 'Cycling' for details.

Norfolk Wildlife Trust ⌀ norfolkwildlife trust.org.uk/home. Norfolk's wildlife preservation charity that manages & protects its nature reserves, including Hickling Broad ❺.

RSPB ⌀ rspb.org.uk. The nationwide bird charity, with many reserves across East Anglia, including several on our routes, such as Cley ❹, Holkham ❸, and Hollesley ⓯.

The Suffolk Coast ⌀ thesuffolkcoast.co.uk. The official tourism website to the coast of Suffolk, with useful information about cycle routes, as well as places to stay & eat.

Suffolk Historic Churches Trust ⌀ shct. org.uk. This church preservation charity has information about Suffolk's astounding collection of 500 medieval historic churches. It also runs an annual 'Ride and Stride' fundraising bike ride.

Suffolk Wildlife Trust ⌀ suffolkwildlife trust.org. A wildlife preservation charity that manages & protects nature reserves across Suffolk, including Alde Mudflats Nature Reserve, near our Orford Loop route ⓮.

Visit Cambridge ⌀ visitcambridge.org. In the absence of an official visitor website for Cambridgeshire county, this is a handy guide to the city, including information about local tours, accommodation and events.

Visit Norfolk ⌀ visitnorfolk.co.uk. The official visitor website for Norfolk, with a huge array of information about where to go, stay & eat, & what to do – including cycling routes, bike hire & organised cycling tours.

Visit North Norfolk ⌀ visitnorthnorfolk. com. The official visitor website for the north coast of Norfolk, with a wide range of information about where to stay, eat out & activities, including details of cycle routes & the long-distance Peddars Way.

Visit Suffolk ⌀ visitsuffolk.com. The official visitor website for Suffolk, with an excellent range of tips about what's on, where to stay, cycle routes & bike hire.

FURTHER READING
Books on East Anglia
Cambridgeshire & The Fens by Lucy Grewcock (Bradt Guides, 2021, 328pp). This new book adds Cambridgeshire & the Fens to Bradt's award-winning Slow Travel series – the biggest series of UK regional travel guides,

now over 20 titles strong. No other title offers the range & depth of information on this varied, beautiful & surprisingly undiscovered region. Cambridge itself attracts visitors, students, professionals & academics from around the world, but beyond the city lie towns & villages, wide-open spaces, gentle waterways & wonderful cycling & walking country that comparatively few take time to discover. Engaging & unexpected, this informative guide captures both the stand-out highlights & lesser-known attractions of this underrated part of East Anglia.

Norfolk by Laurence Mitchell (Bradt Guides, 2018, 264pp). This second edition of Bradt's *Norfolk*, part of its distinctive Slow Travel series of guides to UK regions, remains the only full-blown standalone guide available to this county of contrasts, from the medieval city of Norwich to the watery wilderness of the Broads & the sweeping beaches of the north Norfolk coast. As well as featuring the region's main sights, it covers places & aspects of the region not detailed by other guidebooks & has a special emphasis on car-free travel, walking, local food & pubs. It also includes personal anecdotes & the views of local people as well as tapping into the Norfolk-based author's considerable knowledge of the region.

Suffolk by Laurence Mitchell (Bradt Guides, 2018, 224pp). This second edition of *Suffolk*, part of Bradt's distinctive Slow Travel series of regional UK guides, remains the only full-blown standalone guide to this gentle but beguiling county. Written by expert local author Laurence Mitchell, this guide explores the heart of the region & discovers what makes it tick & offers a very personal view of the county, providing up-to-date information on the best places to visit, stay & eat, covering not just popular sights but focusing also on those places beyond the usual tourist trail. There are also plenty of options for car-free travel: walking, cycling, riverboats & local buses & trains. Written in an entertaining style & offering a personal narrative, authoritative information & interesting anecdotes, this is the ideal companion with which to discover this charming corner of England.

East Anglia by Peter Sager (Pallas Guides, 2003). This weighty & erudite tome casts an insightful eye on the architecture, landscape, people & art of East Anglia. An excellent companion to general travel guides, illustrated with colour & black-&-white photos, diagrams & maps.

Akenfield: Portrait of an English Village by Ronald Blythe (Akadine Press, 1969, 287pp). Written in 1966–67, based on Akenfield – a made-up name for the country village in the heart of Suffolk, this modern classic draws meticulous but undoctored portraits of the lives of farm workers, teachers, doctors, blacksmiths, saddlers & a district nurse. Blythe creates a vivid image of life in one of the most traditional rural regions of England as it was then, but with warning signs of changes coming (see *Return to Akenfield*, below).

Return to Akenfield: Portrait of an English Village in the 21st Century by Craig Taylor (Granta, 2003, 288pp). This 2006 follow-up to Ronald Blythe's original *Akenfield* revisits the inhabitants of this mythical/quintessential rural village, seeing how the 21st century has changed & is changing their lives today. Through the villagers' own voices – from priest to publican, farmer to schoolteacher – Taylor's account gives a deceptively profound view of our transformed countryside.

Bike books

The Big Book of Cycling for Beginners by Tori Bortmann (Rodale Books, 2014, 290pp). Although it was published back in 2014, this comprehensive book covers everything from safe-cycling guidance to tips on buying your first bike, what to wear & even the best nutrition for cyclists. US cycling consultant Bortmann also gives confidence-boosting insights on the benefits of cycling to our physical & mental health. A recommended read to help you get started as the latest cycling boom sweeps the UK.

Bike Repair Manual by Chris Sidwells (Dorling Kindersley, 2021, 176pp). A handy, pocket-sized manual with DK's trademark illustrations. With clear tips on practical maintenance, accessible even for the complete beginner, it also includes an overview of different types of bikes & accessories, for adults & children.

ACKNOWLEDGEMENTS

Firstly, many thanks to Rob Marshall of komoot navigation app, for guiding me through this magical maze – you have taught a stubborn old dog some nifty new tricks. Thanks to Joel Pailes and Andrew Middleton of Norfolk County Council, the UK lead of the EU EXPERIENCE project, for sharing your vision to bring more off-season visitor activities to this beautiful county. To John Seton, of the Cambridge CTC, part of Cycling UK, thanks for all your help, particularly for keeping me going on our ridiculously rain-soaked ride from Cambridge to Ely. Many thanks to Pete Waters, Phil Eke, Kayla Dunne, Asa Morrison and everyone else at Visit East of England, for all the information and advice.

To Alice Greenacre and Callum Leslie of Forestry England, thanks for all your support and information about the wonderful wilds of Rendlesham, Thetford and Tunstall forests. And to Steve T of the Tunstall Rendlesham Off-road Group, thanks for help sorting out the forest trail map. To Simon McGrath of the Camping and Caravanning Club, thanks for welcoming me to the immaculately clean, but natural and peaceful Sandringham campsite. To Barry and Matthew Denny at Maglia Rosso, possibly the most complete one-stop cycling outfit in Suffolk; one day I must go back and join one of your group rides.

To Joshua Ward and everyone at Sutton Hoo, what an amazing site! You and your colleagues really bring it all to life with your enthusiasm and inside knowledge. Now I know where Edith Pretty hid the treasures from their daily dig. To Will Affleck of Original Cottages, thanks for all the information and the hospitality – I will always remember the rotating pod in Mallards' emu paddock! And to Ann and Joe, Imogen and Peter, Ben and Sarah, Ian and Sue, thank you all for letting me drag my muddy boots through your lovely homes (hope I cleared up properly on the way out).

To Rachel Parkes and Alison Rickett of the Nature-Friendly Farming Network, thanks for all the inside information on this excellent holistic alliance of nature and farming. To Rachel Frain and Rebecca Lyon of the Norfolk Wildlife Trust, many thanks for showing us around the Cley Marshes and Hickling Broads reserves. Here's hoping Hickling's cranes and swallowtails thrive and prosper, along with all your other wonderful resident wildlife.

Sincere thanks to Bradt Guides, for giving me a second opportunity to get on my bike and share my wanderings through another beautiful corner of the country. In particular, thank you to Anna, Claire, Hugh, Deborah and Adrian. And a special, huge thanks to Adrian Dixon and Laura Pidgley, my brilliant and supportive editors. I'm still hopeful that one day I can drag you both and all the Bradt team out on the road with me, and we can put these rambling routes to the test.

Lastly and, of course, most importantly: my deepest, loving thanks to my wonderful wife Caitlin. You have patiently supported me through two of these books now, put up with my smelly shoes drying off by the boiler and picked me up from the back of beyond whenever my knees failed me.

COVID-19

Please note that work on this book was completed during the Covid-19 pandemic. Because of the impact of the crisis on tourism, some businesses or services listed in the text may no longer operate. We will post any information we have about these on bradtguides.com/updates. And we'd of course be grateful for any updates you can send us during your own travels, which we will add to that page for the benefit of future travellers.

INDEX

Page numbers in **bold** indicate main entries; those in *italics* indicate maps.

accommodation 19-20, **206-16**
Archer, Fred 168
Aylsham 69-70

bikes
    equipment and accessories 14-15
    hire 20, **218-21**
    maintenance 13-14
    on public transport 15-16
    types of 12-13
    safety 16-17
Boudicca 24, 33, **36**
Brecks, The 11, 47, 103, **108**
Broads National Park 11, 55, 63, **87**
Bungay 93
Bungay Saints Trail 7, **92-101**, *94*
    accommodation 211, 213, 214
    food and drink 100-1
    getting there 99
    tourist information 101

cafés *see* food and drink *under individual trails*
Cambridge 183-6, 196
Cambridge to Ely trail **182-91**, *184*
    accommodation 215-16
    food and drink 191
    getting there 190-1
    tourist information 191
Castle Rising *23*, 26-9
churches and cathedrals
    All Saints, Horsey 59
    Bungay Saints 100
    Ely Cathedral 190
    King's College Chapel, Cambridge 183
    St Andrew, Wickhampton 77-8
    St Botolph, Freethorpe 75
    St Botolph, Iken 141
    St Felix 26
    St George, St Cross 98
    St Gregory, Heckingham 85
    St John the Baptist, Reedham 78
    St Laurence, Castle Rising 28
    St Margaret, Newgate 48
    St Mary, Moulton St Mary 76-7
    St Michael & All Angels, Ingoldisthorpe 31
    St Peter, Chillesford 143
    Walsingham Abbey 42
Cley Loop trail 47-53, *48*
    accommodation 206-7, 209
    food and drink 52-3
    getting there 52
    tourist information 53
Cley-next-the-Sea **47-9**, 51-3
cycle hire
    Cambridgeshire 214-16
    Norfolk 206-10
    Suffolk 210-14
cycle trails and footpaths
    Bure Valley Path 63, **70**
    Guided Busway Cycleway 16, 193, 197, 199
    Icknield Way **12**, 25, 167
    Lodes Way 187
    Norfolk Coast Path 39, 43
    Norfolk Coastal Cycleway 11
    Peddars Way **12**, 24, 31, 33, 113
    Suffolk Coastal Cycle Route 11
    Walsingham Way 63
cycling
    further information 222
    safety 16-17
    what to wear 15

Debenham 125-6

East Anglia **10-12**, 18, 223-5
Ely 189-91
Eye 121-2, 127-8
Eye to Debenham Loop trail **120-9**, *122*
  accommodation 211-13
  food and drink 128-9
  getting there 128
  tourist information 129

food and drink *see entries under individual trails*
further reading 222-5

Grafham Water Loop trail 9, **200-5**, *202*
  accommodation 214-16
  food and drink 203-5
  getting there 203
  tourist information 205
Great Bircham Loop trail 6, 18, **30-7**, *32*
  accommodation 206-8
  food and drink 35-7
  getting there 35
  tourist information 37

historic sites, gardens and houses
  Anglesey Abbey 186
  Bronze Age burial mounds 33
  Castle Rising 26-8
  Grime's Graves 11, **108**
  Holkham Hall 40-1
  Houghton Hall 33-4
  Hunworth Hall 51
  Raveningham Hall and Gardens 89-90
  Sandringham House 23-6
  Seahenge 36
  Sutton Hoo 36, 146-7, 153
  Warham Camp 39, **44**
  Waxham Barn 57-8
  Wyken Hall 114

HRH, the Prince of Wales 25
Holkham 40
  Holkham Bay 39-40
  Holkham Hall 40-1
  Holkham National Nature Reserve 43
Holt 51
Houghton Mill Loop trail 9, **192-9**, *194*
  accommodation 197
  food and drink 156-7
  getting there 156
  tourist information 157

Ixworth 111
Ixworth Millers' Trail 7, **110-18**, *112*
  accommodation 211-12
  food and drink 117-18
  getting there 117
  tourist information 118

Lavenham 157-9
  Guildhall 162
Lavenham Loop trail 8, **156-63**, *158*
  accommodation 212-14
  food and drink 161-3
  getting there 161
  tourist information 163
Loddon 85

maps 19
Marriott, William 70
Marriott's Way trail 7, **62-71**, *64*
  accommodation 208
  food and drink 71
  getting there 70-1
  tourist information 71
Moulton Loop trail 8, **164-9**, *166*
  accommodation 215-16
  food and drink 169
  getting there 168
  tourist information 169
mountain biking 17

see also individual trails
  Rendlesham Forest 150-3
  Thetford Forest 102-9
  Viking Trail 141-2
museums and galleries
  National Horse Racing Museum 174
  Norfolk and Suffolk Aviation Museum, Flixton 98
  Shell Museum, Glandford 49
  Sutton Hoo 147-8
  William Marriott Museum, Holt 70

National Cycle Network (SUSTRANS) 11, 18, 222
Newmarket 9, 18, 175
Newmarket Jockeys' Trail 9, **170-81**, *172-3*
  accommodation 215-16
  food and drink 180-1
  getting there 180
  tourist information 181
Northern Broads: Hickling to Horsey trail 6, **54-61**, *56*
  accommodation 205-8
  food and drink 61
  getting there 59
  tourist information 61
Norwich 7, 63-5

Orford 139-40
Orford Loop trail 8, **138-45**, *140*
  accommodation 212-13
  food and drink 144
  getting there 144
  tourist information 145
Orford Ness 145

pubs *see* food and drink

railways
  Bure Valley Railway 69-70
  Mid-Suffolk Light Railway (The 'Middy') 124-6
  Wells and Walsingham Light Railway 42
  Whitwell and Reepham Railway 67
Reedham 78-9
Reedham Broads Loop trail 9, **72-80**, *73*
  accommodation 207-10
  food and drink 80
  getting there 79
  tourist information 80
Reedham Ferry 74, 83
Reepham 68-9
rivers
  Chet 85
  Deben 121, 125, 148
  Waveney 83, **86**, 93, 121
  Yare 83, 86, 90

Sandringham 18, 23-9
Sandringham Loop trail 6, 18, **22-9**, *23*
  accommodation 206, 209-10
  food and drink 28-9
  getting there 28
  tourist information 29
Sea Palling 55-6
Shingle Street 10, 149-50
Southern Broads Loop trail 7, 18, **82-91**, *84*
  accommodation 207-9
  food and drink 90-1
  getting there 90
  tourist information 91
Snape Maltings 142
Southwold 135-6
Sutton Hoo 147-8
Sutton Hoo and Rendlesham Forest Loop trail 8, **146-55**, *147*
  accommodation 212-14
  food and drink 154-5
  getting there 153-4
  tourist information 155

Thetford Forest trails 7, **102–9**, *104*
  accommodation 211–13
  food and drink 109
  getting there 107
  tourist information 109
trains *see individual trails*

Walberswick 131–2, 136
Walberswick to Southwold Loop trail 8, **130–7**, *132*
  accommodation 213–14
  food and drink 137
  getting there 136
  tourist information 137
Walsingham Abbey 42
websites 20, 222–3
Wells and Holkham Loop trail 6, **38–45**, *39*
  accommodation 207–9
  food and drink 45
  getting there 44
  tourist information 45
Wells-next-the-Sea **38–9**, 42–5
where to stay *see* accommodation

wildlife parks, nature reserves and forests
  Alde Mudflats Nature Reserve 141
  Cley Marshes NWT 47, **50**
  Dunwich Forest 132
  Fen Drayton Lakes, RSPB 196–8
  Grafham Water 204
  Hickling Broad 55, 57
  Holkham National Nature Reserve 40, **43**
  Horsey Gap 58–9
  Rendlesham Forest 150–3
  Thetford Forest 103–9
  Wicken Fen National Nature Reserve 187–8
windmills and watermills 79
  Cley Windmill 48–9
  Great Bircham Windmill 31
  Holton Postmill 133
  Horsey Windpump 59
  Houghton Mill 195
  Letheringsett Watermill 49
  Pakenham Watermill 115
  Pakenham Windmill 116

INDEX OF ADVERTISERS

Camping and Caravanning Club 217
Original Cottages 217

Published in association with komoot
First edition published April 2022
Bradt Guides Ltd
31a High Street, Chesham, Buckinghamshire, HP5 1BW, England
www.bradtguides.com
Print edition published in the USA by The Globe Pequot Press Inc,
PO Box 480, Guilford, Connecticut 06437-0480

Text copyright © 2022 Huw Hennessy
Maps copyright © 2022 Bradt Guides Ltd; includes map data © OpenStreetMap contributors
Photographs copyright © 2022 Individual photographers (see below)
Project Manager: Laura Pidgley
Cover research: Ian Spick

The author and publisher have made every effort to ensure the accuracy of the information in this book at the time of going to press. However, they cannot accept any responsibility for any loss, injury or inconvenience resulting from the use of information contained in this guide. All rights reserved. No part of this publication may be reproduced, stored in a retrieval system, or transmitted in any form or by any means, electronic, mechanical, photocopying, recording or otherwise without the prior consent of the publisher.

ISBN: 9781784778781

British Library Cataloguing in Publication Data
A catalogue record for this book is available from the British Library

Photographs Photographers credited beside images & also those from libraries credited as follows: Alamy.com (A); Dreamstime.com (DT); Shutterstock.com (S); Wikimedia Commons (WC)
Front cover Top: St Benet's Mill, Norfolk Broads (Tom Mackie/AWL Images); Bottom: Cycling at Castle Rising, Norfolk (Visit East of England)
Back cover King's College Chapel, Cambridge (Pajor Pawel/S)
Title page Thetford Forest, Suffolk (High Lodge/Forestry England)

Maps David McCutcheon FBCart.S and Daniella Levin

Typeset by Ian Spick, Bradt Guides
Production managed by Zenith Media; printed in the UK
Digital conversion by www.dataworks.co.in